Moving People, Moving Images

Cinema and Trafficking in the New Europe

William Brown

Dina Iordanova

Leshu Torchin

St Andrews Film Studies

St Andrews

First published in Great Britain in 2010 by
St Andrews Film Studies in collaboration with College Gate Press
99 North Street, St Andrews, KY16 9AD
http://www.st-andrews.ac.uk/filmbooks
Series: Cinema and Transnational Discourse

A CIP Catalogue of this book is available from the British Library

ISBN: 978-1-906678-03-6

This book is published with the assistance of the Centre for Film Studies
at the University of St Andrews. St Andrews Film Studies promotes
greater understanding of, and access to, international cinema and film
culture worldwide.

University
of
St Andrews

The University of St Andrews is a charity registered in Scotland, No.
SC013532

Cover design and pre-press: University of St Andrews Reprographics Unit.
Front cover illustration: The road to Tentsmuir, © Leshu Torchin, 2009.

Typeset in Helvectica Neue 9½pt
by Chandler Book Design
www.chandlerbookdesign.co.uk

Printed in Great Britain by the
MPG Books Group, Bodmin and King's Lynn

Moving People, Moving Images

Cinema and Trafficking in the New Europe

St Andrews Film Studies

St Andrews

Acknowledgements

The authors would like to thank the following, without whose help this book would not have been possible:

Ruby Cheung, Lars Kristensen, Serazer Pekerman, Duncan Stewart at the University of St Andrews Reprographics Unit, Yosefa Loshitsky, Carrie Tarr, Daniela Berghahn, Laura Rascaroli, Claudia Sternberg, Yana Hashamova, Anikó Imre, Katarzyna Marciniak, and Isabel Santaollala.

Dina Iordanova would also like to thank Slobodan Šijan, Želimir Žilnik, Nezih Erdogan, Deniz Bayrakdar, Georgi Dyulgerov, Dimitris Kerkinos, Marian Tutui, Pavle Levi and Nevena Daković for helping with insights and access to material.

Leshu Torchin would like personally to thank the following for their conversation, insights, and support: Elizabeth Ashford, Faye Ginsburg, Kirsten McAllister, Michael McCluskey, Sean Quinn Walpole, Nilita Vachani, Belén Vidal, and Nick Higgins and his inspiring project, *The New Ten Commandments* (2008), which includes a short documentary on the subject of human trafficking in Glasgow.

Work on this volume has been funded in part through grants received over the years from the Leverhulme Trust, the AHRC, the Carnegie Trust for the Universities of Scotland, and from the British Academy.

About the Authors

William Brown is a Lecturer in Film Studies at the University of St Andrews. He has published on various topics in various journals and edited collections, including *animation: an interdisciplinary journal, New Review of Film and Television Studies, Studies in French Cinema, Studies in European Cinema, The British Cinema Book 3rd Edition* (ed. Robert Murphy, Palgrave Macmillan, 2009), *Cinema, Identities and Beyond* (eds. Ruby Cheung and David Fleming, Cambridge Scholars Press, 2009), and *Film Theory and Contemporary Hollywood Movies* (ed. Warren Buckland, Routledge, 2009). He is the joint editor of *Deleuze and Film* (with David Martin-Jones, Edinburgh University Press, 2011), and is seeking publication for a monograph on film theoretical approaches to digital technology and cinema, tentatively entitled *Supercinema*. He also runs an online blog community, Cinema Salon (cinemasalon.ning.com), and is an occasional filmmaker.

Dina Iordanova is a native of Bulgaria where she obtained advanced degrees in Philosophy and German. Having since 1990 lived and worked in Canada, the USA, and England, she is now Professor and Chair in Film Studies at the University of St Andrews in Scotland, where she founded the Film Studies programme. Today she directs the Centre for Film Studies and the Leverhulme Trust project 'Dynamics of World Cinema' (http://www.st-andrews.ac.uk/worldcinema). Iordanova has published extensively on the cinema of Eastern Europe and the Balkans: with the BFI, she has published *The BFI Companion to Eastern European and Russian Cinema* (2000), *Cinema of Flames* (2001) and *Emir Kusturica* (2002); with Wallflower Press, she has published *Cinema of the Other Europe* (2003) and *Cinema of the*

Balkans (2006); and she has published *New Bulgarian Cinema* with College Gate Press (2008). She has edited special issues of *Third Text*, *Framework*, *South Asian Popular Culture*, *Kinokultura*, as well as the collection *Cinema at the Periphery* (Wayne State University Press, 2010), on matters of cross-cultural representation and transnational cinema. More recent work is focused on film festivals, business models and global distribution patterns of film. Iordanova created the concept of the *Film Festival Yearbook* (*FFY*) series, which she also publishes through St Andrews Film Studies and College Gate Press (*FFY1: The Festival Circuit*, 2009, *FFY2: Film Festivals and Imagined Communities*, 2010). She writes a blog, *www.DinaView.com*.

Leshu Torchin is a Lecturer in Film Studies at the University of St Andrews. Her research focuses on the use of film, video, and the internet in social advocacy and human rights activism. This interest has fuelled her study, *Creating the Witness: Genocide in the Age of Film, Video and the Internet*. She has published in a range of journals including *Third Text*, *American Anthropologist*, and *Film & History*, as well as in the edited collection *The Image and the Witness: Trauma, Memory, and Visual Culture* (eds. Frances Guerin and Roger Hallas, Wallflower Press, 2007).

Table of Contents

Introduction   1

Part One: Landscapes

Negotiating the Invisible (William Brown)   16

Foreign Exchange (Leshu Torchin)   49

Making Traffic Visible, Adjusting the Narrative (Dina Iordanova)   84

Part Two: Close-Ups

The Bus   118

The Guardian Angel   126

When Mother Comes Home for Christmas   134

Wesh wesh, qu'est-ce qui se passe?   142

Poniente   148

Spare Parts   155

Promised Land   163

Sex Traffic   172

Ghosts   180

It's a Free World…   186

Import/Export   191

Love on Delivery and *Ticket to Paradise*   197

The Silence of Lorna   204

Taken   211

Traffic Jam: Film, Activism, and Human Trafficking (Leshu Torchin)   218

Bibliography   237

Filmography   247

Index   251

Introduction

What is trafficking?

Within the context of *Moving People, Moving Images*, trafficking can be understood not as the illegal drugs or arms trade, but as the illegal and forced migration of people across the globe: that is, trafficking is, here, *human* trafficking.

Human trafficking, henceforth referred to predominantly as just trafficking, is one of the most pressing issues of the contemporary era, although information about trafficking can be difficult to obtain and unreliable when found. The European Union (EU), the Organisation for Security and Cooperation in Europe (OSCE), and the G8 nations addressed the issue in 2000 (Morrison & Crosland 2000), with the UN Protocols on trafficking and smuggling being signed in Palermo, Italy, in the same year (Laczko 2005). Inter-governmental Organisations (IGOs) and non-governmental Organisations (NGOs), such as the UN High Commissioner for Human Rights (UNHCHR), UNICEF, the International Organisation for Migration (IOM), and the Anti-Slavery International all have anti-trafficking programmes in place (Morrison & Crosland 2000). However, in spite of the efforts of these organisations to make it visible, trafficking remains largely invisible to the general public, even though it takes place under the noses of the developed world, where all lives supposedly are held to be equal.

Trafficking can signify various different practices. The 2000 United Nations Trafficking Protocol gives the following definition of trafficking:

> the recruitment, transportation, transfer, harboring or receipt of persons by means of threat or use of force or

other forms of coercion, of abduction, of fraud, of deception, of the abuse of power, or of a position of vulnerability or of the giving or receiving of payments of benefits to achieve the consent of a person having control over another person, for the purpose of exploitation. Exploitation shall include, at a minimum, the exploitation of prostitution of others or other forms of sexual exploitation, forced labour services slavery or practices similar to slavery, servitude or the removal of organs (quoted in Kara 2009: 4).

From this definition, we can see that the most widely recognised manifestation of trafficking is the illegal sex trade, in which, typically, women are forced into prostitution, sex slavery and mail order marriages, a phenomenon that has also been labelled the 'Natashas Trade' (Hughes 2001; Malarek 2004) on account of the large number of women forced into this business from the countries of the former Soviet Union – although women often come from other parts of the globe as well. However, as the above definition suggests, trafficking can also take on other guises: the illegal traffic of children; the exploitation of illegal immigrant labour forces, the worst examples of which, as bonded labour or debt bondage, can be considered a contemporary form of slave labour; and the illegal trade of body parts and organs for quasi-legal but typically urgent transplants ('human farming'). In addition to the forms of trafficking explained above, and perhaps contrary to some literature on trafficking, particularly that (majority of literature) which views trafficking not as a question of migration, but as a question of human rights, *Moving People, Moving Images* does consider as trafficking various aspects of 'conventional' illegal immigration; that is, while illegal immigration does not always result in the exploitation of humans in the various manners described above, illegal immigration does often involve the professional smuggling of migrants across borders. People smuggling is here held to constitute a form of trafficking.

Researchers admit to the 'absence of reliable statistical data' (Lee 2007: 14) concerning trafficking, a lack of reliability that is in part a result of the continued debate and thus lack of clarity concerning the 'proper' definition of trafficking (does it include 'mere' smuggling?, is it concerned only with forced prostitution?, etc.). However, with more research into trafficking comes more, and more reliable, statistical data concerning this phenomenon – although we might also recognise that gathering and disseminating data alone may not be enough, since data alone perhaps constitute a form of voyeurism, while trafficking demands a political response, in short regarding how one might 'combat' trafficking (Kelly 2005).

The figures that we provide below confirm the lack of reliability with regard to statistical data about human trafficking, but whether we believe even the smallest estimates regarding the number of slaves in the world today, the number of people trafficked annually, the number of women trafficked annually, the number of people trafficked specifically in or across Europe, the number of women working in the European sex trade, and the number of sweat shops in North America, the severity of this problem should become clear. There are reported to be 27 million slaves in the world today (Bales, Trodd & Williamson 2009), although some estimates claim that there are as many as 200 million (Ruggiero 1997), a figure that, if at all accurate, suggests the enormous size of this 'industry,' an industry that is pan-global (or transnational) and more often than not criminal (trafficking has often been identified as a business for organised crime networks; Salt 2000; Goodey 2003; Ballesteros 2005; Kelly 2005). According to the US State Department, between 600,000 and 800,000 individuals are trafficked internationally every year across international borders, while millions more are trafficked internally (Kara 2009: 17). Other studies tentatively suggest that as many as 4 million people are trafficked worldwide each year (Morawska 2007: 94). Estimates regarding the number of women trafficked each year range from 500,000 to between 5 and 10 million. In the European Union, which forms the focus of this book (and which is predominantly referred to simply as Europe), there were in 1996 believed to be some 200,000 to 500,000 women working illegally as sex workers, while organisatons that purport to monitor the trafficking of women claim that at least half a million women are trafficked into/across Europe every year, and anywhere between 20,000 to 50,000 women are trafficked into the USA every year. In 1999 there were reputedly 22,000 'sewing shops' in the USA that involved exploited and illegal labour forces (Taylor & Jamieson 1999). Again, while many of these statistics overlap and/or seemingly contradict each other in terms of precise figures, all point to the scale of trafficking as a problematic industry, which sees human beings reduced to what Kevin Bales (2004) has termed *disposable people*.

Trafficking and cinema

It is not with the aim of diminishing the very real nature of this problem that we shall discuss trafficking as represented in contemporary cinema. On the contrary, by trying to understand the nature of trafficking not necessarily from a statistical but from a theoretical point of view, and by addressing how one might understand the practice of making, distributing and exhibiting films about trafficking, we should like to encourage a critical engagement with this widespread and contemporary issue. If the reader feels compelled to find out more about trafficking in the contemporary world, then they should perhaps refer to the bibliography at the end of the book and to the websites of the organisations mentioned above (UNHCHR, UNICEF, IOM, Anti-Slavery Interational). Throughout *Moving People, Moving Images*, however, we shall be looking at specifically filmic representations of trafficking – analysing these films against the statistics of real life trafficking, considering how they help to refine and/or complicate our understanding of trafficking, and examining the ways in which films can be and often are used in anti-trafficking campaigns.

To look only at filmic representations of trafficking may to some suggest a refusal to engage with the real world phenomenon that is trafficking itself. But, while this book hopefully can inform our understanding of trafficking as a very real phenomenon, it is precisely the possibility or otherwise of representing on film and bringing to the attention of the general public the typically invisible and contemporary slave trade that is the central issue of *Moving People, Moving Images*. For it is the shared position of all three authors that social problems can be and are represented through films (even if often in a problematic manner). We also hold that films can and do function as powerful tools in raising awareness of serious issues like trafficking, and that films can even play a pivotal role in helping to bring about the end of human trafficking. A film seen by tens, hundreds, thousands, perhaps even millions of people, can have a much greater impact than a white paper read by only a handful. While films about human trafficking might initially be considered as 'disposable' as the people that are kept in bondage (and some films may well be 'disposable,' as will be discussed), we should like to argue that films can also be considered as playing a key role in providing a solution to trafficking, and that films perhaps play an *indisposable* role in providing that solution, especially when films are used in anti-trafficking campaigns.

If trafficking and human slavery are not new, nor are films on the subject – although slavery of course predates cinema by several millennia. *Otobüs* (*The Bus*, Tunç Okan, Switzerland/Turkey, 1976) and *Andjeo čuvar* (*The Guardian Angel*, Goran Paskalvejić, Yugoslavia, 1987) are two pre-1989 films that deal with human trafficking, and there are extended analyses of both of these films in the second section of the book, Close-Ups. It is since 1989 and the end of the Cold War, however, that the world has seen an unprecedented boom in migration, which in turn has escalated the problem of trafficking and turned it into a serious social concern – as is reflected by the dozens of films that have been produced on the topic in recent years, and several of which are also discussed in detail in the Close-Ups section. These include: *Otan erthei i mama gia ta Hristougenna* (*When Mother Comes Home for Christmas*, Nilita Vachani, Greece/India/Germany, 1994), *Wesh wesh, qu'est-ce qui se passe?* (Rabah Ameur-Zaïmeche, France, 2001), *Poniente* (Chus Gutiérrez, Spain, 2002), *Rezervni deli* (*Spare Parts*, Damjan Kožole, Slovenia, 2003), *Ha-Aretz Hamuvtachat* (*Promised Land*, Amos Gitai, Israel/France/UK, 2004), *Sex Traffic* (David Yates, UK/Canada, 2004), *Ghosts* (Nick Broomfield, UK, 2006), *It's a Free World...* (Ken Loach, UK/Italy/Germany/Spain/Poland, 2007), *Import/Export* (Ulrich Seidl, Austria/France/Germany, 2007), *Fra Thailand til Thy* (*Love on Delivery*, Janus Metz, Denmark, 2008), *Fra Thy til Thailand* (*Ticket to Paradise*, Janus Metz, Denmark, 2008), *Le Silence de Lorna* (*The Silence of Lorna*, Jean-Pierre and Luc Dardenne, Belgium/France/Italy/Germany, 2008), and *Taken* (Pierre Morel, France, 2008).

The effect that the collapse of the former Soviet Union has had on human trafficking, particularly within the European context, leads us to suggest that trafficking is linked to matters of roaming labour, poverty (which, in particular, seems to remain unrecognised by political science writing on the post-communist period), and to the profound social shifts that are happening in the former Soviet Republics. The mainstream narrative of human trafficking does not include these considerations, an imbalance that we hope to adjust in the course of this book. Furthermore, trafficking is most often considered as a side effect of globalisation, and while globalisation, together with the proliferation of new media and transnational telecommunications networks, features prominently in our consideration of films dealing with human trafficking, we also take in a different approach, one that is suggested by the films themselves. Rather than giving a global overview of trafficking, most films dealing with the issue focus on the side effects, offering a narrative where individual strategies of survival are the centre of attention. Although this 'personalisation' of the problem is sometimes derided (as if a depersonalised approach to this human issue were not somehow complicit in the very process of depersonalisation that trafficked peoples often endure), we hold that it is through these narratives that a greater understanding of the issue – together with the encouragement of urgent responses to it – can be established.

Moving People, Moving Images

If Close-Ups, the second part of *Moving People, Moving Images*, is dedicated to the close textual analysis of 15 key films that deal with trafficking, the first part, Landscapes, deals with the issue from a variety of theoretical and analytical standpoints.

In 'Negotiating the Invisible,' William Brown offers up an extended analysis of how cinema can represent trafficking. If the bonded labour of trafficked peoples is a necessarily invisible but required and perhaps even desired element of the contemporary European economy, how can films make visible this problem? Brown understands human trafficking, within the context of Europe, to be the continuation via other means of the colonial/imperialist project, except that now the labour force provided by trafficked humans is *internal* to and hidden within Europe rather than located in the colonies. This reaffirms Europe as a/the centre to which Europe's 'others' (i.e. non-Europeans) wish to travel and where they wish to work, and as a result it justifies an attitude of 'Eurocentrism' when we consider trafficking within Europe. Furthermore, if trafficked humans are hidden within Europe, it becomes difficult for trafficked humans not only to be seen, but also to see each other – and the ability to see and talk with each other is a necessary but at present non-existent condition that will allow trafficked humans to claim equal rights alongside 'real' Europeans. For this reason, all films about human trafficking are made by observers of this phenomenon, rather than by those who have lived through it themselves. This is a key problem in representing trafficked humans in cinema: since trafficked humans do not have the means to represent themselves (because they are being held in slavery), then are films about trafficking always doomed to be voyeuristic and to 'other' these people who are among Europeans in Europe?

Furthermore, the representation of trafficking poses significant challenges to those 'outside' (i.e. the non-trafficked/non-trafficking) observers who make films on the matter. Since it is an illicit practice, the networks and processes of trafficking are difficult to monitor. Securing testimony adds to the challenge, as victims fear repercussions – whether from the host nation that threatens deportation or from the traffickers who threaten retaliation, if not to the trafficked subject, then to his or her family. There are, however, extraordinary cases in which footage is procured, as in the case of Gillian Caldwell's *Bought and Sold: An Investigative Documentary about the International Trade in Women* (USA, 2009). The documentary, which is further discussed in the final chapter of this book, features secretly taped clandestine operations as well as interviews with victims and experts, and has become a centrepiece in a wide-ranging campaign to promote awareness and response. However, such films are rare, and the task of visualising operations and the suffering of the victims more often falls to feature narrative cinema, which, even as fiction, still bears some degree of an indexical relationship to the lived world (Sobchack 1984). That is, however attenuated the link, the films refer to the real-life phenomenon of trafficking, even as they shape the representation thereof according to agendas ranging from border anxiety to human rights activism.

The negotiation of these representational challenges informs the decision to include both documentary and fiction films in the second chapter, 'Foreign Exchange,' by Leshu Torchin. Torchin does not formally segregate these two modes of filmmaking, in part because of the relatively small number of documentaries discussed, but also in order to suggest that all films exist on a continuum of indexicality with varying, and often fraught, positions concerning the nature of visible evidence, in particular, here, with regard to the representation of trafficking. The very challenges in disarticulating the two modes reflect challenges of representing trafficking. Films like *Last Resort* (Pawel Pawlikowski, UK, 2000), *Import/Export*, and *Ghosts* blur the distinction between truth and fiction by taking real-life people to perform their own conditions, whether as pornographers, prostitutes or day-labourers. This practice highlights the liminal nature of trafficking and the attendant challenges posed to its representation.

Obscuring and problematising presentations of truth dovetail with the fracturing effect of traumatic experience upon straightforward narration (Caruth 1996; Felman & Laub, 1991). Such a strategy calls to mind what Janet Walker (1997: 806) has called the 'traumatic paradox,' which refers to the way trauma can 'produce the very modifications in remembered detail that cultural conventions invalidate in determination of truth.' Although the aforementioned films adopt a realist style in their depictions, and although they may be drawing on non-actors as a means of establishing an authoritative truth-claim, their interaction with fiction points to the challenges and negotiations involved in the representation of the traumatic experience, which 'simultaneously defies and demands our witness' (Caruth 1996: 5). This interplay of fiction and non-fiction may provide an opportunity for increased visibility and insight. Responding to the 1950s public affairs promotional film *Why Braceros?* (USA, c1959) with the science-fiction inflected mockumentary *Why Cybraceros?* (USA, 1997), Alex Rivera uses the liberating power of the interplay of fiction and non-fiction to call attention to the tacit understandings and invisible pathways that link legitimate economies with human trafficking. The discussion of *Ghosts* in Close-Ups develops this thread, noting how the merger of fiction and non-fiction provides a means for thinking through the complexities of visualising trafficking and in understanding its place within both formal and informal economies.

Notably, even the straightforward, realist documentaries addressed in this book point to the challenges of visualising the circuits and experiences of trafficking. In keeping with the classic characterisation of documentary as a creative treatment of actuality, the documentaries discussed here draw on cinematic strategies to form connections; *Life and Debt* (Stephanie Black, USA, 2001), for instance, uses *mise-en-scène* to express the confinement of those working in free trade zones, creating an ironic juxtaposition between the 'freedom' of the market and the slavery-like conditions of its participants. *A Decent Factory* (Thomas Balmès, France/Finland/ UK/Australia/Denmark, 2004) confronts the challenges of rendering violations visible in its chronicle of Nokia's visit to one of its factories in China. Attempting to assure ethical treatment of their Chinese employees, the visitors find only borderline cases that defy clear categorisation as either actionable violation or acceptable practice. Documentaries, then, despite their privileged ontological status, or indeed because of it, can hint to the deeper challenges that are both representational and ethical. How can trafficking be represented, and more to the point, how can newer, and possibly less visible manifestations of trafficking be represented in film?

Torchin engages these questions in an examination of filmic representations of trafficking and the ways in which these express and comment upon the often invisible and occasionally harmful forces of globalisation. If since its invention cinema has reflected and perhaps even played an instrumental part in globalisation, then it should come as no surprise that there have been films about modern slavery since at least 1910. The latter half of the 20th century, meanwhile, has been marked both by radical border permeability, especially since the collapse of communism and the deregulation of transnational economic flow patterns, as well as by a concomitant defence of human rights, particularly through transnational alliances such as the European Union and the United Nations. The chapter therefore outlines the ways in which films about human trafficking represent transnational networks and the human cost of global capitalism, including through its dark underbelly, international organised crime. Torchin also underlines how many films treat trafficking as a human rights issue, not just in terms of their content, but also through their deployment within social justice movements seeking to mobilise political change. Furthermore, while the chapter focuses on films dealing with the European context, the chapter references films and videos from and about Asia, the Caribbean, and the Americas – which is in keeping with a subject that transgresses borders and invites global attention.

In 'Making Traffic Visible, Adjusting the Narrative,' Dina Iordanova offers something of a synthesis of the previous two essays. She takes up again the notion of (in)visibility in her discussion of how certain films depict (Western Europeans') growing awareness of trafficking, as well as making a strong case for the ways in which a wider awareness both of cinema and of the discourses employed in Film Studies can serve as tools for making a difference in a real world where images, especially moving images, have become so integrated into everyday life. Iordanova also investigates the use of spaces in many trafficking films, suggesting that the routes taken by trafficked individuals often pass through liminal spaces or, after Marc Augé (1995), through non-places that do not otherwise feature in the mainstream consciousness, a consciousness that is indeed shaped by cinema and television. Iordanova follows her consideration of the representation of space with a consideration of the representation of traffickers and trafficked peoples, identifying the stereotypes and the exceptions to those stereotypes across a range of films. She then engages in how such representations relate to the real-world issue of coercion or consent, especially with regard to trafficking from the former Soviet Union: to what extent do trafficked peoples know what they are getting into? This is an issue closely tied to gender, which also plays a role in her final section regarding the validity of film and Film Studies in helping us to understand how issues like trafficking are represented and mediated. Since images play a key role in raising awareness about the invisible problem of trafficking, looking at how these images represent the sexes, particularly women, is of pressing importance.

Although each chapter has its own set of concerns, key themes run throughout these and the shorter essays in the Close-Ups section. These include the issue of movement (in a world where privileged Westerners move so freely, trafficked peoples have great difficulty in moving, and often do not move at all when held in bondage), and the body (similarly, in a world where privileged Westerners do not use their bodies to produce anything, the labour of the trafficked individual is almost always *physical* labour). Furthermore, all three essays deal in part with space and place and the tension between centre and periphery in a world where people (try to) move about so much, as well as on the (possible) role(s) that cinema can play in raising awareness of and enabling change in response to human rights issues like trafficking. Finally, each essay also broaches the issue of visibility: how can and do films make visible a problem that is largely invisible?

The essays each deal with a large number of films, and all three make mention of the 'canonical' films that recently have dealt with human trafficking, namely *Last Resort*, *Dirty Pretty Things* (Stephen Frears, UK, 2002), *In This World* (Michael Winterbottom, UK, 2002), and *Lilja 4-ever* (*Lilya 4-ever*, Lukas Moodysson,

Sweden/Denmark, 2002). Given the amount of critical attention that these films have received, and since they all feature in each essay (albeit in different ways), we have chosen *not* to write about these particular films in the Close-Ups section. In keeping with the desire to 'make visible' other, perhaps less obvious films that deal with human trafficking, we have decided to include in this section analyses of the 15 other films mentioned above. These films come from a wide range of national and/or transnational contexts, with films whose action predominantly takes place in Austria, Belgium, France, Greece, Israel, Slovenia, Spain, Switzerland, the UK, and Yugoslavia. While set mainly in Europe, the films also deal with people involved in trafficking from all corners of the globe and from a range of races, religions and ethnicities. Finally, these films also span a range of genres and styles, including action films, documentaries, re-enactment films and social realist films.

Moving People, Moving Images ends with an overview by Leshu Torchin of how governmental and non-governmental organisations use films in their attempts to publicise and to implement initiatives against human trafficking. This chapter, 'Traffic Jam: Film, Activism, and Human Trafficking,' also provides information about the key initiatives that have been launched by filmmakers concerned with trafficking (e.g. Guy Moshe), as well as organisations that turn to film as a means for combating trafficking, especially through Public Service Announcements. Finally, Torchin looks at how film festivals have also begun to be used as a means of raising awareness about this critical social issue.

In the spirit of aiding in this activism, we have supplied details of websites for organisations that use film in a variety of ways to combat human trafficking. We hope that, even if in only the most modest of manners, *Moving People, Moving Images* itself can also help in the effort to eradicate this widespread problem.

Part One
Landscapes

Negotiating the Invisible

William Brown

Who needs trafficking and slavery? (Europe does)

Slavery is perhaps as old as human society itself. Its permanence as a(n often invisible) fixture in the history of humanity does not serve to justify the practice through trafficking of exploitation, both economic, physical and/or sexual, with which trafficking most commonly seems to be associated. However, the enduring nature of slavery and trafficking does serve to highlight the persistence of imbalances of power in the world: the contained slave is forced to provide unpaid or exploited labour for the cruel master. The continued onset of globalisation in the form of globalised capital, the creation and consolidation of the European Union, the end of the Cold War and the collapse of the former Soviet Union, intensified mass migrations of peoples from the so-called Third World to 'Western' or 'First' and 'Second' World nations, sometimes also referred to as the 'global North,' and the enormous social changes brought about by developments in telecommunications, transport and computer technologies, have all contributed to imbalances of power that are quantified typically as imbalances of economic wealth. An individual migrant may be highly educated and even relatively prosperous (see Kelly 2005), but, in needing (for non-financial reasons) to leave her country of origin – and in an illegal manner – she may find herself forced into the contemporary slave trade through trafficking. This is not to say that this hypothetical woman is not economically independent, therefore – at least, she may be economically independent *before* being forced into the slave trade via trafficking. But once engaged in the slave trade via bonded labour or debt bondage, she is deprived of power through economic exploitation (she is not paid [enough] for her labour), as well as, in the worst cases, through the removal of her human rights.

While illegal immigration and the subsequent use of human smugglers may not be motivated for financial reasons, therefore (one might illegally be smuggled across borders for political reasons), to come to be exploited in the contemporary slave trade and/or the inability legally to earn a living in the country entered, suggests a loss of power that is signified through a loss of economic power, as much as such a process might equally involve physical and sexual abuse. The reason for framing this argument through the concept of money/economic power is not to offer a xenophobic account concerning perceived hierarchies of wealth ('they come here to steal our money'), but rather to suggest that trafficking, from the perspective of the trafficker and/or the slave trader, (more often than not) involves the exploitation of the human beings that act as their 'cargo' or labour force. However, I do not simply want to suggest that a trafficker *de facto* exploits the people that he traffics; rather, I should like to suggest that this imbalance of power, this exploitation of immigrants who may have illegally entered into other territories for a multiplicity of reasons (many of which are discussed elsewhere in this volume), is based as much upon the viability of – and perhaps even the necessity for – an exploited labour force in the country or region in question (let us, for the sake of argument, be specific and say in the European Union), as it is upon those diverse reasons that motivated the (illegal) migration in the first place.

Of the workings of contemporary capitalism, Slavoj Žižek writes that

> the inherent structural dynamics of civil society necessarily give rise to a class which is excluded from the benefits of civil society, a class deprived of elementary human rights and therefore also delivered of duties towards society, an

element within civil society which negates its universal principle, a kind of 'un-Reason inherent to Reason itself' – in short, *its symptom* (1997: 46).

The psychoanalytic framework that Žižek provides for describing this 'symptom' is not as important as the process itself (although I shall refer back to the term 'symptom' later). This process is something that Daniela Flesler, drawing on the work of Michael Hardt and Antonio Negri (2000), has also identified with reference to Europe. Flesler writes:

> In the specific case of Europe, the opening of internal frontiers and the striving towards transnational integration goes hand in hand with the closure of its external frontiers to those perceived as threatening... Those who transgress the gates are criminalised, even when their labour is required for capitalist production itself (2004: 103).

In other words, Europe 'needs' disposable people as much as these people need – for whatever reason – to flee their country of origin, and it is a deep paradox that these 'required' people are systematically deprived of their rights institutionally (they are illegal immigrants with no rights in the eyes of the law), while being exploited/treated like (sex) slaves by those very people 'good' enough to take them in/ help them to get (t)here. With no legal support and with exploitation through slave labour as their only 'safe' option for subsistence, it should come as no surprise that some illegal immigrants, faced with the prospect of passive victimisation through bonded labour, turn to criminal activities, becoming active in and potentially perpetuating the very processes/trades (trafficking and slave labour themselves) passivity to which is what they sought to avoid in the first place.

Invisibility

When considering human trafficking into and within Europe, a deeper understanding of this phenomenon might be brought out by considering trafficking within the historical context of colonialism, and its progression through postcolonialism towards contemporary imperialism.

Fredric Jameson has argued that in the modernist era

the epistemological separation of colony from metropolis, the systematic occultation of the colony from metropolis, the systematic occultation of the colonial labour on which imperial prosperity is based, results in a situation in which (again using a Hegelian formula) the truth of the metropolitan experience is not visible in the daily life of the metropolis itself; it lies outside the immediate space of Europe, in the colonies. The existential realia of the metropolis are thus severed from the cognitive map that would alone lend them coherence and re-establish relationships of meaning and of its production (2003: 700).

I shall later discuss in greater depth the question of visibility as it relates to the representation of trafficking in cinema. At present, however, I refer to Jameson in order to suggest that trafficking to and within Europe, particularly as manifested through bonded labour and forced prostitution (which here I also consider a form of bonded labour), constitutes a new form or the continuation of colonialism by other means, even if this 'colonialism' is only tacitly (and not explicitly) endorsed – through the creation of the very conditions that enable it – by the host nations that do not do enough to eradicate it. That is, the sweat shop, the brothel and the so-called 'kiddie dungeon' all function, like the colony, as 'the truth of the metropolitan experience

[that] is not visible in the daily life of the metropolis itself.' Now, given that, as far as *Moving People, Moving Images* is concerned, these sweat shops, brothels and dungeons often *do* exist either within the metropolis or, at the very least, within Europe, it is possible to identify trafficking as different from colonialism. But the invisibility of the sweat shop, etc., involves the same process of the 'systematic occultation of the labour on which imperial prosperity is based,' and it is for this reason that the comparison between trafficking and colonialism is useful.

What is more, those unfortunate enough to have found themselves the victims – whether consenting or coerced – of contemporary trafficking as understood here are demonised in much the same way as the colonised were by the inhabitants of the metropolitan centre, and this demonisation is based upon the economic reality of (enforced) poverty. As A. Sivanandan says in the construction of his argument that 'poverty is the new black,' 'they demonised the "coloureds" to justify colonialism. Today they demonise asylum seekers [and, by extension, both traffickers and, more pertinently, the trafficked] to justify the ways of globalism' (2002: 2).

As a term used to describe the end of the colonial era, postcolonialism privileges European colonialism as its *raison d'être*, and for this reason it can be construed as a term that is Eurocentric (Higbee 2007a). Although the term is problematic, therefore, postcolonialism has historically offered a corrective to the process of exploitation as institutionalised by colonialism. However, no such corrective is formally or even theoretically in place for the victims of what I shall characterise as the 'imperial' practice of trafficking.

In fact, without wishing to imply that there is more bonded labour in Europe than in the rest of the world (there is not), it is perhaps inevitable that invisible bonded labour should take place within Europe precisely because postcolonialism and other 'liberating' discourses and practices have made the Third World more 'visible' (to Europeans). If the labour force that was the Third World was invisibly exploited during colonialism, and if postcolonialism sought and seeks to make visible and to bring to an end that exploitation (which does continue), then in the imperialist era, it is logical that some of that exploitation should be brought into Europe, rather than kept in the now-exposed Third World, precisely because within Europe it can be kept invisible. In other words, if imperialism has replaced colonialism, then part of the imperialist project has been to bring the 'Third World' into Europe so that the illegal but demanded ('required') taskforce that bonded labour supplies can be kept hidden and invisible (even if there is as much, if not more, bonded labour outside of Europe as well).

And yet this unfortunate progression is overlooked by many theorists. Perry Anderson writes that 'the normalcy of servants' allowed for 'a distinctive upper-class mode of life right down to the end of the 30s' (1984: 106), but in suggesting that there is no longer a servant class within Europe, he discounts precisely those who do still persist as 'servants' or, worse, slaves for a European *bourgeois* existence. In addition, when Gilles Deleuze argues that 'capitalism is no longer involved in production, which it often relegates to the Third World, even for the complex forms of textiles, metallurgy, or oil production' (1992: 6), he of course points to continuing exploitation in and of the Third World, but he also overlooks the way in which many centres of production, such as sweat shops, exist within Europe. And yet one can forgive Anderson and Deleuze their oversights, not because to overlook the contemporary slave trade saves one from silent complicity with it, but precisely because the world of trafficking and the trafficked, not least within Europe, remains *invisible*.

Matters of Eurocentrism and the Transnational

If postcolonialism is a term that risks Eurocentrism, in that it foregrounds the colonial at the expense of those that colonialism exploited, suggesting somehow that postcolonialism only exists because the colonialists have authorised it, then the texts cited above from Anderson and Deleuze might also smack of 'unthinking Eurocentrism' (Shohat & Stam 1994) because they fail to recognise Europe's continued involvement in otherwise invisible processes of exploitation within Europe. In effect, as befits a globalised planet in which the formerly strict boundaries between nations have been eroded, the exploitation of humans via imperialist practices no longer respects geographical borders (exploitation happens 'over there' in the Third World), but instead becomes ubiquitous. Exploitation less identifiably becomes a matter of geography, then, and more a matter of what I shall term class: if traffickers/slave drivers in Europe hold their labourers prisoner, be that through miserable wages, systems of debt, or through literal incarceration, those labourers are treated as if they belonged to a perceived 'Third World' *class* of citizens, even if physically/geographically they exist within the so-called 'First' or 'Second' Worlds.

And yet, if Anderson and Deleuze respectively suggest that class is no longer an issue, and that geography is, then they might be redeemed in the face of recent developments in the understanding of space and place as theorised through and represented in the concept of the transnational, especially as articulated within Film Studies. That is to say, in opposition to the Eurocentric notions of centre/Europe and periphery/colonies, there has arisen the study of films that deal precisely with peoples who migrate between these two supposed poles of contemporary existence, as well as those who occupy liminal spaces that cannot easily be identified as belonging to one or the other. For example, Dina Iordanova argues that

East and West, North and South, centre and periphery are no longer useful as meaningful grid coordinates, and entrenched spatial division lines gradually become void of meaning. The hierarchy of places is subverted and changed 'from below,' revealed in films that come from all possible corners of the world and made by directors who work independently from one another. This discourse on place is no longer a prerogative of the 'centre' reflecting on its 'margins.' What formerly was deemed a 'periphery' is endowed with new vitality that challenges the traditional narratives of locale and movement and replaces them with new takes on place and itinerary (2001a).

One should perhaps be grateful for a 'transnational' cinema that is, after Ulf Hannerz (quoted in Bergfelder 2005), transnational in that it transcends national boundaries rather than simply being or belonging to multiple, distinct nations. However, while slavery and the human trafficking that enables it are a global 'epidemic' (Bales, Trodd & Williamson 2009), in the European context it becomes hard to ignore the difference between centre and periphery when trying to conceptualise this phenomenon – as represented in contemporary cinema, and perhaps in and of itself – because the predominant direction of trafficking would seem to be from margin ('Third World') to centre (Europe). In other words, if trafficking is itself a global 'pandemic' (see Laczko & Gozdziak 2005), then research into it perhaps remains Eurocentric (and necessarily so for Europeans?). Anderson and Deleuze cannot help being Eurocentric; they are European, after all.

It is worth lingering on this perceived directionality of trafficking through the introduction of evidence from films. Most films dealing with the issue of trafficking in particular, but also with illegal immigration in general, depict the journey of human beings from non-European and poorer countries to Europe. Many of these have been named in the Introduction and/or are covered in the Close-Ups section of this book, but I might also mention: *Cartas de Alou* (*Letters from Alou*, Montxo Armendáriz, Spain, 1990), *La Promesse* (*The Promise*, Jean-Pierre and Luc Dardenne, Belgium/France/Luxembourg, 1996), *La vie nouvelle* (*A New Life*, Philippe Grandrieux, France, 2002), and *The Transporter* (Corey Yuen, France/USA, 2002). Even if the initial motivation for leaving one's homeland is not economic opportunism (making money in Europe), but something else, in particular economic *necessity*, which is a factor discussed in the subsequent chapters and throughout *Moving People, Moving Images*, the impression given by such accounts is that Europe is the destination/centre, while the place left behind is peripheral/marginal. As much is emphasised by the frequent impossibility of a return home, or that the (enforced) return home somehow involves 'failure' – although Nick Broomfield's *Ghosts* (UK, 2006) in particular might operate contrary to this in that the surviving cockle picker, Ai Qin (played by herself), seems happier back in China than she did in Morecombe Bay. Eurocentrism is also emphasised by the way in which characters sometimes prefer seemingly to endure slave labour and/or to die than to return home – as if even such terrible conditions are *still* better than life in the Third World. Perhaps the impression that even death in the First World is better than life in the Third comes about through one or more of several possible failures on the part of the filmmakers. Firstly, the filmmakers might fail properly to convey the characters' inability to escape those who keep them in bondage, or, secondly, they might fail to make clear the reasons for which the characters trafficked *cannot* return home. That is, the filmmakers might fail to explain that the characters miss home and would prefer to be there, but that a return for them is, for any of a number of reasons, impossible. On account of these potential shortcomings, there is a risk that these films, whether directly or otherwise, reaffirm Eurocentric beliefs (for the European audience, arguably the prime audience for which these films are made), namely that Europe is 'better' than the Third World, that Europe is the 'centre' where all from the periphery wish to live, or whither they wish to escape because life back home is 'so bad.'

This Eurocentrism can also be seen reaffirmed in the counterpart to the trafficking film, which I might define as the 'gap year' film. That is, films in which characters travel from the developed world/Europe to the Third World, not because they have to, but out of choice. Here, the protagonists function in part as tourists, even if they work in their country of destination. They are tourists because they always return home (to the West). Examples might include *The Beach* (Danny Boyle, USA/UK, 1999), *Shooting Dogs* (Michael Caton-Jones, UK/Germany, 2005), and *The Last King of Scotland* (Kevin Macdonald, UK, 2006). The Eurocentrism of these films is affirmed not just through the decision to have the problems of a country (Thailand, Rwanda, Uganda) seen through the eyes of a Western protagonist, but also through the fact that the Western protagonist ends up leaving his country of destination in order to return home – the implication being that one cannot hope to resolve the problems in such places and that life is 'better' back home. In effect, for (Western) Europeans, nomadism is a luxury and an *escape* from the sedentariness of life; it is neither a necessity nor, as those coerced into slave labour might construe their fate, an arbitrary punishment for trying to leave home (for more on 'nomadic' tourism in European cinema, see Mazierska & Rascaroli 2006).

In his consideration of national identity and the idea of European unity, Anthony D. Smith posits that '[t]here is the prospect of an increasingly affluent, stable, conservative but democratic European federation, facing, and protecting itself from, the demands and needs of groupings of states in Africa, Asia and Latin America' (1992: 76). I do not have space at present to consider what these African, Asian and Latin American groupings might be, but Smith's argument that

Europe might need to protect itself is indeed suggested by the illegal nature of immigration into (the) Europe(an Union), as well as by the bonded labour of trafficked peoples, which exists as a phenomenon *internal* to Europe in order to confirm its economic superiority (slaves as a new servant class) and its own centrality (everyone wants to get in). Even though immigration, slavery and nomadism are pan-global phenomena, the resurrection of the new 'Iron Curtain' that surrounds 'Fortress Europe' (Prout 2006) serves only to prioritise Europe's own sense of centrality. Immigration in general may serve to 'suggest that there has rarely been a space that can be defended against an *outside* of which "Europe" is the *inside*' (Elsaesser 2006: 647), and it may lead people to question the notion of centre and periphery (Iordanova 2001a, quoted above), but trafficking, and the illegal slave trade that often is its direct consequence, cannot but paradoxically reaffirm Europe's sense of its own centrality. Not because the illegal entry of those smuggled into Europe does not blur the rigid borders that separate Europe's 'insiders' from these 'other' outsiders, but because, once allowed into Europe, their presence is suppressed in the form of slavery; their very invisibility, the failure to recognise or to remember them, in spite of the fact that trafficked humans are the supply for a European demand (Taylor & Jamieson 1999), reaffirms Eurocentrism, for having slaves that are in one sense invisible is (again, paradoxically) to make visible one's 'superiority'/power. Power can only exist as a relative phenomenon: one is more powerful than/ superior to someone else. Trafficked humans are invisible – in that they are not recognised – but they are also visible in that their very existence is and must be quasi-recognised in order to satisfy the European's Eurocentric sense of power (power *over* someone else).

As Isolina Ballesteros argues,

> [t]he issue of migration is driven by a restrictive agenda
> that is based on the distorted perception that Europe has

become a magnet to the world's dispossessed and on the unrealistic view that there is no real structural demand for labour in EU countries ('invasion psychosis')....
In spite of empirical evidence that demonstrates that immigrants raise productivity and make the countries more competitive internationally... they are collectively used as scapegoats (2005: 3).

This paradox, that trafficked humans/contemporary slaves are invisible (they have no rights; Europeans do not recognise them except, on occasion, in a paternalistic manner), and yet also visible (Europeans know that they exist, from every nanny who is paid less than minimum wage, to prostitutes held prisoner in brothels in London's East End), helps Europeans to create a sense of their own power. It is also key to the issue of trafficking that is here at stake: Europeans are complicit in the perpetuation of this imbalance of power. Threatened by the entrepreneurial spirit of illegal immigrants who are perceived as taking 'European' jobs and money in quasi-legal ways (legal work performed by illegal immigrants), perhaps Europeans are secretly glad even that traffickers exist in order to minimise through exploitation, slavery, humiliation, violence, etc., the 'theft' to be performed by these illegal immigrants whose services they in fact 'require' (Hardt & Negri 2000: 122). Enforced poverty and humiliation is indeed the outlet for the European's (the human's) lowest urges, their hatred (slaves as 'scapegoats').

A centre without a centre

If European films dealing with trafficking reaffirm Europe as centre (to Europeans), they do not necessarily reaffirm Europe itself as having a centre. Drawing on Marc Augé's much-cited *Non-Places: Introduction to an Anthropology of Supermodernity* (1995), Verena Berger and Daniel Winkler (2006) affirm that films such as *Letters from Alou*, *Pummarò* (Michele Placido, Italy, 1990), *La faute à Voltaire* (*Blame it on Voltaire*, Abdel Kechiche, France, 2000), and *Quando sei nato non puoi più nasconderti* (*Once You're Born You Can No Longer Hide*, Marco Tullio Giordana, Italy/France/UK, 2005) depict 'irregular migrants' working and living in non-places such as Europe's subways, parks and airports, and in places usually under-represented in cinema, such as the Parisian *banlieue*, the Spanish countryside, and Italy's island of Lampedusa. Non-places, 'anonymous' zones that proliferate in the contemporary world, or during the period that Augé terms 'supermodernity,' do not belong identifiably to centre or periphery, but somewhere in between. As a result, they blur easy definitions of centre and periphery within Europe (even if Europe as a whole continues to project itself as a/the centre). However, while Berger and Winkler identify how non-places figure in many contemporary narratives of irregular migration and labour, they perhaps fail to take Augé to task for his own Eurocentrism. Augé posits that to be in a non-place grants one temporary anonymity. He continues: '[n]o doubt the relative anonymity that goes with this temporary identity can even be felt as a liberation, by people who, for a time, have only to keep in line, go where they are told, check their appearance' (Augé 1995: 101). However, I shall argue against Augé that what in non-places is liberation for some (Europeans) is incarceration for others (those trafficked), and that, given that contemporary slaves must remain invisible/anonymous, it makes sense for them to occupy and to be held in these non-places. Not that these non-places have been designed for the purpose of housing peoples that Europe wishes to keep invisible, but the use of such non-places to house these 'invisible' people does serve to suggest a 'natural' affinity of one to the other, a process that in turn serves to naturalise trafficking and exploitation: exploitation is necessary for Europe's conception of itself as powerful centre, but if formerly this exploitation took place elsewhere in the invisible colonies, now, in the imperial era (if I can call it such), this exploitation also takes place *elsewhere within* Europe – in non-places.

This is not to suggest that 'Europe' exists as an easy unity. Far from it, since, as Smith points out, (Southern and Eastern) Europe still has its own 'internal peasant classes' whose ability to derive a sense of European identity is indeed up for debate (1992: 72). Smith also argues that the proliferation of 'large-scale "European" music festivals and travelling art exhibitions... testify [not only] to a new "European spirit"... [but also] as expressions of local pride, be it in Edinburgh, Spoleto, Moscow or Leeds, in the Royal Academy or the Louvre or the Prado' (1992: 71-72). Here there is a sense in which the global is accompanied by the local, such that globalisation is perhaps better referred to as 'glocalisation' (Bauman 1998). And yet, I would argue that the disappearance of a centre within Europe, simultaneous to the affirmation of Europe's sense of self as global centre, is also a logical function of the rise of exploitative labour conditions. For, while Europe's self-promotion as centre serves to reflect its own sense of power, a sense of power enabled by the existence of an internal servant/slave class upon whose labour Europe in part depends, the lack of an identifiable centre within Europe not only serves to make these trafficked peoples invisible (they exist in non-places), but it also serves to hide any sense of shame Europe might feel for this knowing-unknowing exploitation (we know it happens; we don't know where it happens) by depriving both the exploited and those who seek to eradicate the exploiters of any easy target. Since the contemporary slave trade always happens elsewhere, even, or rather especially, within Europe, Europeans can never find it, even if they might denounce it. Even if this is not a deliberate policy (it is not one), this seems to serve as an unconscious mechanism enabling Europeans always to deny any association with the contemporary practice of trafficking, even if they know that it exists.

Another mechanism that serves to cover over, or to make invisible trafficking the very (in)visibility of which serves to reaffirm a European sense of centrality (even within a Europe that has no 'centre'), is an illusory sense of kinship that one might feel for those trafficked. This sense of kinship is not uniquely one raised by cinematic identification (I understand better the plight of trafficked humans by seeing films that represent them), although this is an issue to which I shall return. Rather, this kinship is again one brought about by the conditions of (super?)modernity. As much already seems to be implied in Augé's argument that non-places can be empowering through a sense of anonymity for the European citizen. Forced to stand in line, to obey rather than to choose, the European feels liberated in non-places, a process that has as its counterpart the myth that the illegal immigrant forced to work for less than minimum wage (i.e. the contemporary slave) is similarly *liberated* by being in Europe and by not being at home.

Of the contemporary age, Michel de Certeau (1984) argues that '[t]here is no longer an elsewhere… Consumers are transformed into immigrants. The system in which they move about is too vast to be able to fix them in one place, but too constraining for them ever to be able to escape from it' (quoted in Bukatman 1993: 212). De Certeau's argument that there is no longer an elsewhere might seem to contradict the argument above that trafficking always already takes place elsewhere. However, I should contest that the transformation of consumers into immigrants, who are constantly on the move, serves to highlight the way in which Europeans might come to project some sense of kinship with the trafficked person: the European can believe that they and the trafficked person are both nomadic peoples who travel within the 'system,' albeit that the European consumer travels for leisure (to consume) and the trafficked person may travel to find work (to produce). However, the false kinship between European and trafficked person takes on another layer of meaning when the invasion of computer technologies into the home is taken into consideration. The ability always to be online and in touch with everyone else does not so much suggest a liberation from work (one can work anywhere, even on the beach), as the colonisation of leisure time by work, as the enslavement to work. In other words, if everyone is a nomad or a migrant, in an online world everyone is also always working. Like the trafficked human who is forced to work impossibly long shifts in the sweat shop, the European can argue (and thus justify the treatment of the trafficked human) that they, too, are slaves to their work. In other words, contemporary slavery is always elsewhere, because the labour conditions of the master (labour colonises leisure, such that labour and leisure become indistinguishable) are 'equal' to that of the slave. That is, the master can justify the enslavement of the slave by arguing that, in a world where everyone is always working, there is no slavery at all (or, conversely, 'everyone in Europe is already a slave, so welcome to Europe, slave!').

The disposable body

What this kinship glosses over, however, and which makes it illusory, is the difference in mobility between trafficked person and European, a difference that is centred upon questions of the body and upon the nature of labour in the contemporary world. I have already cited Gilles Deleuze (1992) in pointing out that production is deferred to the Third World in the contemporary era. Trafficked humans in Europe, meanwhile, are forced to labour in sweatshops and brothels that exist *within* Europe. Although prostitution is not necessarily a form of 'production,' it does constitute, however problematically, a form of physical labour, as do sweatshops, farms, etc., and while physical labour does persist in Europe (farming, construction work, etc.), it is work that, in Western Europe if not elsewhere, is increasingly 'devolved' (again, problematically) to Europeans from the former Eastern Bloc (Poland, etc.), to non-Europeans who work at competitive rates (illegal and entrepreneurial immigrants carrying out legal work), to non-Europeans who are exploited (illegal immigrants carrying out legal work but engaged in employment in an exploitative manner, i.e. poorly paid, if at all), to non-Europeans who engage/are engaged in quasi-legal work (e.g. prostitution), both in an entrepreneurial manner (self-motivated, well paid) and in an exploitative manner (coerced, poorly paid, if at all). Without spending too long picking through these various forms of labour, I should say that they are united by their physical nature, requiring the presence of a body (or, in the case of online sex rooms, the image of a body) in order to be fulfilled. This can be compared to the European *bourgeoisie* that decreasingly engages in physical labour (and this is not to overlook the plight of those non-immigrant labourers – builders, etc. – who, typically in the specifically national context, find themselves undercut by 'foreign' competition and perhaps seriously deprived of income), and which increasingly performs 'symbolic' labour, which can be conceptualised by the production, reproduction and distribution of signs – in the form of texts, sounds and images – via their computer screens and other contemporary interfaces. The body is no longer required to be present at the site of labour (although the convention does persist that one 'goes to work'), precisely because the work is not physical (and thus the site of labour does not even exist as such). Although they are not the only ones to carry out physical labour that requires the presence of the body – and although not all those who are trafficked carry out this form of labour – we might hypothesise that trafficked people perform physical labour/labour that requires the presence of the body, be it legal, quasi-legal or illegal. Compared to the nomadism of the contemporary 'consumer,' therefore, the trafficked person is not just enslaved by work, but enslaved physically by work, sometimes in the most horrendous ways imaginable.

Permanently to be working is to devalue labour, in that there arises an imbalance between time spent working and remuneration (one is supposed to work a set number of hours in the week, a number of hours that matches one's salary, but one inevitably works longer hours; or one works longer hours in order to supplement one's otherwise insufficient wage). Again, that this devaluation of labour exists both in 'normal' society and for the trafficked person suggests the possibility of kinship or identification, but the foregrounding of the body in the case of the trafficked person suggests a difference in work that the myth of bondage (everybody is a slave) glosses over. In effect, the European is a slave to the system, while the trafficked person is a slave for the system, a person who undergoes a much more dangerous form of bondage (dangerous precisely because it involves labour that marks and affects the body) so that the European can remain in their 'safe'/abstract 'bondage.' The invisibility of the trafficked person, however, means that the European can make the following observation: 'The devaluation of labour implies the obsolescence of the body' (Bukatman 1993: 302). It might seem odd to evoke Scott Bukatman's landmark work on science fiction, *Terminal Identity: The Virtual Subject in Post-Modern Science Fiction*, in a work on trafficking as portrayed in contemporary European cinema, but the fate of the body in a technologised society has its inverse in the form of the trafficked person, whose devalued body enables the obsolescence of physical labour for the European *bourgeoisie*. In effect, since the trafficked person is invisible, so too is their physical labour.

The invisibility of labour brings to mind an anecdote supposedly told by Emir Kusturica, and referred to by Slavoj Žižek in his criticism of Kusturica's film *Bila jednom jedna zemlja* (*Underground*, France/Yugoslavia/Germany, 1995):

Kusturica refers here to the old European fairy-tale motif of diligent dwarfs (usually controlled by an evil magician) who, during the night, while people are asleep, emerge from their hiding-place and accomplish their work (set the house in order, cook the meals), so that when, in the morning, people awaken, they find their work magically done (Žižek 1997: 39).

Involved here is all the rhetoric of the (advertently or not) exploitative European who remains ignorant of/ignores the *real* work carried out by the 'sub-human' slave class ('dwarfs'), construing its achievements as 'magic' because the European's own body, in the technological age that we currently inhabit, is obsolete.

Tension regarding the obsolescence of the (Western/European) body is manifested in several possible ways. Bukatman explains how '[v]iruses and parasites demonstrate vulnerability of the body to invasion from without; telepathy and physical projection break down the dichotomy between public and private; subjectivity and temporality collapse; man merges with machine: we have arrived in a zone without borders' (1993: 268). In other words, anxiety concerning the obsolescence of the body is articulated in science fiction cinema – and in mainstream cinema more generally – through fears concerning the *penetration* and *fragmentation* of the body, which is imagined as having previously been an integrated and unified whole. Needles, machines, bodily dismemberment: all seem to reinforce the same 'crisis' of the body in a technological age where physical labour has indeed been devalued. And the flipside to these manifestations of contemporary anxiety concerning the body comes in the form of ultra-mobile heroes, who can perform impossible feats of agility and dexterity, or who celebrate the exceptional mobility enabled by transport and/or telecommunications technology: travel and instant contact with other human beings on the other side of the planet.

The anxiety concerning the break-up of the coherent body can be understood not just according to the technologisation of society, but also as a result of the disintegration of formerly fixed national borders and identities, wherein it is not so much a machine or a virus that will penetrate the protagonist's body, but legal or illegal immigrants who enter the nation to disrupt the national body. For example, in Imanol Uribe's *Bwana* (Spain, 1996), the illegal immigrant (Emilio Buale), who has just come off a clandestine boat trip from Africa to Almería in the south of Spain, is seen as a threat to the masculinity of Madrileño taxi driver Antonio (Andrés Pajares). The immigrant, referred to in the literature as Ombasi, arrives at a time when Antonio's advanced mobility is threatened (he loses the spark plug to his taxi, which consequently will not start); and Ombasi's physical presence, which becomes the object of affection for Antonio's wife, Dori (María Barranco), threatens to compromise Antonio's own physical 'superiority.' It is notable that only when Ombasi is attacked by a group of neo-Nazis does Antonio manage to restart his taxi, and he drives away, abandoning Ombasi to his assailants, presumably because to help him would continue to remind him of his reliance upon transport/technology for mobility, and his physical obsolescence (Antonio is useless when pitted against nature, while Ombasi is able to start fires, etc.).

Concomitant to the obsolescence of the European (here, Spanish) body is the exoticisation of the foreign body, which is mythologised as whole and strong. Certainly, Ombasi/Buale is muscular, but the representation of his character as he basks naked in the sunrise suggests some sort of fetishisation of the other that smacks of a patronising exoticisation, an exoticisation that is reinforced by Uribe's decision not to have translated in the form of subtitles the words that Ombasi speaks in his native language, even if the intention of this technique is to convey the Spaniards' inability to comprehend and/or to assimilate this other. (For more on *Bwana*, see Santaolalla 1999.)

Jameson notes that 'each mode of production generates its own unique and specific temporality; the premise no doubt posits the primacy of labour time, implying that the temporality of a given type of production has a more general influence on the way time is conceptualised and lived in the rest of the society' (2003: 707). Jameson's emphasis on labour might go against the argument posited above that labour has been devalued for the Westerner/ European, while labour does remain relevant for the trafficked person, whose work often remains physical (and unpleasant) in nature. Or rather, if each mode of production produces its own temporality, then herein lies the difference between the European who is a slave to abstract labour and the trafficked person who is a physical slave for the European's system of abstract labour. A mode of production that is abstract and technological in nature produces a different temporality to one that remains physical. In Jameson's words, the present becomes, for the European 'symbolic' worker, 'self-sufficient and autonomous and independent in quite a different fashion from [the] dimensions of past and future' (2003: 711). This 'reduction to the present'…

> …is also a reduction to something else, something rather more material than eternity as such. Indeed, it seems clear enough that when you have nothing left but your temporal present, it follows that you also have nothing left but your own body. The reduction to the present can thus also be formulated in terms of a reduction to the body as a present of time (2003: 712).

Again, Jameson's argument that the body is reaffirmed as the only measure of time might seem to contradict the notion that the Western/European body is 'obsolete' in the technological era. However, the reduction of experience to the body would paradoxically reaffirm its own obsolescence: with only the body to experience the world, and with no past or future shaping our experiences, it would make sense that it is at this moment that the body is most under threat. Dislocated from the world, unhinged from a perceptible relationship with past and future, the body is isolated, alone, useless, and thus obsolete.

But of what relevance is Jameson's argument to my consideration of trafficked peoples in contemporary cinema? Being marked as other, either by the camera or by society itself, the trafficked person retains an enforced association with the past. That is, the trafficked person is denied access to the perpetual present of the Euro-centre, precisely because their body retains/ is forced to retain an association with its past, a trend that finds its most extreme and thus most tangible expression in the form of racism (difference based on visible differences in skin colour), but which also manifests itself across cultures, accents, styles of dress and so on. And it is an enforced temporality or mode of existence that sees as its offshoot the inducement of nostalgia for the homeland, nostalgia that serves only to intensify the association of past to present for the trafficked person (and the immigrant, legal or otherwise, more generally), and which allows the European further to 'other' the trafficked person (and the immigrant more generally) for not belonging to the same temporality as him.

It is an irony inherent in this system that the trafficked person is locked into an 'old' and immobile form of labour (incarceration in sweat shops, on farms, in brothels), itself another association with the past imposed upon the trafficked person that enables both the perpetual present of the European and his ability to view the trafficked person as irrevocably 'other.' Simultaneously, it paradoxically traps the trafficked person into a temporality that involves both perpetual labour (forced always to work), but which has a past (a time before slavery) as well as a potential future (a time freed from slavery). It is a further irony that the labour of the trafficked person is physical in nature – it involves the body – in such a way that it permits the obsolescence of the European body. Devalued, the trafficked body has use, while the useless European body has pure surplus value. Trafficking in the contemporary era suggests the Marxist revolution gone horribly wrong: use has become wholly divorced from (perceived) value; in fact, the two seem to be inversely proportional. Paradoxically, by perpetuating slavery, which in some respects might constitute the very historical bedrock of capitalist production and consumption, Europeans can through trafficking live in the 'post-capitalist' age at the 'end of history,' living, like the thinkers in Fritz Lang's *Metropolis* (Germany, 1927), separated from and blind to the workers that perpetuate the luxury in which they *un*thinkingly abide. The moment in history in which humans can 'abandon history' is based upon the necessarily invisible perpetuation of historical forms of society (slavery) and 'historical'/physical forms of labour (including prostitution).

In this light, trafficking can be seen to constitute the perpetuation of colonialism in imperialism, but it is a colonialism/imperialism that is internal, or which involves the importation (and occultation) of labour, rather than the outward looking form that was invisible to the colonialist residents 'back home,' but plainly visible to the colonised. Isolina Ballesteros makes a similar point in relation to prostitution: '[t]he proliferation of prostitution networks, that include importing "exotic" women as well as sending sexual tourists to "exotic" countries (mainly Cuba and the Dominican Republic), have contributed to the perpetuation of a cliché ingrained in the colonial imagining of "Otherness"' (2005: 9).

With regard to enforced prostitution networks, not only do we see here the perpetuation of sexism in the form of the exploitation of women for the benefit of masculine pleasure, but the arguably masculine agenda behind the liberalisation of European societies can perhaps be recognised in literal form. Taylor and Jamieson point out that

Herbert Marcuse saw the developing commercial exploitation of sexual desire of that period [the 1960s] (the highpoint of *Playboy* magazine) as evidence of what he called 'the repressive toleration' of a capitalist society – the establishment of a delimited zone of purported 'liberation' in an otherwise alienated and firmly regulated social and economic landscape (1999: 264).

This is not to provide an overdetermined reading of liberalisation as being authored/authorised uniquely by men, but it is to signal that the entrapment of women in systems of enforced prostitution, arranged marriages, 'mail order brides,' and so on, all of which relate directly or indirectly to trafficking, as a 'liberalisation' that in fact has at its core the continued repression of the female. Without wishing to offer a reactionary argument along the lines of 'faithful and lifelong monogamy is best,' I would like tentatively to suggest that liberalisation can be read as involving the continued repression of women; and while some (European) women are also liberated through this process, perhaps enforced prostitution (and paedophile rings) are the manifestations of the darkest and most repressive aspects of this 'liberalising' trend in European society.

Speed/slowness

Liberated, the European body can move freely through the globe, in a perpetual state of tourism, enabled by transport and telecommunications technologies. The mobility of the European is characterised by its sheer speed. Meanwhile, the trafficked person may have been able to travel – though typically in closed, windowless and dangerous containers – but she also finds herself rendered immobile and trapped in her place of destination, an immobility rendered all the more ironic given that the trafficked person is surrounded by transport technologies, such as trains, 'planes and automobiles, which travel from place to place via the non-places that are nodes of mobility such as the Metro station, the airport and the service station. The internet may allow virtual travel and freedom of mobility, but even those who are forced to offer up images of their bodies online, as happens to Olga (Ekateryna Rak) in *Import/Export* (Ulrich Seidl, Austria/France/Germany, 2007) and as may happen to Tanya (Dina Korzun) in *Last Resort* (Pawel Pawlikowski, UK, 2000), are rendered immobile, imprisoned in small rooms in which these and other women must cavort, trapped furthermore by the immobile and small-scale frame of the webcam. The rooms only have one window, a computer screen, and this window does not let in light but the aggressive gaze of the libidinous male.

If the extreme mobility of the European is characterised by *speed*, then a film that wishes to represent sympathetically the plight of the immobile trafficked person might do well to be characterised by its inverse, *slowness*. Herein I shall draw distinctions between the various kinds of films that involve depictions of trafficking in the contemporary era. Mainstream European films reflect the ease of mobility of their characters by being fast-moving and involving intense excitement as created by the speed of cutting, even when these films take human trafficking as their theme. Examples include *The Transporter* series (various directors, France/USA, 2002-2008) and *Taken* (Pierre Morel, France, 2008), all of which are produced by Luc Besson at EuropaCorp. These films do not take into any real account the fate of the trafficked person, instead preferring to reflect the hyperkinetic experiences of its mobile heroes. As such, these films might be deemed 'irresponsible' in their inability to see trafficking as anything other than an exciting quest in which the European hero might become involved, a technique that leaves the trafficked person as an exotic other. More 'artistic' portrayals of trafficking, however, might be slow and involve barely mobile cameras so as to reflect the plight of the trafficked persons. Examples might include

Import/Export, *Last Resort* and *Ghosts*, although I should like briefly to discuss a different film, *Dernier maquis* (*Adhen*, Rabah Ameur-Zaïmeche, France/Algeria, 2008).

Adhen is about a group of immigrant workers at a palette factory on the outskirts of Paris, near Orly airport. Although their legal status as immigrants is not made explicitly clear, one suspects that the workers are not working legally (even though the work that they do is legal and necessary), since they are exploited by their boss, Mao (Rabah Ameur-Zaïmeche), who does not pay them regularly or enough, but who instead tries to pacify them by constructing in the factory a mosque (and problematically choosing for his workers an imam [Larbi Zekkour] that will do Mao's bidding). Set in the shadow of Orly, the take-offs and landings from which constantly affect the soundscape of the film, the workers lead, after Giorgio Agamben (1998), 'bare' lives in a makeshift village. Characterised by immobile frames and long takes of the characters working, this 'slow' film culminates in three mechanics, whom Mao wishes to lay off, going on strike. The unnamed mechanics (played by Salim Ameur-Zaïmeche, Abel Jafri, and Sylvain Roume) barricade themselves into the palette factory and, in the build-up to their confrontation with Mao, they drive around in small fork-lift trucks. Driving the fork-lifts is understood as being one of the most exciting aspects of work at the factory, and so the mobility that the fork-lifts enable for the mechanics is presented as a joyful release from the immobile lifestyle that they otherwise typically lead. (Mao, on the other hand, drives a nice-looking saloon car.) Not only is Ameur-Zaïmeche's film 'slow,' therefore, but what mobility it shows its characters as having does not need to be enacted as some climactic release of tension (even though the film does have a 'climax' in the form of the strike), but instead is deliberately understated, in order more forcefully to remind viewers of the immobility that these exploited peoples face. And all the while, heard but never seen, the Europeans fly overhead in their ultra-mobile 747s, inversing the relationship between 'trafficked' person and European, in that here the European is invisible, if heard, while normally it is the trafficked person who remains invisible to the European.

In contrast to the Besson-produced films, Ameur-Zaïmeche's *Adhen* can be understood as a film that tries in its form to reflect and/or be sympathetic to the plight of exploited humans that are its subject matter/content (even if these humans are not literally slaves here; they feel that they can and do go on strike, after all). However, I should like to end this chapter by exploring further these notions of visibility and invisibility and how they relate to film form, particularly as a film's form might be understood as making it 'sympathetic to' the plight of trafficked humans or not.

Who can speak?

Ameur-Zaïmeche is perhaps the strongest of a new generation of *beur* directors in France, a second generation French-Algerian making films that reflect upon the experience of those who exist at the margins of French society. As has been made clear in work by Carrie Tarr (2005; 2007) and Will Higbee (2007a; 2007b), France has a strong tradition in allowing immigrant filmmakers to make films about their own experiences, a tradition that can also be seen in Austria, Germany, Sweden and Switzerland. In certain parts of Europe, however, this phenomenon is barely to be seen. In Spain and Italy, for example, films such as *Letters from Alou*, *Bwana*, *Saïd* (Llorenç Soler, Spain, 1998), *Poniente* (Chus Gutiérrez, Spain, 2002), *Ilegal* (Ignacio Vilar, Spain, 2003), and *Pummarò* and *Once You're Born You Can No Longer Hide*, are made by non-immigrant (i.e. 'white') filmmakers (see Santaolalla 2000; Berger & Winkler 2006) and, as a result, these films express a Eurocentric anxiety, in either a literal or a figurative manner, over the instability of national identities within Europe and perhaps even over the instability of European identity itself. Films such as *The Promise*, *Last Resort*,

Dirty Pretty Things (Stephen Frears, UK, 2002), *In This World*, *Lilja 4-ever* (*Lilya 4-ever*, Lukas Moodysson, Sweden/Denmark, 2002), and *Le Silence de Lorna* (*The Silence of Lorna*, Jean-Pierre and Luc Dardenne, Belgium/France/Italy/Germany, 2008) may, in the light of Europe's unstable identity, endeavour to critique the efforts for Europe to retain a stable identity in an era when the flow of labour and capital itself extends beyond the borders of the European Union, or they may seek to offer the perspective of the trafficked person. But in spite of all of these kinds of films, there persists a problem when it comes to the representation of trafficked peoples.

This problem can be articulated as a question: can there be a film made by a person trafficked into Europe, or *must* trafficked peoples be represented by the Europeans that are complicit in their fates? For a trafficking film to be made by a trafficked person, the trafficked person must by definition be liberated from their imprisonment/slavery. Although Bales, Trodd and Williamson (2009) point out that most bonded labour is temporary (there is no point keeping slaves for any longer than is necessary/profitable), human trafficking and the bonded labour that is often its consequence are often terminal (the act of smuggling humans across borders alone results in at least 10,000 deaths by drowning, suffocation, etc., each year; see Berger & Winkler 2006). Furthermore, given the invisibility of trafficked people, to allow a trafficked person to make a film would be to ask for the impossible: that Europe properly recognises and legitimates their existence in Europe. As has been discussed, this may theoretically if incomprehensibly remain intolerable to European society, which relies upon their invisibility to persist in its own *bourgeois* luxury guilt-free. *Beur* filmmakers in France have been legitimated thanks to a postcolonial movement that took years to come to fruition, and yet it is hard to conceive of how trafficked peoples might arrive in the same position, since they are systematically kept invisible and illegal not only from legal residents but, perhaps more importantly, from each other, by a system that needs to keep them invisible and illegal, since visible and 'legal' methods of oppression (old-fashioned colonialism and systems of slavery) ultimately proved relatively unsuccessful and had in large part to be abandoned (as the postcolonial movement has tried to prove; that the oppressed could see each other surely helped to foster the solidarity required to create a 'movement' in the first place). Contemporary slavery is systematically kept illegal, but it is paradoxically this illegality that enables it to persist invisibly within the system. As such, it seems very hard to conceive of how one can make visible the invisible, except in the controlled manner that currently predominates. That is, by having European filmmakers make films about trafficked peoples on their behalf. Such films make human trafficking just visible enough that we know that it exists, but a possible upshot/fear is that trafficking is not so visible that we have to do anything about it. That is, and perhaps contrary to Leshu Torchin and Dina Iordanova's arguments in the next two chapters and in the final 'Traffic Jam' section, trafficking continues to exist *elsewhere*: on the non-place that is the cinema screen, as opposed to all around us in the here and now.

For these films might possibly make trafficking visible to those Europeans that are complicit in its perpetuation, and they might also serve a preventative measure in alerting potential victims of human trafficking to the dangers that it involves (something suggested by Dina Iordanova in 'Making Traffic Visible, Adjusting the Narrative'), but how can films about trafficking possibly make visible the plight of trafficked people to those invisible people that are the trafficked people themselves? By trying to conceptualise the audiences of such films, one may argue for a radical critique of any film that deals with trafficking. As follows: how can a human slave find herself in the position to watch a film about human slavery if, indeed, she is a human slave chained to a bed? Film may indeed work as a means of uniting disparate peoples by communicating to them/making visible the collective nature of their shared struggle, but in the case of trafficked humans, who are kept invisible to each other even if not invisible to us, it becomes hard to conceive quite how cinema can serve this function. If, as Alec G. Hargreaves has argued about *beur* films, which, '[w]hile catering for the majority ethnic public... can also send signals to minority ethnic spectators, which may not be picked up by the rest of the audience' (2000: 344), this does not seem possible for the trafficked person in the audience of a film about trafficking, because the trafficked person perhaps cannot get to see that film in the first place. If postcolonial cinema could only denounce colonialism after the fact (hence the name: *post*colonial), then can a cinema denouncing trafficking exist if there is not yet a post-trafficking era in existence, an era, arguably, that Europe unconsciously does not want to exist? By making films that denounce trafficking in Europe, do Europeans not in fact make films for European (and not trafficked) audiences, films that act as the release valve of our collective and guilty conscience regarding our continued complicity in this system of exploitation? In this respect, might one argue that exploitative films such as those produced by Besson are more honest about trafficking, in that they exploit trafficking for profit (as a subject matter) in the same way that humans are trafficked and put into forced labour for the benefit of Europeans, than are films that intend to denounce trafficking and yet which inadvertently (and in spite of their no doubt good intentions) hush the voices of/speak for those who should be given the liberty to speak for themselves? Indeed, perhaps the inability properly to speak for the exploited and trafficked peoples existing within Europe is manifested by the descent into genre filmmaking that is characteristic of many of these films, of which Besson's action flicks are the best/worst examples? *Dirty Pretty Things*, for example, as much as being a critique of human farming, is also a thriller, as are *Ilegal*, *The Silence of Lorna*, and *La fuente amarilla* (*The Yellow Fountain*, Miguel Santesmases, Spain/France, 1999), which is about illegal Chinese immigrants in Spain. Similarly, films like *Poniente*, which deals with the exploitation of farm workers in the south of Spain, resorts to melodrama (centred of course upon the European character and not the trafficked immigrant). As Ballesteros (2005) says of that film, the melodrama of immigrants targets a passive and voyeuristic audience in search of catharsis (the purgation of bad feelings, perhaps even of guilt), as opposed to wishing to bring about any genuine social change.

Returning to Žižek's psychoanalytic use of the term *symptom*, the theorist contends that

> [t]he leftist political gesture par excellence (in contrast to the rightist motif 'to each his or her own place') is thus to question the concrete existing universal order *on behalf of* its symptom, of the part which, although inherent to the existing universal order, has no 'proper place' within it (say, illegal immigrants or the homeless in our societies) (1997: 50; emphasis added).

In other words, the leftist agenda of liberating others is always already paternalistic in nature. Even 'leftist' films dealing with trafficking, then, involve what Miriam Hansen (1991: 76) would describe as the commodification of and profit from immigrant experience. Perhaps this paradox of intolerable visibility is best elucidated through a consideration of the events that inspired *Poniente*. The film ends with a (dramatic/melodramatic) attack on the illegal immigrants working on the local farms, by, among others, the local farm owners themselves, a climax that is based on similar events that took place in El Ejido in 2000. That the real event received much media coverage goes to show that it is only when Europeans try to get rid of what is already invisible in Europe that it is made visible. However, in *Poniente* it is not in the name of *helping* the immigrants that the locals engage them in combat, but with the aim of eradicating them, of making them not permanently visible, but permanently *invisible*. Critically speaking, one might argue that there is a similar paradox created: if to try to make invisible that which is already invisible paradoxically makes it visible, then perhaps trying to make visible through films that which is invisible paradoxically makes it even more invisible.

This is not to malign any filmmaker that tries to raise awareness of this problem, but simply to point out the problems inherent in representing cinematically a problem that typically remains invisible in contemporary Europe. What becomes visible is not the problem that the films explore, but the films themselves, as typified arguably by the way in which they are mobile and travel freely across borders, especially those more 'mainstream' or 'festival' films such as the Besson-produced or the Dardennes brothers films. One wonders whether a film about human trafficking is possible, in perhaps the same way that a film about the Holocaust has, according to Jean-Luc Godard, similarly been impossible; the way in which filmmakers have resorted to genres in depicting this problem perhaps reflects the unease one feels in the face of such a task. How to make visible what is invisible? And how to do so in a way that might do good as opposed to harm?

And yet, if there are 200 or 27 million slaves worldwide at the present moment in time, more than has existed at any other point in recorded human history (Bales, Trodd & Williamson 2009) then the contemporary slave trade, as enabled by human trafficking, does constitute not only an epidemic or a pandemic, but perhaps also a new and unrecognised holocaust. As such, it merits the attention of each and every one of us that, by doing nothing about it, is complicit in its perpetuation. Jameson has said that the holocaust reveals

> not so much death and human finitude as rather the
> multiplicity of other people; it is the spectacle of that
> multiplicity of lives that is then starkly revealed by the
> horrors of the trenches or the mass executions and not
> some metaphysical condition to be brooded over by
> priests and philosophers or impressionable adolescents
> (2003: 709).

And yet, for all that Jameson might be correct in his assertions above, he is perhaps mistaken to follow them by saying that '[i]t is the explosive fact [of the holocaust] that now sweeps these comfortable categories [race and biological inferiority] away and confronts me with an immense multitude of others, which I am called upon to recognise as equals or as freedoms' (2003: 709). For trafficked humans are neither visible, nor free, nor recognised as equals. In the face of this gross injustice and the perpetuation of inequality in the contemporary world, perhaps we must, regardless of the problems inherent in them, make and watch films as a small part of our collective effort to recognise and eventually to destroy the contemporary slave trade, a slave trade enabled by the trafficking of humans. Trying to resist the comforts of genre filmmaking (comfortable because we can cope with what it shows to viewers since it is recognisable on account of its generic status), filmmakers must make films that are unrecognisable, that shake, shudder and tremble audiences out of their silent complicity with the contemporary slave trade. Paradoxically, filmmakers must make films that run the risk of being invisible, perhaps films that are, impossibly, invisible. If this can be achieved with film, then perhaps film can change the world.

Foreign Exchange

Leshu Torchin

The previous chapter addressed the profound challenges of representing the real-life phenomenon of human trafficking. Such problems are enhanced by broader questions of representation: can one ever adequately represent such a massive trauma? This question opens up the practical, narrative, formal, epistemological, and ethical challenges to this endeavour, recalling the work of Holocaust scholars who have engaged this question in another context (for instance, Friedlander 1992). While not arguing for comparison, the previous chapter and this one recognise the challenges of representation in the case of human trafficking. The phenomenon of trafficking is subject to divergent reports while its victims frequently lack access to control the means of their narration – if they survive the situation at all. At the same time, representations of trafficking exist on screen, and these can provide means of visualising anxieties over the global transformations that continue to enable this international crime.

In her examination of anti-trafficking campaigns, Kamala Kempadoo (2005) notes a correlation between surges in globalisation and social panics around sexual slavery. Building on this observation, this chapter argues that films about human trafficking offer a platform for expressing anxieties about globalisation. Commonly understood as the vast and accelerating interpenetetration of nations, people, capital, commodities, ideas and information (Brysk 2002: 1; Appadurai 1996), the phenomenon of globalisation complicates previously held understandings of nation and identity, and challenges ready comprehension. As Arjun Appadurai notes, '[t]he new global cultural economy has to be seen as a complex, overlapping, disjunctive order that cannot any longer be understood in terms of existing centre-periphery models' (1996:

32). Ironically, although trafficking is a largely invisible operation, films about human trafficking visualise these flows and chart out the new forms of transnational interaction whilst emphasising the stakes of these new circuits and relationships. Films about sex trafficking and people smuggling centre on the movement of people, frequently taking up a framework of criminality – prostitution, illegal or irregular immigration, organised crime – in exploration of abuses and threats in a globalising world. Other films move away from this framework in order to position human trafficking – both movements and abuses – within a context of economic globalisation. These films not only address the flows of people, but also begin to visualise the unseen flows of finance, technology, and labour across the globe, pointing out the human cost in these new forms of transnational enterprise.

Early Globalisation and the White Slavery Film

Evidence of the relationship between globalising activity and human trafficking appears early on. The turn of the 20th Century, a period characterised by the development of international communication technologies and a rise in immigration, also saw a distinct cycle of films, theatrical dramas, and novels about white slavery on both sides of the Atlantic. In Denmark, Aarhus Fotorama produced *Den hvide slavehandel* (*The White Slave Trade*, Alfred Cohn, Denmark, 1910) with its ostensible success leading Nordisk Films to remake the film as *Den hvide slavehandels sidste offer* (*The White Slave Trade's Last Victim*, August Blom, Denmark, 1911) a year later. The excitement carried over into the United States, where films like *Traffic in Souls* (George Loane Tucker, USA, 1913) and *The Inside of White Slave Traffic* (Frank Beal, USA, 1913) were released to great success (Lindsey 1997; Staiger 1995).[1]

---

[1] According to Shelley Stamp Lindsey, both films 'generated close to US$5,000 apiece in weekly box office grosses, suggesting that upwards of 15,000 New Yorkers saw the pictures each week.' In addition, *Traffic in Souls* was 'a hit the day it opened in New York... where it played to three packed houses... despite the 25-cent tickets' (1997: 351-2).

Traffic in Souls purports to tell the story of the '50,000 girls who disappear yearly' in a narrative that combines the tragedy of a single American girl's abduction with multiple scenes of the coercion of migrants into forced prostitution. These latter scenes broaden the film's focus beyond the individual melodrama to provide a wider landscape of concern, gesturing to the border crossing that might have provoked social and moral panic. An early scene shows the deception of two recent Swedish arrivals, who are handed information about an employment agency that is nothing more than a front for a white slavery operation. Set and filmed at Ellis Island, the camera captures the arrival of real-life immigrants in a lengthy sequence more associated with actuality films. It is into this documentary setting that the two Swedish women, clad in traditional costume, wander and are subsequently duped. The gestures to borders and their crossings are two-fold. Taking place at a famed centre for international immigration, the formal composition troubles the borders between documentary and fiction, as the two minor heroines stumble into and then out of an actuality film. An abduction sequence of a rural migrant at Penn Station replicates these crossings, both on screen with a scene set in a site of interstate exchange, and in the generic tension generated through the combination of documentary and fiction. The 'quasi-documentary presentation' (Brewster, cited in Grieveson 1997: 153) allows for a representation of traffic that crosses both state lines and generic borders.

The promise of titillation combined with the edification of a social issue film may have enhanced the appeal of this genre, but this genre also tapped into anxieties regarding numerous changes in the social and cultural landscape. The preoccupation with movement is most striking as the film features points of arrival and departure, suggesting clear discomfort with the women's mobility that took them from private spaces and into a public workforce. Disrupted borders and its consequences were represented on screen as attempts to police those borders manifested off screen with a set of security-based laws. The Chinese Immigration Act (1894) sought to limit all Chinese immigration, restricting international movement to men. Meanwhile, this gendered limitation met a racialised imagination, giving rise to stories of foreign men kidnapping white women. It is hardly a surprise that the Mann Act (officially known as the White-Slave Traffic Act of 1910), restricting the transport of women over state borders for 'immoral purposes,' should have been enacted in the following years.

Contemporary Globalisation and Human Trafficking

The above case illustrates the ways in which film, and in particular films about human trafficking, supplies the means for visualising the concerns and processes of globalisation. In the past decades, these flows of people, technologies, capital, images, and modes of governances have accelerated and expanded. The formation of transnational alliances, whether in the United Nations or the more recent European Union, has eroded the stability of state sovereignty and national borders. The collapse of communism, the rise of global economic institutions, and a recent peak in international trade contribute to migration and financial exchange. But as has been discussed earlier, while the effects are felt, the systems themselves are frequently invisible. Moreover, these circuits contribute to a new landscape whose mapping may no longer be so straightforward, as noted by Appadurai above.

Appadurai proposes a framework for approaching and understanding this complex field, advancing a model of 'scapes' or 'dimensions of cultural flows.' These include: ethnoscapes, the flow of people; ideoscapes, the flow of political ideas; financescapes, the flow of capital; technoscapes, the spread of technologies; and mediascapes, shared images and networks of image delivery systems. These 'scapes' remap the world, opening the field to the amorphous and isomorphic qualities of the modern global economy. This model, with its allowances for numerous flows and varying directionality, offers a way into mapping out human trafficking and paths of new slavery within the contemporary global economy. Moreover, like the contents it endeavours to chart, the model itself is open to change and the addition of new flows, enabling its continued practicality.

Appadurai's scapes haunt the discourses around trafficking, with the ethnoscape holding greatest prominence courtesy of the continued anxieties over migration and border security. As has already been explained in the Introduction, the UN Protocol on Traffic offers a detailed definition of trafficking. It is worth repeating it here:

> [The] recruitment, transportation, transfer, harbouring or receipt of persons, by means of the threat or use of force or other forms of coercion, of abduction, of fraud, of deception, of the abuse of power or of a position of vulnerability or of the giving or receiving of payments or benefits to achieve the consent of a person having control over another person, for the purpose of exploitation. Exploitation shall include, at a minimum, the exploitation of the prostitution of others or other forms of sexual exploitation, forced labour or services, slavery or practices similar to slavery, servitude or the removal of organs... (UN Protocol on Traffic 2000: 2).

Siddarth Kara, who discusses this passage in *Sex Trafficking: Inside the Business of Modern Slavery* (2009: 4), suggests that the wording sets up a two-pronged understanding of trafficking, where the processes can refer to 'recruitment, transportation, and transfer' of people, or to their coercion and exploitation, or possibly both. The former understanding appears to dominate. Film scholarship on human trafficking congregates around the subject of shifting ethnoscapes. Writings about irregular migration (Berger & Winkler 2006) or the hidden dimensions of a changing European cultural landscape (for instance, Ferreira 2006; Gibson 2006; Loshitsky 2006) stand at the foreground of this developing field. Films like *Dirty Pretty Things* (Stephen Frears, UK, 2002) capture this imagination with a depiction of a twilight population of the new multicultural London. Characters here seem to be perpetually in transit or traffic: the setting is a hotel, with recent immigrants seeking continued movement (completing escapes from homeland or past lives); meanwhile, the narrative supplies sinister stories of trade, whether in body parts or in prostitution. More recently, *Gomorra* (Matteo Garrone, Italy, 2008) invites attention with its depiction of illegal immigration, a multicultural Italy, and the competition of *camorra* (mafia) controlled sweatshops. At the level of policy, attention to shifting ethnoscapes filtered through a lens of criminality translates into laws and approaches that fail to protect adequately the subject of human trafficking. Rather, the 'tightening of immigration controls [tends] to empower anti-immigrant sentiment and xenophobia' (Kempadoo 2005: xvi), while questions of citizenship and immigration threaten to detract attention from the ways the non-citizen is excluded from protections afforded the citizen (Maher 2002) and even placed at risk by threats of deportation and repatriation (Kara 2009; Kempadoo 2005: xv).

Meanwhile, the bulk of the literature on human trafficking suggests that the necessary investigations of the processes and causes of coercion, and the contemporary manifestation of slavery-like conditions suffer from less attention. Films provide a productive space for this exploration. Films on the subject of sexual slavery graphically capture not only the dimensions of human trade, but also the violent exploitation that follows. As suggested in the last chapter, these stories of forced movement and forced labour place the violation of bodies and borders clearly on display. At the same time, a great many of these sex traffic films express far more concern with shifts in ethnoscape alongside fantasies of their management; moreover, this slavery stays easily limited to the realm of clear criminality, both in the physical trade of the human body and in the work of prostitution.

Such films and formulations raise the spectre of the ethnoscape; however, trafficking films introduce other flows as well. Modern day slavery extends to numerous sectors in the formal economy – agricultural, domestic, and industrial, for instance. As discussed earlier, films do explore this dimension, and in doing so remind us of the hypocrisies in border management in light of the reliance on an unprotected class of labour. Such films suggest that the anxieties and impacts of globalisation arise not only from the changing movements of people, but from the new flows of finance and labour enabled through global institutions and technologies.

While Appadurai's rich model provides technoscapes, financescapes, and mediascapes better to understand these flows, I introduce the concept of the 'labourscape' to assist in further charting and addressing the intersections and complexities of these circuits. The labourscape functions to disarticulate ethnoscapes from trade, taking into account the changes from old to new slavery (such as permanent ownership versus temporary, if brutal, contracts). The labourscape recognises that labour, and not simply humans, can be a fungible commodity traded or trafficked throughout the world (Pangalagan 2002: 99). Most importantly, the notion of a labourscape functions to remind us that not all of those trafficked are mobile; human resources can be exploited and exported whilst people remain confined in their nations. Human trafficking, as I will discuss below, frequently merges with the shifting global ethnoscapes, calling attention to patterns of migration and movement across the world; however, as it is a crime of modern slavery, it is important to remember the element of forced work. This term is a strategic one as well, since deploying a lens of labour opens up issues of economic rights, where otherwise questions of immigration and national identity may dominate. Indeed, a remarkable number of films open the potential for this discussion, as films about human trafficking also offer representations of these often convoluted and enigmatic circuits. More importantly, these films introduce a visceral component into the visualisation of these pathways, reminding us of the human cost exacted in the globalising and modernising developments.

Continuing the argument that films on human trafficking articulate concerns about and components of globalisation, this chapter surveys three basic, if rough categories of human trafficking films. I begin with a discussion of the films on sex trafficking, which centre around ethnoscapes and the dangers of movement for migrants and host nations alike. Like the white slavery films from the start of the last century, these films draw both on highly gendered tropes and on a grid of criminality, a combination that articulates the anxieties around movement and advances fantasies of containment. The next set of human trafficking films broadens the field and develops more complicated arguments around the intersection of migration and economic globalisation; these films shift the focus of threat to formal economies, which affect citizens and non-citizens alike. And in an examination of a recent cycle of films, the final section troubles the traditional understanding of trafficking as necessarily involving the transport of humans. These films sketch out the ways in which labour can be trafficked, or rather exploited, through other flows, including financescapes, technoscapes, and even mediascapes.

Human Trafficking and Ethnoscapes: Criminal Economy

Much as in the early 1900s, fears associated with globalising trends and, in particular, the flow of ethnoscapes, find expression in films on sex trafficking. Also referred to as 'white slavery,' this admittedly archaic term is effective in capturing the racialised component of the presentations. Like the American films made in response to the panic over Chinese immigration, the contemporary films of Europe also find their threat in the East, but this time the former communist bloc nations whose entry into the West has been facilitated by the collapse of communism and the overall opening of borders associated with the European Union. At the start of 2007, British news reporters interrogated bemused Romanian and Bulgarian citizens, wondering when they would arrive in the UK to take advantage of the labour, joining the hoards of Polish plumbers who already inhabited the fevered dreams of Western Europeans. To articulate this menace in unambiguous and clearly criminal terms, films such as *Taken* (Pierre Morel, France, 2008) and *Le Silence de Lorna* (*The Silence of Lorna*, Jean-Pierre and Luc Dardenne, Belgium/France/Italy/ Germany, 2008) introduce Albanian threat, whilst *Human Trafficking* (Christian Duguay, US/Canada, 2005) offers up a Russian criminal mastermind whose sex trafficking empire has branches in New York, Kiev, Prague, and Manila. *Taken* further plays upon multiple fears of border crossing and xenophobia with the introduction of Arabs who import Orientalist titillation to boot. Even in the United States, popular culture focuses on the threat from the East, whereby former Soviet gangsters and Chinese snakeheads, feature as the villains of people smuggling and human trafficking endeavours.[2]

The films act out the encroachment and subsequent management of the borders. *Taken* depicts the abduction, through home invasion, of two American tourists, Kim (Maggie Grace) and Amanda (Katie Cassidy), by Albanian gangsters. The attacks on boundaries are made clear from the outset: Easterners illegally inhabit Paris, forcefully invading ostensibly safe domestic spaces; young women travel on their own, breaking free of any paternalistic maintenance – indeed, both home and nation are breeched in their carefree movement; and finally, at all points, any legal decrees

---

[2] These include, for instance: *CSI: NY*, Season 5, Episode 14 'She's Not There,' first broadcast 11 February 2009; *Cold Case,* Season 4, Episode 22 'Cargo,' first broadcast 15 April 2007; and *Lethal Weapon 4* (Richard Donner, US, 1998), which depicts the Chinese Triad as the ringleaders of a slavery operation.

are violated. It is then no surprise that recovery, of the girl and of the breech, should be achieved through policing. Rescue arrives through Bryan (Liam Neeson), a former CIA Operative, and Kim's father. He arrives in Paris drawing on the assistance of a friend in French Intelligence, Jean-Claude (Olivier Rabourdin), in a search for the girls. After the discovery of Jean-Claude's own collusion in this prostitution ring, Bryan continues alone in his vigilante operation, finding Amanda dead but recovering his own daughter after she has been auctioned off to a Sheikh (Nabil Massad). The girls are punished for their independent travel, and Amanda, who encouraged a scout's attention with flirtation, is punished by death, while the more reluctant and ostensibly virginal Kim is saved in time. The penetration of the bodies and overall criminality of the endeavour (illegal immigration, organised crime, prostitution) compound border anxieties and security concerns, frequently viewing policing and repatriation as necessary measures for prevention and management.

It is admittedly curious that a French film by EuropaCorp should borrow so liberally from America in the assertion of its borders, smuggling in both the (broadly speaking) Hollywood narrative and a transnational (Hollywood) business model. On screen and off, the present day flows of people are apparent. The story adopts an explicitly American hero (albeit one played by an Irish actor), who functions to save France from its corrupt law enforcement and the menacing Easterners who have found their way past national borders. The film echoes *The Searchers* (John Ford, USA, 1956), in which Ethan Edwards (John Wayne) seeks his own abducted niece with both racist and pathological persistence. Seizing on the intertext of the western genre, *Taken* further articulates its own specific nation-building endeavour despite its own transnational economic context.[3]

Human Trafficking continues in this vein. An international co-production with an international cast, the television miniseries

---

[3] Thanks to Belén Vidal for the observation of this comparison to *The Searchers*.

provides a more sprawling narrative style suited to the global character of its subject. In addition, the stories of abduction allow for victimisation of Eastern European women, as well as an American. In Kiev, teenage Nadia (Laurence Leboeuf) applies to a modelling agency and travels to the United States; in Prague, single mother Helena (Isabelle Blais) meets a charming young man who seduces her and encourages her to go on a romantic holiday to Vienna; and in Manila, pre-teen American tourist Annie (Sarah-Jeanne Labrosse) is kidnapped in a busy marketplace before an indifferent native public. All three women cross borders and are sold into an international slavery ring headed, remarkably enough, by a single man, Sergei Karpovich (Robert Carlyle). The fantasy of management begins at a narrative level, as the vast transnational threat is rendered singularly visible through the production of a single villain at the helm. In other words, the broader phenomenon of human trafficking, rendered tangible in this man, unites the women. Further uniting the women and their related stories is Kate Morozov (Mira Sorvino), an officer with the US Immigration and Customs Enforcement agency. This figure and her agency restrict the spread of the dispersed stories on a narrative level, binding them to a single point. Meanwhile, in the narration, the agency captures Karpovich, proving the efficacy of immigration policy or policing in the management of human traffic.

Not only *Taken* and *Human Trafficking*, but also films like *Sex Traffic* (David Yates, UK/Canada, 2004), *Ha-Aretz Hamuvtachat* (*Promised Land*, Amos Gitai, Israel/France/UK, 2004), and *Lilja 4-ever* (*Lilya 4-ever*, Lukas Moodysson, Sweden/Denmark, 2002) depict women held captive and forced into lives of prostitution. Both *Lilya 4-ever* and *Sex Traffic* focus on the stories of young Eastern European women, seduced by promises of romance and a better life, and subsequently sold to traffickers and pimps. *Promised Land* offers a different approach, depicting the women already in transit, subject to the beatings and rape used to subjugate the captured.

The appeal of sex traffic in constructing a human trafficking imaginary is not surprising. As all three authors of this volume note, films about sex traffic capture the slavery and exploitation that complete the definition, providing graphic depictions of the violations enacted on the human body. The women themselves are not only beaten or raped, but also frequently depicted within enclosed spaces, and behind locked doors. The process itself becomes multiply criminalised, as human smuggling and prostitution are embedded in larger matrices of transnational organised crime. An episode of *CSI: NY* entitled 'She's Not There' (original airdate 11 February 2009) gives voice to this sentiment: a character claims that drugs and arms smuggling inevitably accompany these flows of human traffic. This framing discourse asserts human trafficking as a matter of policing and security; what is required is the careful maintenance of bodies and boundaries. As Rutvica Andrijasevic writes with regard to anti-trafficking campaigns, 'the representational strategies… equate women's migration with forced prostitution [and] encourage women to stay at home' (2007: 26). *Sex Traffic* and *Human Trafficking* both offer repatriation scenes: *Sex Traffic* has Elena Visinescu (Anamaria Marinca) return home to Romania and her family, while *Human Trafficking* offers a more literal repatriation as Nadia is returned to the protection of her father. These stories provide a narrative subjugation and confinement of the wandering women, providing a fantasy of managing the unruly wandering body of economic migrants.

Films about mail order brides, a distant relative of the sex traffic film, supply additional cautionary tales about mobility, this time casting doubt onto the women who willingly engage in border crossing enterprises. Including mail-order brides within a discussion of sexual slavery is risky, but these processes can be seen on a continuum of economic exchange. Mail-order brides are not necessarily exploited or violently coerced, and indeed, many of the arrangements are affectionate, as indicated in films like *Fra Thailand til Thy* and *Fra Thy til Thailand* (*Love on Delivery* and *Ticket to Paradise*, both Janus Metz, Denmark, 2008). At the same time, many of the women involved sell themselves and organise a contract that provides subsistence and access to new national resources in exchange for domestic labour and possibly sexual favours.[4] Even as the films introduce the possibility of a woman's agency, which is often lost in victimising narratives, they follow with a suggestion of the threat she smuggles in, effectively replacing the victim with a potential villain. *Birthday Girl* (Jez Butterworth, UK, 2001) features Nicole Kidman as Nadia, a Russian mail-order bride, purchased over the internet by bank clerk John (Ben Chaplin). Soon after her arrival, her cousin Yuri (Mathieu Kassovitz) and his friend Alexei (Vincent Cassel) come to visit and stage Nadia's kidnapping, holding her for ransom and pressuring John to steal from his bank. This is revealed to be a con the three have pulled on men throughout Western Europe, transforming the kidnapped woman into an accomplice, and revealing the true victims to be the Western Europeans whose borders and trust are repeatedly violated.

Similar anxieties surface in *The Silence of Lorna* wherein Lorna (Arta Dobroshi), an Albanian immigrant, seeks permanent resident status through a paper marriage to Claudy (Jérémie Renier), a Belgian heroin addict. A multicultural project, supported by Russian Andrei and Italian-Belgian Fabio, the overall mission to attain an EU passport appears to involve the 'accidental' overdose of Claudy, presenting the Belgian as endangered by these new communities. The film contributes to Belgium's own internal anxieties regarding national identity with a story of foreign threat, brought on by the

---

4 Admittedly, this opens up a profoundly feminist argument that seeks to reintroduce domestic labour and housewifery into an economic framework, but the goal here is not to diminish the value of marriage in general, nor to condemn all mail-order bridal arrangements, but instead to identify the economic underpinnings of these arrangements, particularly as they move across and negotiate national borders.

domestic (Fabio aspiring to the status of crime boss) and the encroaching Eastern European presence.

Both films introduce pregnancy into their narratives, allowing an on screen indication of new partnerships to perform the backstage conditions of films highly dependent on international cooperation. *Birthday Girl* is a British-American co-production featuring a cast of Australian, British and French actors, with interior scenes shot in Australia. *The Silence of Lorna* received funding from a number of international companies, and the publicity materials repeatedly boasted its newfound Albanian actress, who learned French through her engagement with this film. Whether or not the pregnancies are references to the political economy of the films themselves, it remains tempting to read the pregnancies as allegories for the (trans)national future.

In the case of *Birthday Girl*, the provenance of the pregnancy is unclear, but the condition is enough to warrant Nadia's abandonment by her Russian partners. John, however, steps in, and partnered with her, they work to defeat these villains, following them back to Russia. This ending is open to interpretation. The film's tagline reads: 'Before They Share A Future, They Have To Survive Her Past.' It positions Nadia and her Russian background as a problem, but one to be sorted, either through a new united Europe, or through the eradication of the East. The absence of any stable resolution, however, expresses uncertainty about how to proceed or where these new partnerships will go. The ambivalence is even stronger in *The Silence of Lorna*, as Lorna, believing herself to be pregnant by Claudy, retreats to the woods into a grim fairytale existence: the location and the fate of the child (if it exists at all) are unknown.

Although the sex trafficking and mail-order bride narratives appear to highlight the gendered imaginaries of unruly and subsequently managed ethnoscapes, many films do include on screen gestures to the other scapes of the new global economy. *Promised Land* focuses on the minutiae of the trafficking process; while this includes brutality

– the beatings and rapes used to humiliate and subjugate women – the interest rests with the institution of human trade. The film deploys the observational style of direct cinema documentary. The handheld camera in social space impairs the presentation of (titillating) full-body displays and instead turns the viewer's attention to the small interactions and procedures of modern slavery, a possible gesture to the films of Frederick Wiseman and their own records of institutions. Gitai shows not only the violence, but also the labour involved in trafficking women – moving them across borders and preparing them for their internment in a brothel. Although the strategy prevents a full exhibition of bodies, it lays bare the underlying machinations of global capitalism. Other films also link the criminal trade of sexual slavery to broader, and more mainstream global institutions. *Sex Traffic* (discussed in the Close-Ups section) addresses the ongoing scandal of UN Peacekeepers involved in the sex trade in Kosovo, while also indicating the complicity of transnational corporations in forms of global control and exploitation. And even the highly personal drama of *Lilya 4-ever* refuses to cordon off sex traffic from the traffic of other merchandise in the global economy. It is telling that Lilya's first date with her seducer, the one who convinces her to leave Russia for Sweden, and her first day as a prostitute are linked by scenes in a car park, where Lilya eats her McDonald's dinner in the light of the global franchise's glowing yellow sign. This transnational corporation serves as the backdrop to Lilya's movement and life, reminding the viewer at each step that her own trafficking takes place within a well-established circuitry.

The perspectival shift evident in these films advances the women's agency and their status as economic migrants, replacing discourses of immigration and illegality with those of economic social justice. Indeed, by placing these trades in women's bodies within a larger context of transnational enterprise, the films open a space for exploring the links between the criminal act of slavery and the global economy. Although the sex trafficking films participate in this dialogue, another set of films arrive to remind us of the exploitation that takes place within the seemingly legal limits of domestic labour, agribusiness, and factory work. These films, addressed in the next section of this chapter, significantly enhance the understanding of the widespread and embedded nature of exploitation and coercion within the formal economy. Indeed, within this set of films, the financescapes of the new global economy begin to take precedence as the dominant concern.

Ethnoscapes and Human Trafficking: Formal Economy

The illegality of slavery can detract attention from the degree to which this illicit enterprise operates within a formal economy. Root causes of slavery today are often attributed to the modernising and globalising processes that foster tremendous asymmetries in the distribution of wealth (Bales 2004: 12). Siddarth Kara writes:

> The structures of Western capitalism, as spread through the process of economic globalisation, contribute greatly to the destruction of lives this profitability entails. Sex trafficking is one of the ugliest contemporary actualisations of global capitalism because it was directly produced by the harmful inequities spread by economic globalisation: deepening of rural poverty, increased economic disenfranchisement of the poor, the net extraction of wealth and resources from poor economies into richer ones, and the broad-based erosion of real human freedoms across the developing world (2009: 4).

Indeed, economic globalisation can be seen as a factor in two ways: 1) extreme poverty contributes to economic migration, creating a public vulnerable to trafficking operations; 2) multinational and transnational corporations (MNCs and TNCs) exploit local markets and labour, often taking advantage of the lack of rights protection afforded by the host nation. Even the dealings within human trafficking are 'lodged in contractual, wage relations, and principles of free labour power and its market exchange value' (Kempadoo 2005: xx). It is not only national borders that have been troubled in globalisation, but the boundaries between licit and illicit enterprise.

This integration of human trafficking into the mainstream economy is far more hidden, but there are films on human traffic that explore and unpack this dimension. The documentary *Det andet Europa* (*The Other Europe*, Poul-Erik Heilbuth, Denmark, 2006) addresses the issue of immigration in Europe. While fairly standard in style, complete with voice overs and talking heads, the documentary is nevertheless compelling for its argument: undocumented workers are a fundamental and inextricable part of the European economy. The film, for instance, investigates the lives of undocumented African workers who labour in Spain's many greenhouses, growing vegetables that are then sold in supermarkets throughout Europe. Working for below subsistence wages, their labour enables supermarkets to offer low cost produce. The film points out the hypocrisy of immigration policy, which diminishes availability of social protection for the undocumented worker. Instead, these policies foster fears on both sides, and contribute to exploitative work conditions – conditions that feed the larger, legitimate economy.

Like *The Other Europe*, films such as *Massa'ot James Be'eretz Hakodesh* (*James' Journey to Jerusalem*, Ra'anan Alexandrowicz, Israel, 2003), *Ghosts* (Nick Broomfield, UK, 2006), *It's a Free World...* (Ken Loach, UK, 2007), and *True North* (Steve Hudson, Germany/Ireland/UK, 2006) refuse easy presentations of criminality and instead reveal intersections of migration and economic globalisation. In varying degrees, the films explore the nature of financial bondage, and the forms of coercion that underlie even the most seemingly legitimate of economies.

James' Journey to Jerusalem most explicitly presents itself as a case of human trafficking by representing the arrest of James (Siyabonga Melongisi Shibe) and his subsequent debt bondage to Shimi (Salim Dau), the man who posts his bail. This Christian pilgrim, like the women of the sex trafficking films, is made to surrender his passport, ultimately confining himself to the national borders until his debt has been repaid. James' work and living conditions do not fall into the nightmarish tableaux of rapes, beatings and other bodily violations. Instead, the coercion takes a decidedly financial tone, amidst clear discomfort and disempowerment. For instance, James and his flatmates, living in an overcrowded hostel, must pay for their subsistence and any amenity (including television by the hour), signalling an economy that prevents his release. He and the others struggle to repay their debts as well as to meet the hefty financial demands of their accommodation. Outside, James inhabits the everyday world, where he cleans homes, gardens and engages in a variety of odd jobs, including acting as a companion to his employer's curmudgeonly father. Over the course of the film, a powerful and complex web of exploitation comes to the fore: Shimi's wife 'lends out' James for a price to her friends before James himself learns to outsource and traffic in other immigrants' labour. Even the Church, which James attends on Sundays, takes advantage of James and his faith, soliciting donations that both drive James' enterprise and impede his bid for freedom. Here, trafficking does not lurk in a netherworld of dubious morality and clear illegality; it is enmeshed in everyday institutions and practices.

The reliance of mainstream, formal economies on trafficked labour is reflected in *Ghosts* and *It's a Free World....* The first film tells the story of the disaster in Morecambe Bay that claimed the lives of 23 Chinese cockle-pickers. Director Nick Broomfield combines non-actors and re-enactments in his second feature film (one that nonetheless makes documentary-style truth-claims)[5] to focus on Ai Qin (played by Ai Qin Lin) a young woman who has paid to be smuggled into Britain in order to find work to support her family in China. *Ghosts* shows Ai Qin as bound by debt to snakeheads, living in filthy and overcrowded quarters and made to work long hours for below subsistence wages by the recruitment company. Refused the basic protections of the European citizen labourer, these undocumented workers nonetheless play a fundamental role in the European economy. This is expressed eloquently in a sequence where Ai Qin and her colleagues enter Tesco to shop for dinner; there they see bundles of spring onions – likely ones they had picked and prepared earlier that day – that are priced beyond their budget. The sequence stages an encounter of the invisible workers with the fruits of their labour on the turf of the benefiting corporation, illustrating the relationships that go unseen. Unable to make enough money to repay debts and to support their families, the workers are driven to seek out increasingly dangerous forms of work, and in the case of *Ghosts*, this is represented through the disaster that has also been declared one of Britain's worst industrial accidents. This terminology is essential for recognising the place of this tragedy within a larger framework of Britain's economy and the expectations of health and safety protections within the workplace. Exposing the range of threats faced by illegal immigrants, Broomfield refuses a view of globalisation through the lens of stricter border management, and raises questions about obligations within industrial practice.

Ken Loach's depiction of recruitment agencies in *It's a Free World...* brings even greater complexity to this landscape as it challenges simple distinctions of licit and illicit in the conventions of the formal economy. The film follows Angie (Kierston Wareing), who, when fired from her job, decides to start her own recruitment

[5] A discussion of the combined modes is continued in the entry on *Ghosts* in the Close-Ups section.

agency with her friend Rose (Juliet Ellis). They place day-labourers, typically migrants, into low or un-skilled jobs in a variety of sectors. The desperation for work becomes clear as dozens gather in the car park and are crammed into camions headed to factories and hotels; Angie can barely close the door the van is so full. Even so, there are some left behind, signalling not only the demand for work, but that this is a buyer's market. Angie brokers deals between migrants desperate for work and companies who appreciate this desperation for the obedience and hard work it brings. This sector of flexible labour is employed only on a temporary basis, bound by need but without contracts that bring protection and assurance of fair wages and safe working conditions. In the film, the risks and imbalances are made clear when a firm departs, still owing the workers £40,000, and neither Angie nor the workers have any means of recovering the lost wages.

The dangers are intensified for the completely undocumented labourers, the illegal immigrants whose fear of discovery cultivates compliance. A foreman asks Angie to supply him with this clandestine workforce, noting that they work harder, and longer, and without any 'backchat.' There is little danger in hiring illegal migrants, he explains, showing Angie a feebly worded cease and desist letter from the government. They know what he's doing, but rather than act against the corporation, they simply request that it stops. No one, it appears, takes these letters seriously. The threat to the illegal immigrant, however, is made clear when Angie calls the police in the hopes of clearing out a caravan park, a place where she hopes to house her employees. Here, immigration policy does not protect against human trafficking, but might instead facilitate the exploitation of immigrants. Through these events, the film shows the ways that people casually enforce conditions that contribute to institutionalised slavery: it is not always a clear matter of debt bondage to gangsters, or beatings by pimps and slave-holders. Rather, there are slavery-like conditions that emerge in the everyday, in the zones of the legal, as companies and people participate in an economy that adopts principles of deregulation and of outsourcing.

One of the film's strengths is its refusal to demonise Angie, even as she is given to some diabolical acts. She loses her job when she refuses to tolerate sexual harassment. She appears to be haunted by a traumatic past, whether one of violence or dire poverty; indeed, her past disenfranchisement is signalled through her own ambiguous custody of her son. She, too, is desperate and driven to participate in this economy of exploitation simply to get a leg up. This does not excuse her actions, but places them in a comprehensible and familiar, if complex, framework.

True North adopts this economically sympathetic approach in its story of Scottish fishermen who take on board a cargo of Chinese immigrants with tragic results. Director Steve Hudson drew on the real-life tragedy of people smuggling, and specifically the discovery of 60 Chinese immigrants in a cargo hold at Dover in 2000. However, Hudson was also moved by the case of Fraserburgh, a fishing village in Northern Scotland whose local fishing trade was imperilled by the wider globalisation of the industry. As the film's press kit reads, 'with catches declining, quotas increasing, and fishing grounds opened to international fleets, the Scottish fishing industry is being decimated.' This combination of source material addresses the shifting ethnoscape as it calls attention to the economic drive behind people movement – both of the moving and the movers.

The opening sequence depicts the overlapping global flows in an elegant interplay of cuts between the fishing boat and its nets and video taken inside the cargo hold. The intercutting suggests an equivalency of trades, between the trawler seeking to transport and sell fish, and the hold where Chinese migrants are being transported to a new place where they might earn money for their families. The film suggests greater complexity when the ship alights in Ostend, Belgium, where other forms of trade – black market cigarettes and prostitution – also appear. *True North* further enriches the globalised landscape with the depiction of the bar, Sweet Sixteen, shown as populated by date-seeking Eastern European women called 'Svetlanas,' a gesture, even if unintentional, to Victor Malarek's book *The Natashas* (2004).[6] But it is not simply the former denizens of the East who must participate in these twilight economies. The fishing trawler, the *Providence,* is heavily in debt and the haul has been too poor to ensure payment of the mortgage; the family that owns the boat is facing the loss of their livelihood. Desperate to make some money, first mate Sean (Martin Compston) scours the port for alternatives. The film is interested in the flows of people, but places them within a larger context of bigger business, which creates conditions that move people to desperate action.

Contributing to a landscape of moving people, moving materials, and moving capital, is the production of the moving story, or the testimonial to justify entry into Great Britain. The first shot, in video, depicts a man looking straight into the camera, the video and the direct address suggesting a form of testimony to be given. The man tells his story: he was a rural farmer when it was announced that a factory was to be opened on his land. Although he was promised money, none was delivered. Along with other farmers he mounted a protest, but the police came and arrested them; he has spent the last year in a work camp. Following an undersea interlude and the opening titles, another video starts. This man is more hesitant and awkward, providing fewer details in his testimonial. As a small farmer denied the fee promised, he went on strike, but was arrested, and placed in jail. Here, the scene deviates further: an off screen voice asks him for how long he was in jail. The young man looks at a card: 'Five years,' he answers. The off screen voice scoffs; the man is eighteen now, which would mean he

---

[6] Meanwhile, the name of the bar plays with a cinematically enriched landscape, providing a clear gesture to Ken Loach, who directed a film entitled *Sweet Sixteen* (UK/Germany/Spain, 2002), which employed both actors (including Martin Compston) and the narrative strategies apparent in this film.

was put in jail when he was thirteen. 'You need to practice!' the voice admonishes, 'You're no good!' It becomes clear what is happening, and that the migrants are training for asylum. More notably, this training indicates the economy of valued narratives and the disparity between political and economic rights: poverty is not an excusable reason for immigration; rather, there must also be clear political rights infringement in the form of police brutality and incarceration – as we shall see in greater detail in the next chapter.

A third figure comes before the interrogating video: a young girl, Su Li (Angel Li). She is even more hesitant and confused. The off screen voice hectors her in an attempt to prompt the story. 'I'm the policeman. Why do I have to let you into England?' 'So I can earn money,' she asks by way of answer. 'No! You must have a story.' In the process, her own testimony emerges: she needs to earn money. Her family borrowed money to send her away and now she must repay the debt. Although this answer has positioned her as clearly embedded in the slave-like conditions of debt bondage, this is not enough. The off screen voice prompts her again. She adds a story of her mother's new pregnancy, and the fact that this is not allowed – so she must go away and make money. The interrogator makes his frustration known. He will teach her the factory story. It is unclear as to whether another child has prompted the export of Su Li. Indeed, this story, much like the factory story, gestures to the approved asylum-seeking narratives that see the one-child policy and the disenfranchisement of Chinese girls as legitimate concerns. What is significant is that Su Li, by repeating her reasons, places financial matters as the principal motivation for movement – not only poverty, but also now debt. Although she has been placed in the unquestionably illegal state of indentured servitude, the legitimisation for her protection is articulated through discourses of political rights that privilege cases of discrimination and incarceration. The conditions of poverty and the entry into modern slavery do not suffice within this regime.

The division of rights discourse, and the difference in valuation, is longstanding. Economic rights, in terms of the International Bill of Human Rights, refer to labour rights such as the right to work under 'just and favourable conditions' as well as the right to form and join trade unions. The rights also include education, health care, adequate standard of living (food, clothes, housing) and social security. To date, the popular human rights imaginary has been dominated by civil and political rights, which include the protection of the individual self, against torture, arbitrary arrest, unlawful prosecution, execution, invasions of privacy, and discrimination on the basis of religion, race, or gender. These can also include slavery, torture, and relate to crimes against humanity. These abuses are readily framed as violations and seen as subject to political and juridical intervention. Economics rights pose more of a challenge. Their violations do not always fit into the victim-perpetrator paradigm used in other rights representations. And the effects of these violations, such as extreme poverty, are frequently framed as misfortune remedied by philanthropy rather than structural change. Although slavery fits into the former class of rights, it is, as many of these films indicate, a condition brought about by economic violations. And, as I will discuss below, just as enmeshed are the slavery-like conditions, rather than slavery, that arise from poverty and which flourish where labour protections and basic subsistence are denied.

By miming interrogation in the event of capture, the video sequence points to the fine distinctions informing the construction of legitimate reasons for migration. Although seeking asylum for political and civil abuses is reasonable, finding ways to manage poverty and support one's family is substantially less so. Nevertheless, as the film's brutal voyage reveals, both situations, political and economic, enact forms of coercion that can result in bodily harm and death. *True North* seeks to establish the economic migrant as a figure in need of protection, not punishment. When the fishermen's desperate efforts to circumvent detection lead to the death of the Chinese in the cargo hold, immigration policy and security measures are implicitly questioned. These laws provide security for whom? As the film reminds us, the movement of people and the pressures to move them are driven by greater, pressing economic issues: extreme poverty, and the crisis of local business within global industry. The work of violence and coercion is just as much subcontracted in this system, making the chain of responsibility that is implicit in simpler descriptions of human trafficking and slavery (bondage and abuse) less clear to determine, even as they are present.

Human Trafficking: New Labourscapes

The use of the word 'slavery' invites problems. Although human trafficking is frequently referred to as slavery, particularly for its connections to an earlier global trade in humans, new developments bring significant differences. It is, first and foremost, illegal. No longer a matter of permanent ownership, the relationship between slaves and slaveholders is a transitory one. Coercion lies not in ownership, but in forms of debt bondage or contract. The temporary nature of the arrangement renders the person 'disposable' and even less likely to receive the care for maintaining a 'long term investment' (Bales 2004: 14-15). Legal ownership no longer exists, but forms of enslavement and abuse persist. Rather, as Kevin Bales observes, 'the new slavery mimics the world economy... Transnational companies do what European empires did in the last century – exploit natural resources and take advantage of low-cost labour – but without needing to take over and govern the entire country' (Bales 2004: 25). And indeed, this is a theme for the next set of films I shall discuss, films that find exploitation and institutionalised slavery in mainstream economies, where nation states and corporations are complicit, invoking, as the previous chapter argued, Europe's colonial empire.

The export of labour forces is a common and accepted practice. Nilita Vachani's *Otan erthei i mama gia ta Hristougenna* (*When Mother Comes Home for Christmas*, Greece/India/Germany, 1996) points out that Sri Lanka's principal export is labour.[7] The film offers scenes from the Sri Lanka Bureau of Foreign Employment, the website of which claims to provide 'Quality & Skilled Manpower for the Overseas Markets.' The Bureau's website includes information about recruitment costs, which are to be borne by the sponsor, a scenario that can create debt bondage. Although the film's protagonist, Josephine, is lucky enough to find a place in Europe, dispatches from Dubai and the United Arab Emirates list cases of abuse, violence, and imprisonment. A Human Rights Watch report from November 2007 details the 'excessive fees' charged by Sri Lankan recruitment agencies, which leave migrants 'heavily indebted.' The workday can last between 16 and 21 hours without any breaks or days off, while the wages are notoriously low for such wealthy countries.[8] Testimonies from domestic workers describe 'forced confinement, food deprivation, physical and verbal abuse, forced labour, and sexual harassment and rape by their employers.' The findings also noted

> that employers routinely confiscate domestic workers' passports, confine them to the workplace, and in many cases restrict their communication, even with their embassy. Some employers also withhold wages for months to years at a time. In the worst cases, the combination of these practices traps Sri Lankan domestic workers in forced labour ('Human Rights Watch Exported and Exposed' 2007).

---

[7] According to a report from Third World Network, '[t]here are 500,000 migrant workers, mainly in the Middle East, who contributed Rs.35 billion (US$ 0.7 billion) to the national coffers in 1994 – over 50% of them are women, working as maids' (Seneviratne n.d.).

[8] In 2008 a minimum wage was finally established for Sri Lankan workers (Menon 2007).

The plight of migrant labourers involved in state-run work initiatives is chronicled in Stephanie Black's *H-2 Worker* (USA, 1990), which takes its name from the H-2A temporary agricultural program that brings 'nonimmigrant foreign workers to the US to perform agricultural labour or services of a temporary or seasonal nature' (United States Department of Labor n.d.). *H-2 Worker* depicts the lives of Jamaican and Caribbean workers who come to Florida for six months out of each year to cut sugar cane by hand. Black repeatedly draws connections between the old slave trade and this work situation. The workers live in overcrowded barracks, receive little subsistence in terms of food, wages (which are below the American minimum wage), or necessary medical care, while on-the-job injuries are given inadequate treatment. Meanwhile, deportation hangs over these men as a threat. At each step, the film links the old and new plantations, perhaps most so when pointing out the history of the H-2 programme, which began in 1943, shortly after, the website argues, the 'US Sugar Cane Corporation was indicted for conspiracy to enslave black American workers.'

Black connects this form of coerced and exploitative labour to international trade laws and practices. Namely, she observes that the US government's aggressive subsidisation of domestic sugar production impedes Third World sugar importation whilst encouraging Third World labour importation. A similar argument develops in Black's next documentary, *Life and Debt* (USA, 2001), which explores the impact of global financial institutions – the International Monetary Fund (IMF) and the World Bank – in Jamaica. The film argues that these global lenders have not produced development in Jamaica as promised. Rather, the pressure to privatise has led to increased interest and cutbacks of aid, forcing Jamaica into economic dependence and impeding rights to an adequate standard of living and just and favourable working conditions. In other words, debt bondage to global economic institutions leaves entire nations open to exploitation. Black makes this argument apparent throughout the film, particularly in the segment on Free Trade Zones, areas throughout Kingston that are available for use by foreign companies at low prices. These sites bring in materials tax-free, benefit from Jamaican labour to manufacture goods, and then immediately transport the completed goods to overseas markets. Interviews with the labourers support claims of exploitation and the abuse of economic rights. The wages are low, even withheld. Efforts to organise or strike result in blacklisting; in fact, the Jamaican government, in order to maintain this source of income, has prohibited unionisation in the Free Trade Zones.

The images that accompany these stories remind the viewer of the human cost and the spectre of violence in these scenarios. The living conditions of the women interviewed are evidently substandard as they stand before threadbare homes. The subsistence level and the disparity of distribution are evident throughout the film, which counterpoints the tourist's Jamaica with that of the locals. One sequence shows a flourishing local chicken plant devastated by the dumping of low-grade American chicken parts. Substandard food floods the region, as there are no trade protections. The checkpoint at the Free Trade Zone is adorned with barbed wire, a sight that hints at confinement and menace, and contradicts any trace of freedom in this space. This imagery filters the violation through the charged lens of political rights, prompting recognition of the human cost of these economic policies.

Trafficking Labour: Mobility and Confinement

Through the Free Trade Zone sequence, *Life and Debt* broadens the concept of confinement amidst rapidly accelerating global flows. Although the Jamaican economy is integrated into the international marketplace, the Jamaican people are bound by the nation's debt to the IMF and World Bank, and are compelled to work in exploitative conditions. Disparity and asymmetry within formal economic policy comes to the fore in this discussion of globalisation, leaving behind the concerns over illegal immigrants and transnational organised crime.

As films like *Vers le Sud* (*Heading South*, Laurent Cantet, France/Canada, 2005) suggest, the threat of movement can be located in the flow of tourists, who, like their colonial predecessors, arrive to exploit local resources. Cantet's film disrupts the traditional gendered narrative of women imperilled by globalisation in its portrait of three white European women who come to 1980s Haiti to indulge their sexual desires. As per the films of John Sayles, each character is given an opportunity to provide a meditative speech on their circumstances. Many of the Haitians provide statements that align the violence of colonialism with the economic interactions between tourist and native. Albert (Lys Ambroise), headwaiter at the resort, recalls his family's resistance against the earlier American occupation; today's occupiers, he states arrive armed with money. Another character compares gifts to the shots fired from a machine gun. Although slavery as such does not exist, the coercive forces of capital are made known throughout. Two European women battle over Legba (Ménothy Cesar), who 'belongs to everyone' – a phrase that indicates his state of servitude. Legba's girlfriend, Maryse, is a domestic worker outside the resort who also faces a violent lack of choice; she is a live-in maid who must sleep with her boss and his son. While no one in the film is explicitly a slave, the formal economic conditions replicate the relationships of the past, contributing to the compelled exploitation of those without money.

A recent cycle of documentaries has taken up this issue of economic globalisation and the exploitation of local labour, recognising that the transnational movement of finance may pose greater threats than the movement of people. *Mardi Gras: Made in China* (David Redmon, USA, 2006) juxtaposes scenes of carefree revelry with scenes of life in a Chinese bead factory, complete with long hours, low pay, and exposure to toxic materials. The contrast in cost is revealed as one woman figures she earns one penny for each twelve necklaces she makes, with monthly pay topping out at US$62. The filmmakers tell the factory workers the price of a strand: a day's wages for these labourers.

A *Decent Factory* (Thomas Balmès, France/Finland/UK/ Australia/Denmark, 2004) also visits China in a story that follows Nokia's internal ethics advisor and a British ethics consultant on a trip to Shenzhen to audit the operations of a factory making parts for Nokia phones. Nokia, a company based in Finland, takes advantage of the lower costs of manufacture and wages. However, on this tour, they learn that the conditions in these workplaces would not be supportable within the legal framework of Europe. In effect, the basic subsistence level and labour rights demanded in Europe are not met in these factories, and the European company benefits from this arrangement. The sequences here do not provide scenes of tragic violence, such as the industrial disaster at Morecambe Bay or the beatings and rape of women forced into prostitution; these scenes do not even provide extreme examples of sweatshop labour, with underage girls toiling for nothing. The film is more elegant in its ethical inquiries. Like the fictional employees of *It's a Free World...*, coercion and exploitation arrive in the absence of contracts and in the economic need of the workers who risk losing their jobs should they complain. And there are causes for complaint. The young women, rural migrants, live in cramped, monitored dormitories with eight girls lodging in a single room, the rent for which is automatically deducted from their paycheques. Their income is further limited by a less-than-minimum wage, disguised by the imaginative accounting of the factory management; the pay is hardly augmented by the involuntary overtime or the six-day workweeks of twelve-hour shifts. The health and safety conditions are equally dismal, if not as threatening as the nightmare scenarios of sexual slavery and brutal sweatshops. Toxic chemicals are stored in the place where the workers make their tea; when the visitors observe this danger and bring it to the attention of the crew, the manager demands the bins are stored in the kitchens. Beyond the 'break room,' the women work without magnifying mirrors, straining their eyes over detailed work. Most startling, and best expressed through cinema, is the sound: the factory environment is a deafening one, and the workers have no protection from it. Conversation cannot be heard by anyone – on and off screen alike.

These violations fall short of the horrifying visions supplied by body farming films, sex traffic films, and even those investigations into global capitalism such as *Darwin's Nightmare* (Hubert Sauper, Austria/Belgium/France/Finland/Sweden, 2006), which reveals the devastating effects of the fishing industry at Lake Tanzania. Nevertheless, they call attention to the exploitation of workers that arises out of the flows of finance and labour that benefit European corporations. In addition, the lack of grave abuses contributes to this ongoing and asymmetrical relationship: these interactions are not clearly actionable, and not so readily ended or avoided. The film's coda articulates the ambivalence of these circumstances. Hanna Kaskinen, retired head of the ethics department at Nokia, is unable to reconcile what she has seen with her mission. She explains this as she walks along a snow-covered path, along which she spots some dog waste. Maintaining her distance, she attempts to manage this blemish on the landscape from a distance, poking and burying it with her ski pole. She finally manages to toss the waste out of sight into the nearby shrubbery. Out of sight might be out of mind, but the film's work reminds us of these connections and relationships, of the ugliness that mars the transnational economic ecosystem, and the spectre of slavery that haunts the European landscape.

While financescapes loom large in present-day renditions of

human trafficking, so too have technoscapes entered the fray. Alex Rivera's short film *Why Cybraceros?* (USA, 1997) plays upon the hypocrisy of American anxiety over Mexican immigration, in spite of its reliance on Mexican labour.[9] The film adopts a public affairs mockumentary style, based on *Why Braceros?*, a promotional film produced by the California Grower's Council in the late 1950s. That film explained the need for Braceros, a form of temporary immigrant labour that likely served as a template for the H-2 programme. Rivera's short, meanwhile, follows the same line of explanation and defence, explaining the value of such assistance for American production before revealing the twist: the Mexican workers can telecommute as they operate robots via the internet. Like the outsourcing of labour to markets overseas, this solution sidesteps any obligation to the workers and tends to border security as a primary concern. As Rivera's website explains: '[t]he Cybracero, as a trouble free, no commitment, low cost labourer, is the perfect immigrant. The Cybracero is the hi-tech face of the age-old American Dream.' Rivera has since built on this idea with his film *Sleep Dealers* (Mexico/USA, 2008). In a dystopic future, the borders to the USA are closed. Instead, major cities in Mexico serve as technological and labour hubs where workers literally plug their bodies into a network to control robots throughout the world. Cybraceros and the workers of this film are pure labour exported through circuits of technology and finance; the shifting ethnoscape is of minimal concern in this portrait, which as Rivera himself states, is a 'realisation of the American Dream': all the labour without the worker.

These fantasies are not so far off, as almost any story of call centres might suggest. The very real use of technologies in restricting movement whilst exporting labour is a feature of two recent films: *Import/Export* (Ulrich Seidl, Austria/France/

---

9   The film can be viewed in full at Rivera's website, *Invisible America*: http://www. invisibleamerica.com/whycybraceros.shtml. The original *Why Braceros?* can also be viewed online at http://www.archive.org/details/WhyBrace1959.

Germany, 2007) and *Last Resort* (Pawel Pawlikowski, UK, 2000). As mentioned in the last chapter, both films include sequences on internet pornography wherein women in one location do the bidding of a man in another. *Import/Export* features a cyber-brothel in the Ukraine, where Olga (Ekateryna Rak) works before moving westward. The women learn German in order better to understand the instructions of the men in a gesture to the cross-border nature of the enterprise. Although untouched, these women conduct labour at the behest of these virtual bosses, most likely also exploited by the present management that runs the show. A similar enterprise runs in *Last Resort*, this one in England but equally populated by Eastern European women; indeed, the business is located beside housing for asylum seekers, where the pornographer deliberately seeks out new workers.

The films perform their own status as a convergence of mediascapes, ethnoscapes, technoscapes and labourscapes. Although these films, unlike many others listed in this chapter, are not international co-productions, their international make-up is evident in the diversity of locations and talent. The sonic landscape testifies to on and off screen transnational dimensions with German, Slovak, Russian, and English all spoken. Most notable, perhaps, is the presence of non-professional actors, particularly in roles relating to sex work. Les, the internet pornographer of *Last Resort*, is played by real-life pornographer Steve Perry, credited here as Lindsey Honey. As in the case of *Traffic in Souls*, the borders between documentary and fiction are traversed in such approaches; even Perry's use of a pseudonym reflects his real work, which also requires a stage name for the credits (he typically works under the pseudonym Ben Dover). *Import/Export* makes the more disturbing connection regarding the potential for exploitation in mainstream and criminal economies alike when Michael (Michael Thomas) attempts to debase a Ukrainian prostitute in front of his son. The woman playing the prostitute is herself a prostitute, not a professional actress; it is unclear from whom this Eastern European woman takes direction: the drunken character or the sober Austrian director. Even if paid well, the spectres of exploitation and the abusive dimension of power now haunt this landscape – the film that will travel the globe in its own border-crossing enterprise.

By this point, I have clearly pressed the definition of human trafficking to the limit, unpacking variations in transportation, coercion, and exploitation. The intent here is not to diminish the suffering of those held captive and/or subject to beatings, rape, and dismemberment. Rather, I seek to open up a more complex overview, where trafficking occurs not only in operations veiled in underground criminality but also in arrangements hidden by distance and state complicity. If the clandestine elements of a criminal trade do not sufficiently obfuscate the circuits and practices of contemporary slavery, its temporary nature does: people pass into and out of exploitative conditions and confinement as the practice itself seems to drift in and out of legality courtesy of economic globalisation. Films on human trafficking become means of visualising these unseen currents, and more importantly, of introducing the human element into the flows of capital, labour, and technology. In this way, these films articulate concerns with globalisation in its present incarnation, and ask us to see globalisation and human trafficking as issues beyond the shifting ethnoscapes tamed and managed through security measures. Instead, they invite new thinking about policies, about the forms of protection required on a transnational level, and about the ways that these global flows affect us all.

Making Trafficking Visible, Adjusting the Narrative

Dina Iordanova

On arrival at Istanbul airport, a place that Marc Augé (1995) might call a 'non-place,' in that it is anonymous and transient, I am welcomed by a large poster in Russian. Most of the people who have disembarked alongside me from London cannot read it; it is not addressed to them anyhow. It is a social service announcement of a free phone number, urging passers-by to memorise it and to use it if needed. But why would they want to do that? The campaign is geared toward Russian-speaking women who are entering Turkey via the airport (a small fraction when compared to those who enter via ports and land border crossings), and who might be trafficked. They are those who are likely to find themselves in unwanted bondage, enslaved by an impossible level of debt that keeps growing as they keep repaying it, or exploited in a way that they have not imagined when taking off for the journey. How many are calling? I have got no way of knowing. Could the young blonde who is lining up in front of me at the immigration control be one of them?

In real life, trafficking remains largely invisible. One just does not realise that someone who appears to move around voluntarily may, in fact, be bullied, intimidated and treated like a slave. The media may report a lack of awareness, but this barely changes anything.[10] Only occasionally may one realise that someone nearby is being exploited or held captive; one may see a girl with a bruised arm shopping at the supermarket or notice some foreign-looking

---

[10] In August 2009, for example, the BBC reported that about 360 children are trafficked annually into the UK. According to *The Scotsman* newspaper, the majority of people in the UK are unaware of the trafficking that is going on around them, and that 500 children are being trafficked into the country every year, one third of whom are brought in for sex slavery (14 August 2009: 1).

families working at the nearby farm, but one might not suspect that something is wrong. Recent cases in places like Austria, Belgium and the USA have shown that situations of detention can last for years without attracting any significant public scrutiny.

It is this invisibility of the traffic in the context of the societies at the receiving end, already extensively discussed here, that makes cinema special when it comes to raising awareness. In this chapter, I will discuss the specific new geography that emerges from the film narratives on contemporary migrations, one that no longer moves within the familiar trajectories of South-North and East-West. I will then scrutinise the typology of representations related to the depiction of those involved in the business of trafficking – the villains and the victims. At the end of the essay, I will make a case for the need to embrace the study of popular representation in the context of contemporary social studies. More than any other art form, film has the power to tell non-traditional and multifarious stories of voluntary and involuntary migrations. In showing the plight and the presence of trafficked people, contemporary cinema brings to light what is invisible and makes it visible.

Even when not at the heart of contemporary narratives, human trafficking has taken a prominent place as a subplot in films that focus on contemporary problems and realities, especially in the cinema of countries on the periphery of Europe. In Ibolja Fekete's *Bolse vita* (*Bolshe Vita*, Hungary, 1996) the two Russian protagonists who end up in Budapest have migrated willingly – yet they see quite a few others who have been brought and are kept there by a trafficking ring. One of the segments in Pantelis Voulgaris' *Ola einai dromos* (*It's a Long Road*, Greece, 1998) is set in a nightclub and focuses on the exploitation of trafficked Bulgarian women who work as go-go dancers and prostitute themselves on the side. Greek cinema in general has released numerous films where the traffic of people from Albania and Russia serves as a backdrop to the main story, and which often are made by younger generation directors such as Sotiris Goritsas (*Ap' to hioni/From the Snow*, Greece, 1993; *Parees/ Pals*, Greece, 2007) and Constantine Giannaris (*Apo tin akri tis polis/ On the Edge of the City*, Greece, 1998; *Omiros/Hostage*, Greece/ Turkey, 2005). The same applies for Turkish cinema, where subplots follow around women trafficked in from the former Soviet Union: *Gölge Oyunu* (*Shadow Play,* Yavuz Turgul, Turkey, 1992), *Gemide* (*On Board*, Serdar Akar, Turkey, 1998), *Rus Gelin* (*Russian Bride*, Zeki Alasya, Turkey, 2003), and others (see Pekerman 2009). The subplot of the fallen trafficked woman is sometimes used to foreground the story of a local person's estrangement from society. This is the case in *Sonbahar* (*Autumn*, Özcan Alper, Germany/Turkey, 2008), where the protagonist, Yusuf (Onur Saylak), has been released after a ten-year jail term for his involvement with leftist anarchists, only to realise that he can no longer reintegrate. His only friend is a young woman, Eka (Megi Kobaladze), who has been trafficked into Turkey from neighbouring Georgia. The protagonists of the Bulgarian film *Dunav most* (*Danube Bridge*, Ivan Andonov, Bulgaria, 1999) live near the Romanian border, where the traffic of humans is part of daily life. In *Leydi Zi* (*Lady Zee*, Georgi Djulgerov, Bulgaria, 2005) the teenage protagonist, Zlatina (Aneliya Garbova), is abducted and confined to a brothel in Northern Greece, which is just an hour's drive south of the border – and yet a world apart from her previous life.

However, European directors who work in the West have also been sensitive to the theme of human trafficking; stories of illicit migrations and of people who have ended up trapped in human bondage have since the 1990s prominently featured as subplots in what one might term European humanist cinema. Gianni Amelio's *Lamerica* (Italy/France/Germany, 1994) was one of the first films openly to address these matters. Using a clever reversal in the story, the director positions his Italian protagonist Gino (Enrico Lo Verso) in the shoes of impoverished Albanians and makes him follow the same (precarious) pathways for getting to Italy that were available to his fellow would-be-migrants, thus making a point about the real human need that drove the influx of Albanians into Italy and other West European countries in the early 1990s. In Michael Haneke's *Code Inconnu*: *Récit incomplet de divers voyages/Code Unknown: Incomplete Tales of Several Journeys* (France/Germany/Romania, 2001) a middle aged woman, Maria (Luminita Gheorghiu), spends her days begging on the sidewalks in Paris and is followed back to her village in Romania where she is shown functioning like a person of clear moral standards, the kind of person who would normally never consider begging had other options for economic survival been available. In Eloy de la Iglesia's *Los novios búlgaros* (*Bulgarian Lovers*, Spain, 2003), a satire that shows resourceful immigrants exploiting naïve well-to-do Westerners, the privileged gay protagonist realises that the sexy macho immigrant he is involved with is, in fact, a heterosexual, who would resort to desperate means (and even smuggle radioactive material) in order to get his family together for a new life abroad. In *Quando sei nato non puoi più nasconderti* (*Once You Are Born You Can No Longer Hide*, Marco Tullio Giordana, Italy/France/UK, 2005) the encounter of Sandro (Matteo Gadola), an Italian boy of privileged background, with Radu (Vlad Alexandru Toma), an illegal Romanian immigrant, results in a genuine bond. It is an accident, an unexpected plot twist, that makes the illegal traffic of dozens of impoverished immigrants get through to Sandro; he would normally not be exposed to the plight of trafficked people. And, of course, there are films where the invisible life of the trafficked is brought to the very centre of the narrative, as seen in acclaimed features by British Michael Winterbottom (*In This World*, UK, 2002) and Swedish Lukas Moodysson (*Lilja 4-Ever/Lilya 4-ever*, Sweden/ Denmark, 2002). In all these instances, cinema is serving a humanist concern by making visible what would ordinarily stay out of sight.

Geographies of Acquiescence: Trajectories and Trails across Non-Places

All books about contemporary migrations and illicit traffic feature maps. Either maps of the world, with pointers coming out of one spot and going into all sorts of directions, as seen on the inside cover of Victor Malarek's book *The Natashas* (2004), where the source of traffic is set in Eastern Europe. Or maps of a part of the world, with an overlay that describes a specific trajectory, as seen in Misha Glenny's book on transnational organised crime *McMafia* (2008: 116). Glenny displays a 'case study,' which shows the itinerary of a Ukrainian woman who has been trafficked as a sex slave: starting off in Odessa, the course of her journey first goes up north to Moscow, from where it takes a sharp turn to the south for a big jump down to the African continent, to Cairo in Egypt, and from there to the east, through the Sinai and Negev deserts, to a place in Israel, Beer Sheba, near the Gaza strip, and from there a further short-haul move up north, to Tel Aviv. The trajectories of other 'case studies,' similarly, do not move east-west, but take off from landlocked areas that, from the Western point of view, appear to be in 'the middle of nowhere' – places like Transdnistria or Moldova, before swinging in unexpected directions to the east and the south, and then passing via places in Turkey and Egypt, the Middle East, and so on.

Whereas common wisdom has it that the desired central destination that attracts most migrants is somewhere in the West of Europe or North America, a view that William Brown critiqued earlier in 'Negotiating the Visible,' it is obvious from these maps that many movements actually take place within the periphery. Migrants do not necessarily move from one central location to another but often simply leave one small town in their home country to turn up in another peripheral location in the new place, and the route largely determines the story. In Goran Paskaljević's *Andjeo čuvar*

(*Guardian Angel*, Yugoslavia, 1987) the itinerary moves from a Roma hamlet near Belgrade in Serbia to the outskirts of Venice in Italy. In Emir Kusturica's *Dom za vešanje* (*Time of the Gypsies*, UK/Italy/ Yugoslavia, 1988) – from a Roma hamlet near Skopje in Macedonia through Slovenia to the outskirts of Milan. In Xavier Koller's *Reise der Hoffnung* (*Journey of Hope*, Switzerland/Turkey/UK, 1990) the migration itinerary is from a village in Turkish Kurdistan to an isolated mountain town in Switzerland. In *Lamerica* the movement is between secluded seaside towns in Albania to provincial Bari in Southern Italy. In *Massa'ot James Be'eretz Hakodesh* (*James' Journey to Jerusalem*, Ra'anan Alexandrowicz, Israel, 2003), as dealt with in the previous chapter, the itinerary goes from the imaginary village of Entshongweni in an unnamed country in Southern Africa to the margins of life in Israel.

Previously stories were told in relation to the global city in the West (assumed as the normative destination) and from the point of view of a Western observer (assumed as the normative narrator). But no longer. The focus of representation switches more to liminal places such as Trieste in Italy or the makeshift tent settlement dubbed 'the jungle' (Sangatte) in Nord-Pas-de-Calais in France, and the narration is devolved to those who are trying to get into 'Fortress Europe' (as best seen in the case of *In This World*). Alice Bardan (2007) even observes a specific reversal of semiotic positioning in the hierarchy of places. In her analysis of Pawel Pawlikowski's *Last Resort* (UK, 2000) she cannot fail noticing that 'the fact that we do not see London is also politically relevant here.' Talking of the representation of East Europeans coming into the West, she remarks: 'We have long been accustomed to films in which the East is configured as a space where individuals feel trapped, subject to a state of uncertain waiting, or as a space from which they are desperately trying to escape. In *Last Resort*, it is England that is cast in this role' (2007: 98).[11] Indeed, in the early years after the downfall of communism, a woman featured in Mircea Daneliuc's *Patul conjugal* (*Conjugal Bed*, Romania, 1993) was shown as threatening to take off for Istanbul as a prostitute: apparently, this was meant to be a reference to an improbable 'apocalyptic' scenario, playing on fantasy images of lusty Oriental men and a destination that subverted the geographical imagination that communism had cultivated indirectly, namely that Romania, even if temporarily estranged in the peculiar geopolitical stranglehold of communism, is a country that belongs to the Western world and is thus superior to the Orient. Back then, prostituting themselves to Orientals was a nightmarish scenario and a threat for 'Westernised' Romanian women – and other Eastern European women for that matter. Just a decade later, however, a Chinese soap opera has featured Chinese men extensively involved with newly arrived blonde East European women (Lu 2000), and a whole bunch of prostitutes from the former communist block are shown merrily practicing in Tokyo in Miike Takashi's *Hyôryû-gai* (*City of Lost Souls*, Japan, 2001). There is a clear consciousness that migration moves are often confined to the periphery, and the reality is sometimes even wilder than the moves seen in film: Vanya, a prostitute of Bulgarian origin, interviewed in Ann-Sofi Sidén's book *Warte mal!,* recounts her trajectory between spots in Tunisia, Cuba, Russia's Far East, and Korea (2002: 102).

Earlier margins, typically classed as 'non-places' (Augé 1995), have become the new junctions where the lives of the protagonists traverse and interconnect. Films are often named after such sites: Merzak Allouache's *Tamanrasset* (France, 2008) is named after the eponymous Tuareg oasis on the border between Algeria and Mali, and which is a key node in sub-Saharan human traffic. On

---

[11] When Bardan says 'we,' she assumes a Western audience, which implicitly remains the audience for *Last Resort*. Ultimately, this is a confirmation that England is where the film itself wants to live – according to Bardan – regardless of whether the film's plot says otherwise for the protagonist and her son.

the surface it appears to be just another desert spot, but it is soon revealed as a crossroads for lively traffic, as witnessed by the fashion photographer Philippe (Denis Lavant), who, while on a photo shoot in the desert becomes an accidental witness to the well-organised underground operation that shifts large groups of African men across the desert.[12] As Bruce Bennett and Imogen Tyler note, 'the border has become a central theme within a range of international films that might be categorised as "the cinema of borders" due to their central preoccupation with border crossing' (2007: 21), a new genre that also subsumes Gloria Anzaldúa's concept of 'uncrossable borders' (1987), where not only national differences but also a range of other hierarchies (class, race, gender, ethnicity) are at play. Border regions come to matter in an unprecedented manner, especially those dividing Schengen from non-Schengen countries in Europe,[13] as seen in films that focus on the crossing between Croatia and Italy, such as *Tvrdjava Evropa* (*Fortress Europe*, Želimir Žilnik, Slovenia, 2001) or *Rezervni deli* (*Spare Parts*, Damjan Kožole, Slovenia, 2003), or on the border between Serbian Vojvodina and the Schengen territory of Hungary, as seen in Želimir Žilnik's *Evropa preko plota* (*Europe Next Door*, Serbia/ Montenegro, 2005). The human traffic along the Slovenian-Italian or Croatian-Italian borders where traffickers cross the woods near Trieste on foot, the Mediterranean crossing between North Africa and

---

[12] The operation is 'underground' also in the literal sense, as the men move mostly during the night and sleep in caves under the ground during the day. Director Merzak Allouache uses the film to put forward a jaundiced take on such witnessing practiced by white affluent Westerners. At the end of the film Philippe's photographed testimony of the trafficking has not led to changes in the fate of any of the smuggled men. Only Philippe has benefited from his witnessing and now enjoys a high profile celebrity status as his images of scared African men caught by his camera in the cave near Tamanrasset feature on billboards all over Paris. Merzak Allouache's latest film, *Harragas* (Algeria/France, 2009), also deals with human trafficking, this time focusing on one of the anonymous key 'non-places' of trafficking, the Mediterranean sea crossing between Algeria and Europe.

[13] The Schengen agreements (1985; 1990) between a range of European Union member-countries made provisions for the free movement of people within the framework of the treaty, thus creating one common European border, which, once crossed, grants to illegal immigrants virtual access to most of Europe.

Spain, or the traffic at the Italian-French border pop up frequently in these films.[14] As seen, for example, in Spanish artist Xavier Arenós' *Schengen* (*The Castle*, 2007), a modern art project that seeks to 'document different economic typologies that spring up around the idea of the border, understood as the great monster of political and economic control in which the human becomes just another commodity' (David 2009: 120). Using the metaphor of Franz Kafka's novel *The Castle*, the video focuses on the dynamics of legitimate and illegitimate flows between North Africa and Spain, and exposes its invisible underground economy. Most suitably, the Lille3000 (France) exhibition, where I saw it, was dedicated to all these 'invisible borders.'

The plots of many traffic films evolve around unusual narrative trails that move between locations that can be designated as 'non-places' (Augé 1995) that, nonetheless, come along with rich emotional references and turn into intense and powerful 'memory sites' (Nora 1996) for those involved in the trafficking process, directly related to the postcolonial exploitation of 'invisible' people as discussed in the first essay of this volume. The narratives move between places that require constant cross-referencing to a map, as these are not places that the normative Western narrator has ever looked up before: stories of trafficking and re-trafficking begin in Benderi (Moldova), Livno (Bosnia), Tiraspol (Transdnistria), Durres (Albania), or Vinnitsa (Ukraine), then go on to no-man's land border crossings at Tivat (Montenegro) or Kmehin (Israel), before ending in equally obscure locales, such as a bar in Karaburun (Turkey) or Co-tai (Macau). If one connects the dots on the map of these places, a specific alternative geography gradually appears. Anonymous and previously unknown border towns become key nodes in the itinerary of anguish and distress.

[14] The border crossing becomes symbolically loaded, note Bennett and Tyler; in such a context, the challenge for Western filmmakers is 'to represent the "intimate others of globalisation" in ways that can attend to the specificity and materiality of lived experiences of borders and problematise, rather than reinforce, dominant Western tropes of visibility' (2007: 34).

Yet the movement and the stopovers in these 'non-places' come along with such arousing intensity that they would easily qualify as '*lieux de mémoire*,' the 'memory sites' of French philosopher Pierre Nora, where space and time collide in a uniquely significant configuration, often linked to a special historical experience or trauma.[15] The lives of those entangled in the traffic get linked to dull spots, somewhere near a highway, like Dubi in Slovakia (prominently featured in Ann-Sofi Sidén's work) or Krško in Slovenia (in *Spare Parts*), where they encounter some of the most harrowing experiences of their lives (as per the scene featuring the extreme terror and degradation of the East European prostitute at the bordertown motel in Ulrich Seidl's *Import/Export*, Austria/France/Germany, 2007). The slave trade takes place in equally undistinguished 'non-places' that stand in as the clearest and most condensed expression of the combination of traumatic memory and deprivation – the notorious Arizona Market in Bosnia, the Lelele in Istanbul, or the nameless spot in the middle of the Sinai desert featured in *Ha-Aretz Hamuvtachat* (*Promised Land*, Amos Gitai, Israel/France/UK, 2004) – places linked to the harrowing moment when the trafficked not only see themselves put up for sale but also learn their (low) price.

How can such unknown places, however, be designated as *lieux de mémoire*, when according to Augé it is precisely the problematic standing of such places in the context of identity and memory that defines them as 'non-places'? 'The distinction between places and non-places,' Augé writes, 'derives from the opposition between place and space' (1995: 78), and it is this acknowledgment

[15] 'If a place can be defined as relational, historical and concerned with identity, then a space which cannot be defined as relational, or historical, or concerned with identity will be a non-place. The hypothesis advanced here is that super-modernity produces non-places, meaning spaces which are not themselves anthropological places and which, unlike Baudelairean modernity, do not integrate the earlier places: instead these are listed, classified, promoted to the status of 'places of memory', and assigned to a circumscribed and specific position' (Augé 1995: 77-78).

of the importance of trajectory and movement that gives the 'non-places' of present day human trafficking the status of 'memory sites.' Pierre Nora describes these 'memory sites' as 'complex things,' and stipulates that 'at once natural and artificial, simple and ambiguous, concrete and abstract, they are *lieux* – places, sites, causes – in three senses: material, symbolic, and functional' (1996: 14). The intention of remembering is particularly important here, Nora remarks; without such an intention, '*lieux de mémoire* would be *lieux d'histoire*' (1996: 15). He also talks of sites of memory that are portable or topographical (1996: 18), and then distinguishes a kind of site that seems precisely to describe the types of location that are seen in trafficking films: places the emotional function of which is 'intended to preserve an incommunicable experience,' and which is 'doomed to vanish with those who shared that experience' (1996: 19).

Thus, the liminal secluded places where the victims of trafficking are stuck are transformed into 'memory sites.' In *Heremakono* (*Waiting for Happiness*, Abderrahmane Sissako, France/Mauritania, 2002), a story of migration which nonetheless is told mostly through the imagery of endless African sandscapes, Abdallah (Mohamed Mahmoud Ould Mohamed) is stuck in an isolated village, Nouhadhibou, on the coast of Mauritania, waiting for a sign to allow him to follow the migration path to Europe like so many others have done before him. The sea washes to the shore the bodies of those who have not succeeded, and yet Abdallah is hopeful that his journey will be better. Other films go even further in showing lives spent in places where one does not 'live': anonymous unmarked spaces, such as the muddy bottom of low tide Morecambe Bay (*Ghosts*, Nick Broomfield, UK, 2006), the interior of a bus that one does not dare leave (*Otobüs/The Bus*, Tunç Okan, Turkey/Switzerland, 1976), the interior of a freight container where a group of trafficked immigrants may suffocate to death somewhere off the coast of Newfoundland (Denis Chouinard and Nicholas Wadimoff's *Clandestines/Stowaway*,

Switzerland/Canada/France/Belgium, 1997), or a spot in the middle of the Mediterranean where a boat is about to vanish in the water with its load of hopeful migrants (*Once You're Born...*). Or, what is probably the most intense 'site of memory' in 'no-man's land' territory, the anonymous waters of the English Channel where the young Kurd Bilal (Firat Ayverdi) is last seen during his desperate attempt to swim across from Calais to Dover in Philippe Lioret's *Welcome* (France, 2009). It is also the place of his death.

The Villains: Patrons and Masters

> When I met Salim on a sunny crisp day in the remotest reaches of Bihar, my mind went blank. He was so ordinary – just a man, wearing simple village clothes. His aspect was common, his moustache trimmed, his hair neatly combed. He spoke without emotion of how he took male children for carpet weaving to the carpet-belt towns of Varnasi and Badoi and female children for sex work in New Delhi and Mumbai
>
> > Siddharth Kara on his encounter with a trafficker
> > on the Nepal/India border (2009: 63).

In films on civil war, helpless women and children are more often the centre of attention than villains. Or at least this was the case with most of the films I investigated in the context of my study of the films related to the Bosnian war of the mid-1990s (Iordanova 2001b). Similarly, most films on trafficking depict situations of victimisation and focus on the sufferers while leaving the victimisers out of the picture. The villains are rarely shown, maybe because of the 'banality of evil' that they carry along (Arendt 1963); they are, after all, just 'ordinary' and 'common' men like Salim, with neatly combed hair and simple clothes. John Picarelli's remark that historically 'traders in human beings were entrepreneurial' (2007: 39) brings to mind Werner Herzog's film *Cobra*

Verde (West Germany, 1987), in which one of these 'ordinary' men, the slave trader in the centre of the narrative, European explorer Francisco Manoel da Silva (Klaus Kinski), is shown relentlessly transporting slaves from the west coast of Africa to Latin America, gradually building his small but intense enterprise.

It is not that the traffickers are completely absent from the films we are discussing. Even if relegated to the shadowy corridors and dark alleys where the films take place, they still figure as secondary characters. When it comes to their portrayal in cinema, most often the mastermind behind a trafficking ring is shown as an enterprising middle-aged male who does not get himself involved in the operation but hires instead a host of bouncers who are to do the dirty jobs. If *The Sopranos* (David Chase, USA, 2000-2007) were a trafficking film, James Gandolfini's Tony Soprano would make for the perfect ringleader: a man of good common sense who knows how to set up the operation, how to outsource the dirty work, and how to make best use of contacts in the right places. Trafficking is, in a way, a transnational business the set-up of which is like the logistics of any other operation, where the attention goes to developing a robust supply chain, and to putting the respective risk management mechanisms in place. The whole process is broken down in functional fragments. It is about securing the transport and the premises, and about ensuring the regularity of supply and demand. There are no moral dimensions to this business; it is all about cash-flow projections, reducing accruals, increasing turnover, and optimising profitability. All those involved in the trafficking process are treated as participants in a deal: those who are trafficked become clients, those who traffic them become service operators, and it all evolves around negotiations over service, price, the terms of payment and delivery, and so on.

'Traffickers are enormously diverse,' remarks Louise Shelley. 'They range from diplomats and employees of multinational organisations who traffic young women for domestic labour to the large organisations of Asia which specialise in human smuggling and trafficking. There is every size of organisation in between the family business and the multinational criminal organisation' (2007: 120). Other researchers have noticed that people involved in the so-called 'shuttle trade' taking place in the context of countries like Greece, China, UEA, South Korea, or Turkey, are often involved in human trafficking, be it as recruiters, pimps or facilitators and that shuttle trade may, in fact, be a front for trafficking and bonded labour (Kelly 2007: 76). When it comes to cinema, one can discover several main categories of villain that dominate: traffickers of specific ethnic origins, women-traffickers, locals recruited from the places where there is an intense traffic of people, as well as petty criminals who are trying to set up in business by building a small traffic operation for themselves.

The first category, presenting ringleaders of specific ethnic origins, quite often shows a member of the same ethnic group who has migrated earlier and knows that there is money to be made wherever movement of people takes place. We see this kind of person in *Time of the Gypsies* where the white suit-wearing and Mercedes-driving Ahmed (Bora Todorović) is the epitome of such 'warlord'-type businessmen. Similar to the Gypsy ringleader seen in *Guardian Angel*, Ahmed lives in a caravan on the outskirts of an Italian city, in a makeshift camp that can be built (or which can disappear, depending on the need) within a few hours. Both these ringleaders are of Romani origin and rely on a network of ethnic contacts that send a constant supply of Romani children that they then use for begging, pickpocketing, and prostitution. The bosses of the trafficking ring are briefly shown in *The Bus*: apparently, like those whom they traffic, they are also Turks of an older migration wave who now sit in a restaurant and receive the bag of money that the driver-executor of the task brings in. Both films are reviewed in detail in the Close-Ups section, since they were among the first to offer commentary on these matters. As mentioned in the previous chapter, in *Human Trafficking*

(Christian Duguay, Canada/USA, 2005), the mastermind behind the large operation is the Russian Sergei Karpovich (Robert Carlyle), a member of a former colonial power who, in line with Russia's earlier colonial experience, has victimised women from across former Eastern Europe in a new, postcolonial configuration.

While logical, the choice of the ethnic identity of the traffic leaders in filmic narratives is indicative of the assumptions about the homogeneity of the audience for which the film is made: the rings are set up by 'others,' the criminals are as foreign as the victims, and therefore the problem that is shown, while awful, does not have much to do with 'us,' the viewers. In this way, cinema seems to assist in the demonisation of ethnic mafias (Albanians, Turks, Gypsies, Russian, Chinese, Nigerian, Romanian), as discussed by various researchers. Barbara Hudson, for example, notes that whole groups of immigrants are demonised because of the media-maintained perceptions that only certain ethnic networks are involved in human trafficking; Albanians, Roma, North Africans, non-white Muslims in general and Pakistanis in the UK specifically are identified as the 'usual suspects' in their respective immigration contexts (2007: 214). Morawska talks of excessive attention being paid to Albanian networks, in a context where the evidence also points to Lithuanian, Russian, and smaller-scale Chinese chains, as well as Polish, Ukrainian, and Israeli rings that traffic people into the UK (2007: 103-105). To Malarek, all known 'principal powers in international organised crime: the Italian Mafia, the Colombian drug cartels, the Chinese Triads and the Japanese Yakuza' are involved in what is essentially a transnational and not ethnically specific trade (2004: 48).

In her discussion of Sister Ping, the notorious chief of a large Chinese smuggling organisation, and of a number of other trafficking networks run by women who are themselves immigrants to the West, Louise Shelley remarks that taking on employment in a trafficking organisation often seems an ideal opportunity for solving the financial difficulties that recent legal immigrants face in the new societies; these people, she underlines, believe they are 'providing a public service' for the migrants who have no recourse to legal means of immigrating (2007: 121-122). Along these same lines, cinema seems to love the category of women traffickers (thus, again members of the same group as the trafficked women). They are role models of sorts: they clearly come from a background that has exposed them to the world of prostitution and human trafficking as run by men, and who have then taken on a daring step and have decided to run the business themselves. They feature in a number of films, often presented in somewhat romanticised or exoticised fashion, with roles often assigned to experienced popular actresses. Take, for example, Marion, the brothel-owner from Nae Caranfil's *Asfalt Tango* (*Asphalt Tango*, Romania, 1999), played by a steely-eyed Charlotte Rampling: this aloof woman travels to Romania to recruit other women to work in the chain of brothels that she runs, and she personally escorts them on the bus to France. Or Anne Parillaud and Hanna Schygulla's characters in *Promised Land*. Both have apparently been involved in prostitution before, but in the present one of them runs the nitty-gritty aspects of the slave market in the desert (leather-clad Parillaud), while the other (Schygulla) is a turban-wearing heavily made-up 'Madam' in an eccentric luxury establishment on the Red Sea. Other films show women who come dangerously close to getting involved on the wrong side, but who manage to preserve their moral integrity and redeem themselves: Helena (Isabelle Blais) in *Human Trafficking*, who becomes an accountant for the ringleader; Lorna (Arta Dobroshi) in *Le Silence de Lorna* (*The Silence of Lorna*, Jean-Pierre and Luc Dardenne, Belgium/France/Italy/Germany, 2008), who has entered a deal to marry a Belgian drug addict for an EU passport and who is involved with the prospective killers of her junkie-husband, whose death will allow her to move upwardly. And then, there are other women who, whilst not directly involved in the trafficking business, effectively support it – like Madeleine Harlsburgh (Wendy Crewson) in *Sex Traffic* (David Yates, UK/Canada, 2004). Madeleine is the wife of the wealthy American businessman whose military services outsourcing corporation is accused of being involved in trafficking in the Balkans. She travels to Italy to visit the homes where rescued girls are sheltered and to meet with victims and social workers. However, her actions are of a morally dubious nature, as the generous donation to human rights organisations involved with the repatriation effort is nothing more than an attempt to cover up her husband's dishonour.[16]

In yet another category, the traffickers simply happen to be locals who take on a job opportunity available to them. Where there is war, there is an opportunity to become a warlord, and where there is a flow of migrants, there is a host of jobs available to service it, from people smuggler to immigration lawyer to judge. In *Journey of Hope*, the traffickers are a bunch of rough Swiss mountaineers, who take a motley group of migrants (among whom is the Kurdish family that is the focus of the action) through the Alps – a venture not particularly different from the logistics of the work performed by Sherpas for Western mountaineers in the Himalayas. In Želimir Žilnik's *Kud plovi ovaj brod* (*Wanderlust*, Yugoslavia/Slovenia/Hungary, 1999), a bunch of young local entrepreneurs has set up an operation that transports cigarettes and people into Italy with a fleet of gliders that take off from a small coastal town in Montenegro. In Pier Žalica's *Gori Vatra* (*Fuse*, Bosnia/Herzegovina, 2003) the ringmaster is the local gold chain-wearing thug Velija (Senad Bašić), who is shown splitting his time between playing tennis and shagging whores, while occasionally

---

[16] There has been extensive documentary writing on the mercenary DynCorp's involvement in setting up notorious establishments like Crazy Horse II and Apache in Bosnia. DynCorp, which serves as a prototype of the corporation in *Sex Traffic*, has often been identified as a key driving force behind the intense slave trade that reportedly takes place at the Arizona Market in Bosnia and behind the general human traffic across the Balkans (see Malarek 2004: 160-179; Kara 2009: 144).

also stockpiling weapons and bribing the police. In Artan Minarolli's *Nata pa hënë*, (*Moonless Night*, Albania, 2004), another bunch of young entrepreneurial locals has organised a boat operation to traffic Albanians to Italy through the Otranto strait. In *Once You're Born...*, the trafficker is a local brute sailing in the Mediterranean. In *Welcome* the traffickers are a gang of Normandy locals who live near Calais, where the main current of illegal migrants hoping to cross into England is concentrated. These kinds of local men, who become gangsters by accident, are at the centre of *Spare Parts*, the only film that is focused entirely on the lives of jobbing traffickers. Rudi (Aljoša Kovacić) and Ludvik (Peter Musevski) have simply taken the jobs that have happened to be available, and they perform them as they would any other job in service or transportation. If there was no stream of people, they would turn to something else; in contexts where no other job opportunities exist, this is, indeed, one of the few areas in which they could be employed.

Last but not least, there are traffickers who belong to a category that I shall tentatively call 'carpetbaggers': broke Western businessmen who have failed at the game in their own countries and who now travel to the countries where traffic originates, like gold-diggers on a hunt for opportunities and after 'emerging markets.' A prototype of a 'carpetbagger' in European cinema is Fiore (Michele Placido) in *Lamerica*: he travels to Albania, scheming to pocket an EU development grant to set up a mock shoe production operation that would exploit cheap labour in a country that is clearly undergoing an economic disaster in the early 1990s, when the action of the film takes place. In Armando Manni's *Elvjs e Merilijn* (*Elvis and Marilyn*, Italy, 1998) the trafficker, Gino (Giorgio Faletti), has taken the time to organise a talent contest in Romania and Bulgaria where he recruits his victims. Somewhat improbably, he eagerly maintains the myth that his recruits are going to land reputable entertainment jobs in Italy, and does so almost to the end, when things rapidly sour and he shows his real (monstrous) face. Another 'carpetbagger' is the sleek and nice looking Andrei (Pavel Ponomaryov) in *Lilya 4-ever*, a baby-faced criminal who uses his pretty looks and good manners to lure teenagers like Lilya (Oksana Akinshina) to fall head over heels in love with him. Becoming a ruthless and exploitative 'carpetbagger' is shown as one of the few opportunities in the trajectory followed by the protagonist of Ken Loach's *It's a Free World...* (UK/Italy/Germany/Spain/Poland, 2007): Angie (Kierston Wareing) is employed by one of the companies recruiting workers from Poland and the Ukraine, where she gains first-hand experience in taking people's money in exchange for shitty jobs and a harsh life in the West. Seeing herself as a victim of sexism and exploitation, Angie soon decides she can exploit people equally well while pocketing all the profits. And she soon proves she can be as bad and treacherous as one needs to be in this business in order to pull it off. Beautiful and committed, she is completely focused on advancing the business and often forgets the human dimension of things.

The Victims: Consenting Adults, Labour Migrants?

There is no question that smugglers take advantage of the migrants' desperation or vulnerability. But are all exploitative offers coercive and is coercion always exploitative? The answer is no... Just because the smuggler's offer is exploitative does not necessarily mean the migrant is coerced. For that to be the case, states need an independent yardstick. If the migrant has no other acceptable options, then the exploitative offer becomes coercive. For instance, if the migrant would starve, or be unable to get medicine for a child unless he or she took up the offer, then the offer would be coercive.

Jacqueline Bhabha (2005)

There seems to be an irreconcilable dichotomy between coerced and consensual, which sets the watershed between trafficked and voluntary migrants, and is based on the perceived involvement of individuals.[17] Those who have willingly become part of a situation where they let themselves be smuggled into a country cannot possibly be seen as victims of trafficking; they appear as active participants in an act of unlawful entry. However, the fact that the migrant has consented to be smuggled – Jacqueline Bhabha notes – does not alter the fact that the same act can be coercive. She believes it is more important to establish the 'moral baseline' (a term coined by philosopher Alan Wertheimer) as to what counts as coercive and what counts as consensual; it is in relation to these matters that the rigidity of the framework applied by policy makers in individual states comes to light (2005). Slavery and slavery-like work are clearly unacceptable human rights abuses, yet the destitution and lack of access to basic economic staples (like food, medicine, and shelter) that lead to enslavement are not considered as factors that may conceivably lead to forced migration.

To Bhabha, the 'abuse of a position of vulnerability,' which is included in the definition of trafficking, can encompass a broad range of situations, as 'poverty, hunger, illness, lack of education, and displacement could all constitute a position of vulnerability.' No state in the world, Bhabha underlines, is required to address social ills originating in other counties, nor is it expected 'to expand lawful access to their territory, or to address the chronic mismatch between supply and demand by increasing supply' by admitting economic migrants to its territory (2005). Yet this may probably be the only radical solution to a range of problems experienced by those who end up as trafficking

---

[17] In 2000, states drafted two new protocols to the UN Convention on Transnational Organised Crime (UN TOC) dealing with trafficking and smuggling. The Trafficking and Smuggling Protocols, more commonly known as the Palermo Protocols, came into force on 23 December 2003 and 28 January 2004 respectively.

victims. In the eyes of sociologists, the background behind the traffic is often summed up by the term 'labour migrations'; some speak of 'roaming labour.' As economic rights are not part of the human rights hierarchy of categories and the abuse of labour rights is, respectively, not regarded as a human rights violation, these matters simply cannot be addressed under the current framework, as Leshu Torchin pointed out in the previous chapter. It is a context where cinema and popular narratives step in to show the true complexity behind matters related to coercion and exploitation, and to expose the underlying factors behind the anxiety and vulnerability of trafficking victims.

Policy makers are generally reluctant to admit that it is international politics that often lies at the root of these migratory problems. The economic globalisation that followed the collapse of the communist system, Siddharth Kara writes, 'unleashed catastrophic increases in poverty levels and civil strife, most directly in Central and Eastern Europe and East Asia'; the situation was 'enhanced by the rigid formula of market economy measures imposed by the IMF on the region' (2009: 25). None of these economic factors, however, is considered as legitimate grounds for the migration of individuals who have been truly coerced to seek a new life elsewhere. Still, as already discussed in the first essay of this volume, affluent countries with developed economies need 'disposable people' (Bales 2004). Trafficked or not, they are all economic migrants who come in to earn money, in whichever way is available to them.[18] It is the legal framework of the receiving country that forces them, on arrival, to enter a game in which they

---

[18] In *A Street without a Name: Childhood and Other Misadventures in Bulgaria* (2009), for example, Kapka Kasabova tells the story of a young Bulgarian woman who hopes to work at a kitchen in the West. She travels to Hamburg, only to realise that she is in the hands of traffickers when she overhears her price being discussed by the Albanian and Bulgarian men with whom she has come to the restaurant (the 'sale' in this instance is for a paltry €1,000). It is a typical situation where the victim has gone to Germany voluntarily and at her own expense, a move triggered by the lack of opportunities at home.

must have a 'story' that fits with what is expected of them in order to 'qualify' as vulnerable victims, a specific 'legitimisation' that could give them easier access to the new society and substantially reduce the risk of their exploitation in the context of the underground grey economy. Within the current legal framework, however, fleeing economic hardship may be prevalent but it is not admissible as a 'story' (as discussed in the last chapter with regard to *True North*, Steve Hudson, Germany/Ireland/UK, 2006); it must be some other form of persecution that these migrants are fleeing from (political, racial, gender-based, and so on). It is thus suggested to migrants to present themselves as refugees and asylum seekers, and they eagerly embrace the opportunity. Immigration lawyers are paid by legal aid schemes in the receiving states to train refugee claimants to tell their story the way it should be communicated; in other words, to present in acceptable categories the experiences that have led them to migrate and to adjust the narrative around prescribed templates. Migrants who do not manage to fit the account of their experiences into a suitably communicable storyline of suffering are categorised as 'bogus' refugees.

Ironically, in a context that keeps a strict demarcation line between coercive and consensual participation in trafficking, the only ones who 'qualify' as true 'victims' would be unsuspecting individuals grabbed from the streets by ruthless traffickers. Such situations, however, are only seen in films showing the snatching of Western girls from affluent families, like the one in *Human Trafficking*, who is snatched from a bazaar, and the one in *Taken* (Pierre Morel, France, 2008), who is violently abducted from a spacious Parisian flat within minutes of her arrival – both unwary and fully blameless targets of organised crime. Everybody else is complicit to some extent: Diana (Diana Bespechni) in *Promised Land* is shown going to a modelling agency in Tallinn to be photographed naked without any coercion. Olga (Ekateryna Rak) in *Import/Export* seeks employment with the internet-sex company of her own free will as well. Women like them, who are pushed into trafficking by economic hardship, cannot easily 'qualify' as victims of trafficking leading to bonded labour and sex slavery as their position of vulnerability is not as clear cut as in the case of the gullible American girls who are seized by force to end up in the same position.[19] Even more, women like Diana and Olga have actively sought out the situation that leads to their current deplorable condition; similarly, the protagonists of *Elvis and Marilyn* have entered a talent contest and have won it, ending up in the paradoxical situation of becoming both winners and victims.

True, there is often deceit involved in getting individuals into the system of trafficking – a false promise of employment (*Elvis and Marilyn*), a phony marriage offer (*Last Resort*), a spurious promise of love (*Lilya 4-ever*) – but it is not as clear cut as the sheer evil trickery that is behind the abductions of American girls in *Human Trafficking* and *Taken*. All the 'dubious' victims of deception appear to take part in the traffic consensually; as Áine O'Healy has shown in her analysis of relevant texts from recent Italian cinema, many films even implicitly suggest 'that the woman herself is partially compliant in her victimisation' (2007: 41).[20] Typically, these are characters that come from impoverished backgrounds that provide no opportunity whatsoever; the very existence of economic hardship (and, by default, their interest in economic betterment) taints their credibility and precludes their capability to qualify as sheer victims. They may be descendents of impoverished families who have ended up with

---

[19] It is probably not by chance that the ringleaders and those enabling the human traffic shown in these films are also presented in an equally clear-cut fashion that successfully qualifies them as villains within established clichés (a devious transnationally-operating Russian Mafioso in *Human Trafficking*; a corrupt French executive in *Taken*).

[20] O'Healy (2007) scrutinises Italian films such as Carlo Mazzacurati's *Un'altra vita* (*Another Life*, Italy, 1992) and *Vesna va veloce* (Italy, 1996), Gianluca Maria Tavarelli's *Portami via* (*Take Me Away*, Italy, 1994), *Elvis & Marilyn*, Corso Salani's *Occidente* (*West*, Italy, 2000), and Giuseppe Tornatore's *La Sconosciuta* (*The Unknown*, Italy/France, 2006).

more children than they can support, as seen in the Romanian film *Maria* (Calin Peter Netzer, Romania/France/Germany, 2003).[21] Their own parents may have sold them into bondage, as is revealed in *Guardian Angel*. Or they may have chosen to get themselves into the traffic, probably thinking that nothing can be worse than what they are already living through, as in *Lilya 4-Ever*. It is often the downcast existence of someone in the family that is depending on them (a baby, a child, an ill parent) that prompts these protagonists to seek options for better financial prospects. In *Journey of Hope* the story begins by showing the impoverished household of the Kurdish family that has no other alternative but to try elsewhere. In *Fortress Europe,* the Russian protagonists are searching for a better economic future. The prostitutes in *Fuse* are escaping a more miserable existence back home. And in *Europe Next Door* the girl from [non-Schengen] Vojvodina in Serbia pays €3,000 to marry a Hungarian guy in order to get a [Schengen] passport, again a situation that would improve her economic prospects. Films show the miserable conditions in which Bulgarian 'Elvjs' (Goran Navojec) and Romanian 'Merilijn' (Edyta Olszówka) live, the despondent dead-end environment of the Moldovan sisters of *Sex Traffic*, the wretched surroundings of the Ukrainian protagonist of *Import/Export,* and so on, thus presenting mounting evidence of the relevance of the economic collapse of the former Soviet bloc to the present-day realities of involuntary migrations.

Indeed, in an overwhelming majority of mainstream films, the plot centres on a young woman who is trafficked for sex; the storyline is uniform and predictable, often moving within a paradigm that combines a degree of fascination for the specific

---

[21] The plot of this film does not take the protagonist into international sex traffic, but only into prostitution confined to clients passing by locally. Impoverished Maria, a mother of seven who is married to an unemployed alcoholic, ends up selling sexual favours by the sheer need to feed her children and in order to fight eviction and starvation. The film was widely acclaimed at festivals across post-communist Eastern Europe, where it routinely won the audience award.

'glamour' associated with the sex industry with a duly expressed (yet insufficiently genuine) moral outrage. O'Healy aptly defines this approach as 'ambivalent,' as it simultaneously constructs the woman 'as both innocent victim and alluring erotic object' (2007: 41). The East European prostitute in French film *La vie nouvelle* (*The New Life*, Philippe Grandrieux, France, 2002), for example, wears a stunning Karl Lagerfeld-designed fantasy outfit during her visits to men in various depressing motel rooms, an approach that makes the film a prime candidate for O'Healy's observation according to which this type of film tends to display 'complicity with the sadistic logic of the diegetically placed perpetrators' and to rely on a passive gaze, which is 'dutifully compassionate though ultimately complicit' (2007: 41). In *Taken*, the abducted girls, all pretty and sweet, are kept in bondage in individual en suite rooms, and they all look dazzling, wearing sexy lingerie, arms up and hands tied to the bed frame, even if withered and dehydrated when the rescuers finally get through to them. And indeed, if I recall correctly, the billboard advertising the free [rescue] phone number at the Istanbul airport also came with a picture of a young blonde girl, thus suggesting that if you are overweight and in your mid-fifties the number is probably not for you... One wonders if this obsession with sex traffic does not help the relative obscurity to which other forms of human trafficking are relegated. One does not see much of the plight of domestics (as revealed in the fate of the Sri Lankan woman seen in *Otan erthei i mama gia ta Hristougenna/ When Mother Comes Home for Christmas*, Nilita Vachani, Greece/ India/Germany, 1996), or carers for the elderly and the disabled (shown in the 2008 Dutch documentary *Caregivers*, by Amsterdam-based Spaniard Libia Castro and Icelander Olafur Olafsson), or those employed in construction (*It's a Free World...*), or in farming (*Poniente*, Chus Gutiérrez, Spain, 2002).

Several visual tropes that recur in the films on trafficking contribute to the ambiguousness of representation. The first revolves around showing a young woman sitting on the side of the road or in a square awaiting a pick-up next to their luggage, then a bus arrives to take her toward her new life – as seen, for example, in *Balalayka* (Ali Özgentürk, Turkey, 2000) where the women are collected from around South Russia and the Caucasus, or in the previously mentioned *Asphalt Tango*, where the women are collected from around Romania. It has all been arranged in advance – documents, payment, the works – and she is now only waiting for the pick-up to happen; there is no doubt that it is all happening consensually. Letting oneself be trafficked appears as a choice. The other visual trope – surrendering one's passport on arrival in the foreign country (seen in *Balalayka*, *Lilya 4-ever*, *Sex Traffic*, *Fuse*, and elsewhere) – also appears as a consensual move.[22] A third recurring motif relates to situations that reveal that even if there may not be full clarity on what one expects, there is a lingering suspicion that one would need to use one's body in whatever one does. In *Tirana, année zero* (*Tirana Year Zero*, Fatmir Koçi, France/Albania, 2001) a young girl proclaims that the purpose of her travel to Paris is to get into modelling. According to Andrew James Horton, however, it is a false declaration: 'she clearly has no contacts in Paris that would keep her on the legitimate side of the business of showing off her body' (Horton 2006: 298). She is most likely to end up using her body in some other way. The same is true for the émigré protagonists of Brazilian *Foreign Land* (*Terra Estrangeira*, Walter Salles and Daniela Thomas, Brazil/Portugal, 1996), whose bodies are used for diamond trafficking, or with the Colombian protagonist of *Maria Full of Grace* (Joshua Marston, USA/Colombia, 2004) whose body is used as a

[22] Louise Shelley (2007) talks of the confiscation of passports as one of the routine first steps taken by traffickers, since without documents the trafficked have no legal status. This measure also has practical implications, for if the trafficked victim escaped, she would not even be able to command the protection of her own country's embassy; as she would have no proof of her citizenship, the crime cannot be investigated. In addition, 'loss of identity is key to the dehumanisation of the victim. (2007: 131).

container for illicit drug traffic. The use of the body in *Elvis and Marilyn* is implied already in the film's very premise – the protagonists are recruited via a contest for celebrity lookalikes, a configuration in which their bodily appearance is key. The bodies of the girls in *Promised Land* are handled and inspected as lifeless goods; Olga's body is treated in a similar way in the scenes of transnational webcam sex in *Import/Export*. These are all set-ups into which the protagonists are shown entering consensually. The judgement on matters of vulnerability, exploitation and coercion is left to the viewers.

On the other hand, a key feature of many of these films is the use of subjective flashbacks meant to allow a glimpse into the inner world of the trafficked, often representing moments of calm and peace referring to a point in time just before the current ordeal has begun. The moustached protagonist of Turkish immigrant saga *The Bus* experiences flashbacks that take him back to the cotton fields of Kurdistan. The trafficked Romani boy in *Guardian Angel* keeps returning to an idyllic vision of a golden afternoon when he sees himself walking by the side of his father who carries a white ram. Lilya keeps seeing an apparition of her teenage friend Volodya (Artyom Bogucharsky), a dream-like visualisation where they are both angels. In *Promised Land*, Diana's story is told in a series of flashbacks that mix up images of home (snowy back yard, a cat), belonging (angelic choir singing in an Orthodox church), and itinerary.

Popular Culture: Do Films Have an Impact?

I was recently invited to give a talk at a research seminar at the Political Science department of a British university. It was an invitation from colleagues working in what I thought of as a related social science discipline that, like my work, focuses on transnational interactions. I thought the talk went well until, in the Q&A period, a woman who had been sitting quietly in the corner of the auditorium, confronted me somewhat nervously: Everything I was talking about, she said, surely sounded interesting as it was about movies and she was entertained. However, how could I make claims about social issues on the basis of the film material that I was working with? This was popular culture stuff; it could not possibly have validity nor, for that matter, social impact. Whatever I was saying, she claimed, would be inconclusive by default, as what was found in films could not possibly have bearing on the social process or other aspects of reality.

I admit I was taken by surprise: it had never occurred to me that one could question the importance of popular culture representations, especially from an 'impact' point of view – after all, a popular TV sitcom or a Hollywood blockbuster has got a much broader public reach (and influence over minds) than a government 'white paper' or a policy initiative that remains known to a handful of specialists.[23]

This encounter, however, was an eye-opening experience; it alerted me to the striking absence of cinematic references from the work of social science scholars. Once I had made the observation, this absence kept popping up when reading the next book on trafficking or contemporary migrations that I would open. Many were studies that, although on contemporary social issues widely represented in cinema, persistently abstained from making any references to films or other texts of popular culture related to these same social issues. So, on the one hand there was a large number of films that address trafficking, either as the main theme or as a subplot in the context of other contemporary concerns, and which were all made by concerned and committed filmmakers. And on the other hand,

[23] Victor Malarek's book *The Natashas* (2004) on the traffic in East European women makes extensive references to the impact of popular culture images. Many of these women, he claims, 'venture off with visions of the film *Pretty Woman* (Garry Marshall, USA, 1990) dancing in their heads' (2004: 18), whereas, in fact, later on in their lives as prostitutes they are made by their pimps to watch over and over again and to 'learn' (as well as practice 'bump-and-grind techniques') from films such as *Striptease* (Andrew Bergman, USA, 1996, with Demi Moore) and *Showgirls* (Paul Verhoeven, USA, 1995, with Elizabeth Berkley) (2004: 61). Thus, Hollywood cinema gets acknowledged as an important contextual reference that directly and powerfully impacts reality.

there were the social scientists, equally concerned and committed to addressing the same themes in their writing. Both scholarship and filmmaking had received their impetus from the recent growth in global trafficking, both were driven by the same social concern. Why was it, then, that they did not seem to intersect or interact? Or, rather, whereas in films an individual story would frequently be 'framed' (prefaced or concluded) by an on screen note making reference to the general social problem (e.g. '20,000 children are trafficked in Yugoslavia every year,' a statement made at the close of *Guardian Angel*), social science studies would remain silent as to the existence of films or other texts that may have presented, in fictional form, the same migratory trajectories and the same human concerns that the study was addressing.

Let us take a closer look at a book to which we have been referring repeatedly throughout this volume: Siddharth Kara's *Sex Trafficking: Inside the Business of Modern Slavery* (2009). It is not a traditional social science book, in that the author, in his efforts to trace trafficking as thoroughly as possible, takes the subject matter close to heart and travels personally around the globe, providing his own reports on the status of sex trafficking as he comes across it in various corners. *Sex Trafficking* would normally be classified as a journalistic book. It often reads like a novel, and often relies on highly personalised accounts. However, it also has claims to being social science because it makes a rare attempt to provide estimates of the size of the phenomenon (something that most sociologists have agreed is notoriously difficult to pin down) and to calculate the global sex trafficking industry's turnaround, revenues, and profits.

Leafing through the pages after reading the book, I see I have made numerous pencil marks in the margins, cross-referencing film titles that have come to mind as related directly to the story and trafficking pathways that the author is discussing

(*Phoolan Devi/Bandit Queen*, Shekhar Kapur, India, 1994, when he talks about the abuse of young girls in India; *Lilya 4-ever* when he talks of the former Soviet Union; and many more). My notes, however, remain confined to my personal copy of the book. Even though the text often reads like an account of familiar film plots, the author himself does not reference a single film. But why is that? Why is it okay for him to refer to personal impressions and encounters, to stories that people tell him, but not to films? Is it possible that Kara is not familiar with any of the numerous documentaries or features that have tackled these same matters? Is it possible that, on his travels, no one made a reference to films and nobody suggested that he could find an interesting representation of trafficking in some work of cinema? Is it possible that Kara, who has included a chapter on Thailand in his study, never came across the acclaimed *The Good Woman of Bangkok* (Dennis O'Rourke, Australia/UK, 1991), one of the first public attempts to raise the awareness of trafficking and prostitution related to Thailand? Is it possible that he, who explains that his initial interest in the matters of sex trafficking was triggered by a visit to war-time Bosnia in the 1990s, is not aware of Karin Jurschick's *The Peacekeepers and the Women* (*Die Helfer und die Frauen*, Germany, 2003), the documentary that shows persuasively how the presence of international troops in Bosnia and the free market zone facilitated and enhanced trafficking? Is it possible that he, who spent time in Moldova and studied the intricate patterns of sex slavery that originate there, was not referred to the widely shown TV series *Sex Traffic*, where the Moldovan sisters Elena (Anamaria Marinca) and Vara (Maria Popistasu) are shown following precisely the same trafficking routes as the routes he describes in his study? How about the story of the Ukrainian named Brigitte, who, Kara reports, 'was well educated with a nurse's degree, but her "pay slip" of thirty-five dollars per month was not nearly enough for her to make ends meet' (2009: 85)? Doesn't this read directly as a plot description of the opening sequences of *Import/Export*, showing the pitiful existence of Ukrainian maternity ward nurse Olga, who is forced to look for ways out of her existence below the poverty line? How about the stories of Balkan child beggars in Italy and Greece that Kara tells (2009: 146-7)? He even talks of organ harvesting, but makes no reference to films that tackle the same issues, such as Stephen Frears' *Dirty Pretty Things* (UK, 2002) and *Spare Parts*, both films internationally distributed and critically acclaimed. Kara talks at length of forced prostitution in North America, but makes no mention of *Human Trafficking*, a production that was distributed widely in the USA by Miramax and by Walt Disney on DVD. This latter production at least should have been brought to his attention, especially as the filmmakers and Kara share pretty much the same concerns.

Given the abundance of these potential references, I wonder if I can speculate that in the course of researching his book, references to a variety of films were most likely brought to Kara's attention, but that it was a conscious decision on his part not to use them in his writing. Why would one avoid referring to films, however? If the book is meant to be part of the global effort to stop trafficking, why is the author shunning all these films that have precisely the same purpose as his book – to raise awareness about a dangerous yet hushed social problem?

Not that this particular author is alone in the approach. I am referring at length to his book mostly because the comparisons and references that could have been made there are so overwhelming (maybe because, like Kara, filmmakers have persistently kept sex traffic as the centre of attention). The picture, however, is the same throughout most of the social science writing on trafficking: it is marked by persistent and obstinate silence with regard to cinematic representations of the phenomenon.[24]

'Real life' material – interviews, statistics, policy documents, reports – seems fine. As soon as it comes to literature and film, however, one enters a 'grey zone'; the 'fictional' not only cannot supply legitimate material for study, but it is not even mentioned nor acknowledged as something that may be informing opinions and thus a factor of social life. Social scientists seem particularly cautious not to mix in popular culture representations; images and narratives are seen as something that cannot possibly have an impact. At the same time, many of the texts we discuss here are not only created with the intention of having an impact on human trafficking in real life, but in fact lead to increased awareness and enjoy an influence that often goes far beyond the impact of the policy recommendations made by some think tank or policy consultancy. Thus, a further factor should be added to the list of reasons for the insufficiency of efforts in combating sex trafficking (besides the poor understanding of its nature, the underfunding of anti-trafficking organisations, the

---

[24] The edited collection *Human Trafficking*, for example, includes a chapter on trafficking into and from Eastern Europe by influential professor Ewa Morawska – with not a single mention of the numerous films that have been made in the region to reflect on the same issue (2007: 92-116). Gabriella Lazaridis' study of migrant women in Greece (2001) makes no references to films, even though *When Mother Comes Home for Christmas*, discussed in our Close-Ups section, had been released and widely commented on in Greece around the time the research was done and could have been referenced. Natalia Shostack's study on trafficked Ukrainian women (2004) is equally silent on the matter of popular culture representations. Maggy Lee talks about the tragedy of cockle-pickers in Morecambe Bay (2007: 18), but no mention is made of Nick Broomfield's film *Ghosts*, released the previous year and shown on British television. In this same collection, Andrea Di Nicola identifies a range of limitations that the research into trafficking encounters: the inaccessibility of traffickers and victims, the ethical implications, the political sensitivity, the descriptiveness, the non-evaluative nature, and the sampling problems of the research. She notes the limited range of data collection techniques and laments the fact that more evaluative, ethnographical approaches do not seem to have been adopted, making pronouncements in favour of participant observation and other anthropological methods (2007: 60). However, the use of cinematic narratives, which could partially alleviate these difficulties in research, is not listed, even though anthropologists have lately made powerful arguments in favour of using feature film narratives in lieu of oral testimonies.

inadequacy of poorly-enforced anti-trafficking laws, and the lack of a systematic analysis of this changing situation): the reluctance of social scientists and policy makers to take advantage of the insights that the analysis of popular representations and narratives of trafficking can offer.[25] Film shapes perception, so we can and should look at films to see what stories people tell about trafficking, who tells them, who receives them and how they are received. In addition, especially where celebrities are involved, film can help raise the awareness of an issue, even if problematically, and this too should be taken into account.

The poster listing a free phone number for victims of trafficking to call at Istanbul airport, which greeted me on arrival there, was yet another manifestation of the same attempts to raise awareness that cinematic narratives install in people's minds. I am not aware of human rights activists distributing leaflets containing studies by migration specialists; I am aware, however, of a number of anti-trafficking organisations that are setting up film festivals – discussed later in 'Traffic Jam' – in the hope that those girls who see the films will not end up involved in the traffic.

---

[25] There are, of course, exceptions to this pattern, usually found in the work of feminist or media scholars who are conscious of the importance of representation and popular culture in any given social context. Collections such as *Been There and Back to Nowhere: Gender in Transnational Spaces* (2000), edited by visual artist Ursula Biemann, bring together interdisciplinary writing from social scientists like diaspora sociologist Avtar Brah, philosopher Yvonne Volkart, as well as Biemann's discussion of her own video projects that focus on the trans-border trafficking of women. The volume on *Transnational Feminism in Film and Media* (2008, edited by Katarzyna Marciniak, Anikó Imre, and Áine O'Healy, each one of whom has also done work on these matters independently) features the writing of Dutch feminist scholar Ginette Vestrate, who expresses the same concerns over a lack of interaction between social theory and the study of representation as an element of the social environment. It is in the work of predominantly female scholars that such an examination is discovered: Sandra Ponzanesi, Yosefa Loshitsky, Ewa Mazierska and Laura Rascaroli, Daniela Berghahn, Claudia Sternberg, Carrie Tarr, Isabel Santaollala, Yana Hashamova, Rutvica Andrijasevic, and others who work on matters of representing migrations in popular media and film.

Part Two
Close-ups

The Bus

Otobüs (*The Bus*, Tunç Okan, Switzerland/Turkey, 1976) opens with a dilapidated old bus travelling through the snowy landscape of Sweden, a scene accompanied by the sad melody of an Anatolian song.[26] The passengers on board are all silent, dark, moustached men, wearing scruffy jackets. It is early morning when the bus arrives in wintry Stockholm; it negotiates the busy arteries of the orbital, passes by the harbour, and then, averting an encounter with a policeman, heads on into the central pedestrian area, a part of town where it is clearly not meant to be, and where it abruptly stops. Hurriedly, the driver, himself a dark, moustached individual, turns to the men on the bus and asks them to pass on their money and IDs. He then puts it all in a bag and instructs the passengers to sit quietly behind the drawn curtains of the bus and to wait until he returns from the police station. According to local custom, he explains, he must first register them and their money. Only then can they go out.

The men on the bus are clearly insecure and intimidated; they understand they should not be seen until all is sorted. The driver leaves in a hurry. The camera cranes up to a bird's eye view of the bus parked in the middle of the square, which itself is in a pedestrianised city centre, the easily recognisable and busy commuter spot of Sergels torg in downtown Stockholm.

For the next few days the men hide behind the curtains of their absurdly parked vehicle while the liberal police do not bother with what appears to be yet another hippy encampment amidst street singers, passers-by and hangers-on. The cosmopolitan feel of

---

[26] I would like to acknowledge the assistance of Serazer Pekerman, who viewed *The Bus* with me and who translated the Turkish dialogue, providing invaluable background commentary that significantly facilitated my understanding of the film. I am truly grateful for her support.

downtown Stockholm is contrasted with the images of terrified illegal immigrants clinging to their 'secure' space within the bus until, a few days later, a policeman notices that the vehicle is still there and makes a call to headquarters to check if anybody is claiming it. The policeman then arranges for the bus to be towed away, at which point the petrified illegal immigrants are discovered inside it. The film ends with a scene showing seven terrified men being removed one by one from the vehicle and taken to the police headquarters. In the build-up to this climax, the would-be immigrants make shy nocturnal forays into the metropolis, which make for an outlandish encounter between a timid Middle East and a corrupt West.

The Bus is the first of many recent examples of transnational cinema raising issues about human trafficking, illicit immigration, and the rift between the lifestyles of traditionalist Islam and the late modernity of the West. On the one hand, the film clearly intends to satirise Western consumerism and corruption, specifically amplified through the chosen point of view that the unadulterated primitives on the bus represent. More importantly, however, it announces the resolute arrival of a 'foreign body' that is determined to infiltrate and to stay, a 'foreign body' that at this point may only observe shyly, but which later on will come to judge, become outspoken, and learn Western ways (but mostly in order to criticise them vocally). *The Bus* is one of the first films to document not only the arrival of these immigrants but also the advent of a major new theme in Europe's social and cultural dynamic. The very image of the dilapidated bus that has been planted absurdly in the heart of the city, in a place as central as Beaubourg in Paris or Trafalgar Square in London, is an allegory of the idiosyncratic yet powerful agenda that these silent and shy immigrants bring right into the heart of the Western public sphere. They may appear totally inadequate but they also seem to possess a sound moral judgement that is otherwise missing in their new milieu. The absurdly staged encounter between these inhibited

Oriental workers and the hurried commuters and the night birds of this Western metropolis is of symbolic value.

Written, edited, produced and directed by Tunç Okan, who also acts in one of the key roles, this is a truly auteurist film, pre-dating by a decade the films that typically are considered the early classics of 'Turkish migrant cinema,' such as Tevfik Baser's *40 Quadratmeter Deutschland* (*Forty Square Metres of Germany*, Turkey/West Germany, 1986), or the films of the first generation of *beur* directors in France. Along with films by other directors, including Aleksandar Petrović, Želimir Žilnik, and Radu Gabrea, who were from the South East of Europe but who worked in the West during the 1970s and who were the first to address themes of *Gastarbeiters*, *The Bus* is a 1970s European transnational film that needs to be brought into the annals of film history. Officially a co-production between Switzerland and Turkey, the film was also funded privately by Okan, who, reportedly, invested in it money he earned while working as a dentist in Sweden. And while the crew involves Francophone and Swedish collaborators, all key roles on the team are kept for Turks – the cameraman is TV professional Güneş Karabuda, while the music is by Zülfü Livaneli, an acclaimed leftist intellectual who later worked on well-known films linked to Yilmaz Güney, such as *Sürü* (*The Herd*, Zeki Ökten, Turkey, 1979) and *Yol* (*The Way*, Serif Gören/Yilmaz Güney, Switzerland, 1982). Even in today's context, *The Bus* remains a rare film in that an immigrant made it and the story is told from his fellow-immigrants' point of view. Thus, even if the (Westernised and educated) director does not necessarily see things in the same way as his simple-minded protagonists, he is in control of a narrative device that allows him to reveal the inner logic of the outsiders' perception of Western society.

Judging from the pensive background music that accompanies them on screen, the men on the bus are most likely Kurds. Even though there are multiple close-ups of their moustached faces, there is barely any individualisation; the men remain indistinct from each other. There is only one professional actor among the group (Tuncel Kurtiz, best known for his recent role as Ali in Fatih Akin's *Auf der anderen Seite/The Edge of Heaven*, Germany/Turkey/Italy, 2007), while the director himself also plays one of the men. The others are real members of the immigrant community, village men playing themselves. They rarely converse with each other – they all feel the same, no need to talk. Their jackets over their sweaters and their thin-soled shoes make them look outlandish; they eat strange food wrapped in newspapers, and they pray on a small carpet: *Allah Emanet!* ('May God protect us').

Even though they suspect they have been cheated, their behaviour is all sheepish obedience. They stick to the security that the bus' curtains offer. That is, until natural urges force them, hungry and thirsty, to venture out into the treacherous territory of the foreign metropolis in search of a toilet. They know it must be late at night when they leave the bus and they expect to be surrounded by total darkness. Instead they find themselves in a brightly lit urban landscape, an outlandish space into which they will creep little by little. Gathered around a garbage bin, they dig out leftovers and eat eagerly, and then they hunt around for more. When a policeman asks them for their papers, they run away along empty alleyways and back to the bus. Not that anyone is chasing them; they, in fact, are quite invisible, even if stationed in the very heart of the city. One of the men stays out all night and is seen the next morning, squatting under a bridge next to the icy Baltic waters in deep melancholy. In an awfully matter-of-fact scene of existential invisibility, he is shown leaning forward and falling over into the water, never to re-emerge, his death unnoticed by the passers-by. The following day the others all cast hungry glances at a nearby supermarket, where whole chickens roast on a spit, just the way they would make them back home. One of the men can no longer control his bladder, and his urine quietly flows out and under the bus;

the excrement of the 'foreign body' is shown as quietly penetrating into, subverting and polluting the public space that has just been cleaned and sanitised according to rules and regulations.

The men's nocturnal forays into the city are, invariably, shown as terrifying encounters with corruption and decadence, which the men confront in silent shock while wandering the empty pedestrian areas of the night, surrounded by advertising images persistently featuring nudity, and by the frozen figures of mannequins displaying lingerie in brightly lit shop windows. A sex shop, a man walking his poodle on a leash, a couple making love in a phone booth, a junkie asking them for a fix: it is all received in dazed silence. They do not know how to ride the escalator, this strange staircase that keeps on moving in the middle of the night.

A handsome young man (played by director Okan) strays apart from the group and ends up alone. A young Swede smiles at him in a public toilet and then takes him under his wing. Carrying a bottle of alcohol, the Swede guides the man down a side alley and to the entrance of a bar. They end up in a brightly lit locale where men and women eat and drink while watching soft porn on a large screen. When the film is over, it is followed by the evening's main event, a gaudy competition in which playboy volunteers undress on stage, revealing the image of their preferred make of car on their underpants. The winner is awarded a trophy: a plaster penis. The next act is a live stage show involving heterosexual intercourse, and which causes excitement among the audience. The young Kurd watches it all in hungry disbelief until the Swedish friend reaches out to grope his newly found dark buddy. Terrified, the young man runs away. In his flight, he manages to drag a piece of meat from the hand of a woman, and eagerly bites into it. Thrown out of the bar in disgust, he is followed by some of the playboys who give him a kicking and who knife him, leaving him for dead.

One of the film's subplots tackles the treacherous bus driver and provides some insight into the trafficker's identity and ethos. Eighteen minutes into the film, after having left the bus at Sergels torg, the driver is seen at Arlanda airport taking a Lufthansa flight. Arriving in Hamburg some time later, he is subjected to a gruesome series of humiliating checks, evidently because he is also immediately identified as another 'foreign body' on account of his darker skin tone, shrill red blazer, and large moustache. His Turkish passport, together with his look of guilt, does not help; the extensive customs scrutiny causes congestion and discontent among the other, 'legitimate' passengers who line up for entry from Sweden into Germany. He is undressed, his clothes scrutinised, his mouth looked into. When the customs officers express interest in examining his rectum, he protests vocally and is finally left alone.

Once out of the airport, a taxi takes the driver to a restaurant overlooking the harbour. Here he hands over the bag with the money to two men in suits. This is the only glimpse we get of the men who actually run the operation, and they look like reputable and established Turkish-German businessmen. The driver, however, remains the only trafficker identified by face and action – a petty player, who by the next morning has lost the money he earned from betraying his fellow-countrymen. Unlike the shy Kurds he has left behind in Stockholm, he is already familiar with all of the agreeable aspects of the Western life of sin: later that night he ends up drunk with two scruffy German prostitutes who drag him into a cheap hotel room in Hamburg's red light district. He boasts that he will go until morning but is fast asleep within minutes, and so the girls quietly sneak out after emptying his pockets.

The Bus is shot with grey and blue overtones and makes great use of its urban setting, both in terms of landscape and soundscape. The chequered surface of Sergels torg, its modernist vertical lines, geometrically regulated figures, an abundance of glass, steel and plastic, its futuristic shop windows, brightly lit public toilets and its pedestrian passages/escalators at night: the place has an alienating feeling. One can only speculate about the shape, taste and smell of the environment that these men come from, but in any case it is probably much more curved and full of natural materials; the angular patterns that surround them, designed by avant-garde architects, hint at a hostile milieu. The director makes a lot of this quasi-sci-fi anxiety; the protagonists could have landed on Mars instead of Stockholm and the effect would have been the same. And indeed, when near the end the bus is lifted for towing, the feeling is as if they are being launched into space.

The syncopated background sound greatly enhances this feeling of spatial unease, starting with the sad rhythm of an oriental *tambour*, and then escalating into a disturbing mixture of distant sounds that make up the soundscape of city routines, together with songs in praise of Jesus, the chant of Krishna followers, and jazz and brass bands. The men's fearfully suppressed coughs are contrasted with the sound of hand-pulled cello strings and crash cymbals, which escalate into a panicky crescendo. Any outside noise the men hear perplexes and terrifies them: a yellow sweeping machine approaches to clean the tyres of the bus, while the men inside are completely terrified, not knowing what may be producing these extraterrestrial sounds. The sci-fi noises of the metropolis are in contrast with the total silence that accompanies some of the key scenes, especially those that involve flashbacks and flashforwards.

The sparingly used subjective visions of the men are a key stylistic element of this otherwise austere film. The black and white idyllic image of a young woman in a cotton field flashes several times to Okan's handsome young Kurd, especially when he becomes the object of sexual advances in the bar; his very masculinity is challenged here, and the flashback to the beloved woman gives some kind of protective security. At the end of the film the surviving immigrants are taken one by one from the bus to the police building; these scenes, which see the protagonists' worst fears come true, are intercut with visions of a vehicle (the bus?)

being crushed at a junkyard. One by one, the men are dragged by two policemen through the geometrically patterned courtyard of the police headquarters; this is repeated six times, for each one of them, with the camera cutting from the man being dragged to the others looking on from the bus, terrified, and then to a flash forward of the bus being scrapped: five, four, three, two, one, until a final very fast zoom into the face and the eyes of the last man, who is dragged through a space overlooked by the rectangular silent windows of apartment buildings. This scene takes place in total silence.

The best-known image from *The Bus* shows a group photo of black-clad and moustached men gathered in front of the bus, this vehicle that served as a Trojan horse installed in the very heart of the Western stronghold. A similar group photograph is the landmark of another film, produced in Sweden just a few years later – Dusan Makavejev's *Montenegro* (Sweden/UK, 1981), yet another immigrant story that tackles the theme of illicit migration from the poorer peripheries of Europe to the riches of Scandinavia; only the individuals who have gathered for the photo in *Montenegro* are Yugoslav migrants who cluster around a Zanzi-bar in a Stockholm suburb. One of them has even got a knife sticking out of his forehead; the photo is made before he is taken in to a hospital so that there is a record of this proud moment.[27] It will take another ten years before Ulf Hannerz identifies Stockholm and other European metropolitan areas as centres of migration, globalisation, and before sociologists start paying attention to the matters of trafficking. *The Bus* is a film that pioneers in discovering and recording what have since become key social trends. It shows an early manifestation of the moral shock experienced by Oriental immigrants, a silent shock that has, by now, grown into vocal outrage.

---

[27] Unlike *The Bus*, however, *Montenegro* introduces the immigrant protagonists through the eyes of a Western housewife, who ends up in their midst by accident and who cannot stop marvelling at their weird yet exciting and exuberant lifestyles. In this way, *Montenegro* can be classified in the long line of films where the 'legitimising' normative gaze of a Western narrator is used in telling the story of immigrants, as discussed in the first chapter of this book.

Guardian Angel

At the end of *Andjeo čuvar* (*Guardian Angel*, Goran Paskalvejić, Yugoslavia, 1987), the legend appears: 'Over 20,000 Gypsy children from Yugoslavia have been left to the mercy of white-slave traders across Europe [in the 1980s].' Using bold statements such as this one, *Guardian Angel* ranks among those European films that alerted the public to human trafficking years before the issue took centre stage in the 1990s. We also include it here because it reveals to a certain degree how, in the process of moulding public discourse, trafficking has at times been pinned on a specific minority group: Romanies.

Guardian Angel is neither the first nor the last Yugoslav film about Romanies. The film comes 20 years after Aleksandar Petrović's acclaimed *Skupljaci perja* (*I Even Met Happy Gypsies*, Yugoslavia, 1967), with which *Guardian Angel* shares cast and crew members, and two years before Emir Kusturica's *Dom za vešanje* (*Time of the Gypsies*, UK/Italy/Yugoslavia, 1988), which also tackles the theme of trafficking and the exploitation of Yugoslav Gypsy children in Italy.[28] While *Time of the Gypsies* closely follows the teenage Roma protagonist Perhan (Davor Dujmović), *Guardian Angel* sticks to the more traditional approach of telling a story about trafficking through the eyes of a normative narrator – the journalist Dragan (Ljubisa Samardzić[29]) – who

---

[28] Kusturica's film has enjoyed greater exposure than Paskalvejić's, not least because Kusturica received the Best Director award at Cannes in 1989. Both Paskalvejić's and Kusturica's films seem to be based on a newspaper story published in Yugoslav newspapers in the early 1980s. The matter of copying Paskaljević is even jokingly addressed in *Time of the Gypsies* when a trafficking ringleader in Italy refers to a film made about him in Yugoslavia (evidently meaning *Guardian Angel*).

[29] Samardzić is one of the most popular actors in Yugoslav cinema. By the time of *Guardian Angel*, he had already acted in more than eighty films, mostly comedies and action films. In the post-Yugoslav period, Samardzić has become a prolific film producer, and has also directed some films.

is perceived as a reliable and trustworthy source. This approach is more in line with the majority of 'Gypsy-themed' films that also present the story through the eyes of an educated stranger who penetrates these tightly-knit ethnic communities. As discussed in the first chapter of this volume, this is also the prevalent narrative strategy for most films about human trafficking, where the story is told from the point of view of a 'legitimate' reporter.

Guardian Angel tells the story of Dragan, who investigates the fate of Šajin (pronounced Sha-yn, and played by Jakup Amzić), a 12-year old Yugoslav Romani boy who, along with other children, becomes a victim of trafficking and exploitation in Italy. Dragan meets a social worker who introduces him to some Romani children that have just been repatriated. The traffic has been going on for a decade now, the social worker says, but even when brought back to their homes in the poorer south-eastern parts of the country, most of the children run away and return to begging. Dragan, who plans to run a series of articles on child trafficking, befriends Šajin, one of the repatriated boys. The son of an alcoholic father and ill mother, he is a talented accordion player, but withdrawn and inhibited. When Dragan attempts to track him down at his home in the Gypsy neighbourhood, he learns that Šajin has not returned home but has instead dashed back to Italy. Dragan realises there must be more to the trafficking than meets the eye, so he undertakes to investigate it in depth: why would one opt for a life of bondage abroad over the chance to return home? He hangs around the Gypsy slums and later on travels to Italy, where he finds Šajin and manages to uncover a lot about the trafficking operation. He brings the boy back to Yugoslavia but, in the process of arranging for Šajin's release from bondage, he loses the boy's trust and friendship. Determined to expose the trafficking ring, Dragan continues to investigate but is attacked and killed in the Gypsy hamlet where he has returned for more clues.

Director Paskaljević's interest lies in exposing the social ills that in contemporary Yugoslavia make such a level of victimisation and slavery possible. The trafficked children are reluctant to talk and to renounce the people who exploit them; none of them is willing to discuss the events that saw them go to Italy to beg, to pickpocket, and for prostitution. On the few occasions that they do talk, the children tell stories about being lured away with promises, and then being smuggled into Italy overnight in the back of a van. They are then trained to pretend to be blind or crippled, and beg amidst the pigeons and the tourists on the piazzas of Italian cities. If they try to run away, they are severely beaten.

Dragan travels to Italy in search of Šajin, but none of the street beggars in Venice is willing to disclose the boy's whereabouts. Still, Dragan manages to find him at an Italian detention centre where he is being held for pickpocketing. It is amazingly easy to get his release – the Italians are keen to get rid of this kind of prisoner. After his release, however, Šajin is more scared than relieved: Musa , the ringleader, is likely to kill him if he finds out about the journalist. With an astonishing maturity, the boy outlines what he sees as the only possible way out: escape is not an option, but if Dragan would consider buying him out, Šajin would be free to return. Dragan, however, dismisses this idea: one cannot possibly pay the traffickers, since they are criminals who need to be opposed, not appeased. At the same time, Šajin does not think of himself as a slave and appears conscious of having obligations to his masters.

While witnessing the transfer of a newly arrived child in a café in Venice, Dragan manages to meet the ringleader Musa under the false pretence of wanting to buy a gun. The black-clad Musa is polite but evasive; he takes Dragan to his headquarters in a campsite at the outskirts of the city and treats him to a glass of Scotch. While pretending he has come to buy a revolver, Dragan observes the comings and goings of various groups of children, but does not even notice when he is stripped of his watch and other personal possessions. Musa makes fun of Dragan; he first provokes him with an offer to sell him a child, then drops him off in the middle of nowhere, telling him to mind his own business. Back at the camp, a boy is tortured for having spoken to the journalist; the other children tremble in fear as they look on. When the next morning Dragan brings the police to the campsite, there is no trace from the Gypsies. Even if the journalist talks about their involvement in firearms and trafficking, there is no proof of any wrongdoing, as the alleged criminals are not even there…

Back in Yugoslavia, Dragan makes several visits to the maze of slums where Šajin's family lives in the hope of untangling the workings of the traffic ring. Here, he is exposed to the reality of contemporary Gypsy life in Yugoslavia: a picture of misery and destitution and a mostly outdoors existence. Countless children and pigs roam the slum's muddy streets, animals and people sharing the same living space. Girls play with rag dolls on a scrap heap,[30] toddlers with naked bums piss around unsupervised, scruffy idle men hang on the corners. People are not exactly hostile, but they are withdrawn and avoid contact with this stranger who, like a typical 'gadjo' (non-Gypsy), has come to marvel at their misery. Even though Dragan claims he is recruiting for a TV talent show, they remain reticent.

It is against the backdrop of this harsh reality of Gypsy life that Dragan's compassionate concern for the fate of Šajin and other Romani children develops. The film locates trafficking as a problem only in relation to the Romani minority, where it seems to be endemic, and places it in direct correlation with the abject poverty that is endemic among the Romanies. At Šajin's house, Dragan learns that the mother died a while ago and that the father is always drunk; two little sisters

---

[30] The scrap heap is a key prop in most films about Romanies. The recent *Dallas Pashamende* (*Dallas Among Us*, Robert-Adrjan Pejo, Germany/Hungary/Romania, 2004) even set the whole film in a Gypsy community located at a giant rubbish dump; a special set was built in Romania for the shoot (see Iordanova, 2008: 305-310).

are left to care for a third child, a deaf and crippled brother; there is no running water or sanitation. Given these circumstances, the line 'Šajin went to Italy' is pronounced with relief; rather than worrying for the safe return of those who have been trafficked out, more children are in fact keen to go away, with the prospect of begging in Italy appearing a desirable option in comparison to current life.

However, Dragan's interest in Šajin is fraught with ethical problems. Yes, his effort to save him is brave, and it is necessary to bring the concern of trafficking to the attention of the wider public. But it is also patronising. His visits to the slums are meant to be similar to the outings of an anthropologist, yet he cannot help adding a moralistic slant to what would be a matter-of-fact record if Dragan engaged in pure observation. His is not the non-judgmental gaze of an ethnographer, however, but more that of an interventionist who is prepared to manipulate and lie in order to 'fix' things. Dragan is determined to find proof that Šajin has been sold into bondage and to expose the whole chain of human trafficking; he is not concerned with understanding the reasons behind the practice but in proving it is taking place and in condemning it in public. In order to get hold of the information he needs, he lies on a number of occasions. While in Italy, he 'bribes' Šajin into talking by treating him to a large bowl of ice cream, taking him to an amusement arcade, buying him an accordion, and even by giving him and his child-prostitute girlfriend Rava a ride around town. As if accidentally, he fails to tell the boy that his mother has died. He is not bothered to protect Šajin's privacy, either. His willingness to help is premeditated and intrusive.[31]

A crawling suspicion, which has been there from the outset, grows into a viable hypothesis: the parents of the trafficked children seem to be complicit in the traffic. It comes across as a monstrous deed,

---

[31] It also becomes clear that Dragan's own 14-year old son now lives with his mother in Switzerland and is barely in contact with the father; this revelation casts suspicion over the whole relationship with Šajin: isn't Dragan trying to play father to someone else's son, having failed to care properly for his own?

which someone like Dragan is incapable of comprehending. When he confronts Šajin's father on this matter, the man flatly denies it: 'I would never do this!' But later on the father apologetically elaborates: 'I only hired him out for a year,' he says. 'I had to.' The father (played by legendary Romani singer Šaban Bajramović[32]) tells Dragan of the apparition of Sajbiya, the guardian angel of the Romanies, who came to him in his sleep and dictated a solution to his problems. Later on Šajin will confirm this account: his father had a vision of Sajbiya, the guardian angel, who told him to get a white ram and to offer *kurban* at his home in order to ensure that his wife would be cured and all problems of the family solved.[33] In order to offer the *kurban*, the father borrowed 10 million dinar from trafficker Musa, agreeing in exchange that he would send Šajin to work for him in Italy for a year.[34] A scene of the ram's offering, the *kurban* gathering, Musa's blessing, and the father singing songs of praise to Sajbiya, is shown in a flashback.

Throughout the film a further and recurrent flashback shows father and son bringing back the ram in the golden light of a late afternoon. It is an image full of serenity and poise. Apparently this has all been done in an effort to save the ill mother, to help the handicapped little brother, and to secure the family's wellbeing within the restricted means available to this class of people. Šajin is not 'trafficked,' then; he is on a mission to help his family. His unwillingness to come back to Yugoslavia was because Sajbiya, the guardian angel, may punish him and his family for breaking their word of honour.

[32] See 'Šaban Bajramović (1936-2008)' (Iordanova 26 June 2008).

[33] *Kurban* is the sacrificial offering of a ram, which is slaughtered and cooked into soup that is then given away to friends and neighbours. Part of a Muslim tradition, making *kurban* is widely practiced among Orthodox Christians in the Balkans as well.

[34] It is difficult to estimate how much is the dollar or sterling equivalent of 10 million dinar, as the film was made in a period when the Yugoslav dinar was undergoing huge inflation. In 1982, 10 million dinar would have come to more than US$150,000, and yet in 1987 (the year of the film's release) it would have amounted to about US$7,700. I am grateful to Slobodan Šijan for helping with these estimates.

Dragan begins to grasp that there is more complexity to Šajin's bondage than he is prepared to delve into, and he persists in treating it as a clear-cut matter: the father has sold his son into slavery, period. Indeed, selling one's child looks like an awful deed. Šajin, however, refuses to take part in the accusations: his father has given his word, he can leave the traffickers only if he is bought out, and not if he is 'rescued'; running away would be below his dignity. Acting in line with the unwritten rules of honour that form part of his underprivileged milieu, Šajin is dignified and truthful. He may be a victim, but he shows more emotional intelligence than the journalist, who single-mindedly pursues the agenda of 'rescue' and 'repatriation.' Dragan has acted manipulatively in concealing the mother's death from Šajin: if the boy knew his mother had died, he might not have wanted to return home and Dragan's repatriation plan would have failed. By doing this, the journalist comes across as morally corrupt. His behaviour, however, is sanctioned by his overarching and socially desirable concern for the trafficked child's wellbeing.

Mila (Neda Arnerić), the female social worker who initially introduced Dragan to the repatriated Gypsy boys, has a different take on it all. While Dragan takes the children's reluctance to talk as a sign of trauma or fear, she knows that they conceal a more complex explanation that is not suitable for public consumption, especially in a country where all members of society are supposed to be equal and socially secure. During her six years on the job, she has learned that most of the children are sold into bondage by their parents. She does not pass judgment, however. She is sceptical of Dragan's chances to get to the bottom of the matter, and even more reserved about his efforts to intervene: the traffic has been going on for more than a decade, and it is not newspaper articles that will put an end to it. 'They are a different world from us,' she concludes with resignation.

And indeed, the birds' eye view of the Gypsy neighbourhood with which the film opens and closes only confirms this view of a 'different world.' Accompanied by soulful Gypsy music, the camera wanders around Šajin's family's poor household, showing father and children asleep, the handicapped boy in a trolley. The father wakes up and looks into the camera – evidently, this is a flashback to the moment of his vision of Sajbiya. Other scenes in the film also depict the specific mysticism that marks the Gypsy worldview. Ultimately, the world of the Roma remains impenetrable; the effort to break the trafficking circuit is doomed from the outset. 'We are treated worse than Blacks in America,' one of the Gypsy men in the local café remarks. 'If the police come, it is only to investigate some robbery, never to help us.' So no wonder they are suspicious of Dragan, especially as it will transpire that they all, at least to some degree, are involved in the trafficking business. They think he has been sent on an undercover mission to spy on them. As it happens, they also kill him at the end of the film: when it transpires Dragan has got closer to exposing the ringmasters, they beat him to death with wooden planks. Dragan has tried to penetrate into a closed world that is beyond his comprehension and he should have stayed out. These people are not joking. For Dragan, trafficking is just an engrossing investigative assignment, but it is a matter of livelihood for them.

When Mother Comes Home for Christmas

Early on in *Otan erthei i mama gia to Hristougenna* (*When Mother Comes Home for Christmas*, Nilita Vachani, Greece/India/Germany, 1996), a Sri Lankan housemaid cares for her European charge as they sit together in a flat in Greece before a television playing the American soap opera, *The Young and the Restless* (CBS-TV, 1973-2009). With understated eloquence and efficiency, the scenario illustrates the mediascapes, technoscapes, and ethnoscapes that Arjun Appadurai describes in *Modernity at Large* (1996). Drawing on the power of film to animate these invisible pathways and hidden lives, the documentary turns its attention to the intersections of migration and labour, and specifically to the economic globalisation that exacts a profound emotional cost on people's lives. To this end, director Nilita Vachani introduces us to Josephine Perera, a Sri Lankan domestic worker who has managed to secure a rare visa home to visit the family she has not seen in eight years. Following Josephine on her journey back, Vachani offers a remarkable look at the national practices of exporting labour and the unseen human costs of this uneven distribution of capital, which results in a vast disparity, both financial and emotional.

Opening with a brief introduction to Josephine, the film turns to a church in Greece where Josephine prays for her family's well being and for the house they might one day share. Her hopes are interrupted by informational titles that expand on the implications of these domestic dreams. Almost one in ten Sri Lankans works abroad since the local economy 'depends on the export of labour,' an export that has since exceeded tea in earnings. The titles outline this economic exchange: '70% of women workers are housemaids in foreign lands. They send their earnings to families left behind.'

This seemingly informal labour economy has institutional and national underpinnings. Twenty-four years ago the state established the Sri Lankan Bureau of Foreign Labour (SLBFE) which, according to its website, 'has given the highest priority to prompting [sic.] foreign employment. Hence, the SLBFE maintains a database that lists jobs available by country and by local recruiting agent.' This public corporation, operating under the jurisdiction of the Ministry of Foreign Employment Provision, finances itself through the fees and commissions paid through recruitment agencies, thereby positioning itself as a legal hub for trade in human resources. The bureau regulates services, provides training, aids in visa acquisitions, and '[protects] foreign migrants'; protective measures include the monitoring of recruitment agencies, the provision of safe houses, and scholarship funds for the children of migrants. While one hesitates to doubt their commitment to care for their mobile workforce, Josephine's story raises questions outside the explicit violence and confinement of trafficking and slavery. In this case, it may simply be care and freedom deferred, indicated by the bureau's curious slogan, 'Our Concern Today, Your Well Being Tomorrow!' Such a slogan speaks to the delays and sacrifices made by Josephine and her family for local interests, interests that may one day result in their well being. And if we understand this slogan as speaking to recruiters, then it also has a grim implication: namely that the nation will supply the domestic product to create a happy consumer abroad.

One finds traces of this promised 'well being' in *When Mother Comes Home....* As Josephine prepares for her trip home by making purchases for her family, a song produced by the SLBFE plays on the soundtrack. 'How lucky I am to live in a foreign land... Return home with treasures for everyone,' a woman sings. The song gestures to the combination of people that benefit from this economy, those being the individuals involved as well as those involved in the larger global exchange economy, especially companies that find ever more consumers for their product. One questions the productivity of an economy that encourages such consumption over development, but there is at the same time some demonstration of investment in a local economy when we learn that Josephine has helped her son, Suresh, to buy a bus to build his own transportation company, an alternative to the government transit system. He is anxious because his local competition enjoys a fleet of eight buses, but Suresh will have more with help from his wife, Chooti.

Immediately following the opening titles, *When Mother Comes Home...* depicts the institutionalisation of an informal economy, showing the training undergone by future housemaids. The women practise vacuuming, baking cakes, and preparing a European tea service. In a more provocative instance, they are trained on how to use condoms, a hint at sexual encounters, wanted or coerced. The sequence begins with a lecture and the demonstrations of a live instructor, who is replaced by the tinny notes of a recorded lecture. The recorded speech charges the housemaids to be clean and tidy, whether working or not. It encourages them to 'show your master or madam that you are working hard... If they see you working hard, they will be very happy. Your future will be a great success.' Even with this display of such official services in Sri Lanka, the personal story of Josephine remains the centre of Vachan's film. As the lecture plays, a trainee housemaid cleans a mirror with other trainees standing in the reflection behind. A match cut joins them to Josephine who wipes down a mirror in Greece, only she is alone; the army of Sri Lankan housemaids is invisible in the European picture. There may be success to come, but from the start, the cost is implied in visions of isolation and exile.

Supported by the government, this export of foreign labour would seem to fall outside the definition of trafficking, which brings to mind force, captivity and slavery. However, aside from arguments that financial and state pressure exert their own forms of coercion, asking one group to make sacrifices for the freedom and comfort of others, there are significant risks involved in this legal trade. As mentioned earlier, a Human Rights Watch report from November 2007, 'Exported and Exposed,' chronicles the abuses suffered by Sri Lankan domestics in the Middle East (Saudi Arabia, Kuwait, Lebanon, and the United Arab Emirates). Some women find themselves at the mercy of recruiters who demand large fees for the opportunity to work, and when the women arrive, they meet with long hours, little pay, and a life 'confined to the workplace' (Human Rights Watch n.d.: 1). The report continues:

> In some cases employers or labour agents subject domestic workers to physical abuse, sexual abuse, or forced labour. While current figures likely underestimate the scale of abuse, the Sri Lankan government reports that 50 migrant domestic workers return to Sri Lanka 'in distress' each day, and embassies abroad are flooded with workers complaining of unpaid wages, sexual harassment, and overwork (ibid.).

Although reports of abuse and enforced servitude sit at the margins of Josephine's story, there are clear mentions of the disparity of treatment. According to Josephine, a Sri Lankan housemaid in the Middle East earns US$100 per month, whereas in Europe one earns US$500 per month. Her experience, as it turns out, is perhaps closer to these circumstances than the film indicates. The SLBFE does not have any trade agreements with Europe, and negotiates primarily with the Middle East and East Asia. According to Vachani, Josephine, who was working illegally in Greece until shortly before the film, had initially gone through the SLBFE to Kuwait on a two-year contract. While there, she managed to pay a ring of smugglers to take her into Greece. There the story becomes one of the few success stories of this trade in people. Her employers, who were 'influential and connected' (Vachani 2009: private correspondence), helped Josephine to procure a work visa by getting her papers as a trained nurse.

Even as she stands out as a rare success story, it is nevertheless one of extreme limitations and sadness: returning home is a rarity, and her family suffers terribly in her absence. Shortly after Josephine is introduced as one of Sri Lanka's primary exports, the film asks us to consider an emotional economy explicitly tied to the financial and global economies. Josephine's son Suresh may enjoy more clear benefits, but her younger son, Suminda, stays in Bosco Boarding House and Orphanage in Halton, Sri Lanka. A heartbreaking sequence animates the dramatic disparities in a capital of care as it compares Josephine's daily tending to her charge, Isadora, with the stark existence of Suminda in Sri Lanka. In Greece, Isadora lies on a soft bed, soothed by soft pastel colours and surrounded by giant stuffed animals. She says her evening prayers in the gaze of a loving father and the doting Josephine. Back in the Sri Lankan orphanage, a group of boys stands in darkness as all their voices join in unison to read out their evening prayer, the words of which are grim even in the best circumstances ('if I should die before I wake...'). Their morning activities continue the stark comparison. The boys move about in an echoing dark space surrounded by walls made of stone, each component contributing to a portrait of a cold and austere life. The contrast continues in a scene illustrating Isadora's morning routine. She is sprawled across her bed as a fluffy cat leaps up to join her. Josephine enters and softly strokes the girl's back, whispering at her that it's morning, and time to wake. In the bathroom, Isadora splashes in the tub, chattering to Josephine, and basking in the joys of this personal attention. Things are not so kind at the orphanage where the boys gather in a dark room, pouring jugs of water on themselves as they are chastised for talking. They dress behind a wire barrier the actual function of which is unclear but whose cinematic function is not: here we find the confinement and callousness that come in this legitimate economy of human servitude. Moreover, Suminda is not alone in this orphanage; his fellow charges directly address the camera, introducing themselves and stating where their parents now work and in what capacity. Yes, it's a boarding house, but it's also an orphanage: whether their parents have been stolen into slavery or are participating in this foreign export system, the children at home are abandoned, and longing for their parents.

The epistolary sequences give further voice to the lack and longing, articulating distance and suffering, as well as the networks of exchange. Suminda writes a letter to his mother, read in voice over as the image track depicts the orphanage. 'Everyone hates me,' he reads, highlighting his own emotional isolation, before he follows with a request that expresses the intersection of financial and affective economies: there are presents he wants for his birthday. A moment that could play in any intimate family drama takes on a greater resonance in this context. Later in the film, when he is with his mother, he confesses to hating the school where he is failing in his education. The lack of emotional security may impact his progress, much as the export of Sri Lanka's resources, human and otherwise, impede its own development. Daughter Norma's letters equally speak to the lack and risk faced by the children at home. Over the course of the film, we learn that she has been practically homeless for the eight years of Josephine's absence. She has run away several times, and has even attempted suicide, but now, in this letter, she expresses her plan to marry, so that she will no longer feel alone and feel compelled to move from place to place. As with her brother, this confession of emotional want is also followed by a list of requests, in this case, three nightdresses and three pairs of shoes.

Josephine's obligations are ceaseless. Over the course of her visit, she meets with the proposed groom, Chandan, and his family to discuss the terms of the arrangement. Although she has volunteered her own assistance, she fears for his ability to provide financial security; it is later revealed in the film that his small bit of land was pawned by relatives so they could go abroad. Even his emotional support is in doubt, as Josephine wonders if Norma won't run away as soon as she leaves again for Greece. Amidst this doubt, she considers finding a way to bring her daughter over to Greece, where she can find work – something that Josephine accomplished years after the film by spending the money she was saving for the family house on people smugglers who brought Norma to Europe (Vachani 2009: private correspondence).

Perpetually delayed gratification is a theme that courses through the film, recalling the off screen promise of SLBFE, 'Our Concern Today, Your Well Being Tomorrow!' Josephine's reunion with her family is laden with painful recriminations over her neglect for as well as her own constant worry over her children's welfare. 'As if I could enjoy tiring myself out,' she tearfully protests, agonising over the implications of the sacrifices she makes. She works for them and yet she also knows how they suffer, something made clear in their exchanges and in observations of the children's outbursts, including Suresh's violent agony over a broken toy. Although on this trip Josephine has aimed to buy a house, as expressed in the opening prayer, this does not happen. And, as noted above, this will not happen as Josephine opts instead to contribute to an economy that depletes her region of young women, providing foreign domestics at the expense of domesticity at home. The great success for hard work is still postponed.

The final sequence of the film is deliberately open-ended, combining the epistolary voice over with glimpses of life in Sri Lanka, thereby communicating the structuring absence of the local economy. Josephine reads a letter to Suresh and his wife, Chooti, over an image of Chooti, who sweeps the bus that Josephine's money has purchased. The voice over notes that two weeks have passed since her return to Greece, but that the days have been filled with work, denying Josephine a moment to herself. 'My arms ache with all the cleaning. Otherwise, I am well.' She laments the speed of her visit, the failure to accomplish her goals, and the time spent 'quarrelling over silly things.' The last part of her letter asks the family to help care for Suminda, as he needs to improve his performance in order to attend a better school. As she reads these last parts of her letter, the camera sits on a train, capturing the movement of departure, the ongoing nature of Josephine's absence, and the hint of global traffic. This personal story reaches out to the broader circumstances, as Josephine notes: 'More and more girls from Sri Lanka cross the borders illegally into Greece and suffer great hardship. I am so lucky to have a visa.' Her observation equally supplies the bittersweet irony that flavours this film: Josephine is lucky. As an economic migrant, hers is a relative success story as she has secured papers and avoided the slavery faced by many. At the same time, her ambition to provide for her family is met with frustration and suffering, both emotional and practical. With sequences such as this, Vachani illustrates the painful personal cost of the global economy and its institutionalised human trade.

Wesh wesh, qu'est-ce qui se passe?

Rabah Ameur-Zaïmeche is emerging as one of the most noteworthy talents in the latest generation of *beur* (i.e. of North African descent) directors in France. *Wesh wesh, qu'est-ce qui se passe?* (France, 2001), his first film, made over the course of several years and featuring mainly the director's friends and family, tells the story of Kamel (played by Rabah Ameur-Zaïmeche himself), who has recently and illegally returned to France after being deported upon release from prison.

Set on the Cité des Bosquets in the Montfermeil area of Seine-St-Denis, a Parisian *banlieue*, *Wesh wesh...?* deals with the phenomenon of the *double peine*, whereby Maghrebi-French convicts serve the double sentence of a stretch in prison followed by deportation, often to a country with which they are entirely unfamiliar, a 'homecoming' that is referred to in the vernacular as going back to the *bled* (the topic of Ameur-Zaïmeche's second film, *Bled Number One*, Algeria/France, 2006).

Wesh wesh...? details Kamel's experiences as a newly-illegal immigrant in France. That is to say, if Kamel's status as a legal subject in France has been taken away from him, and if, following deportation he has subsequently returned to France, which is after all his homeland, then we can see manufactured in Ameur-Zaïmeche's film a situation whereby the state is to an extent complicit in the creation of people smuggling as a practice: had Kamel not been deported on account of his ethnic origins, he would not have had to adopt illegal (if unseen) methods to return home (the film opens with Kamel hitching a ride home – but how he has managed to re-enter France is not apparent).

Wesh wesh...? displays various characteristics that might be deemed commonplace in the *banlieue* film: it features 'the *mise-en-scène* of alienating tower blocks, young *beur* protagonists who face exclusion, discrimination and police harassment on a daily basis and who, with little or no prospect of social mobility, face considerable pressure to enter into the alternative economies of the *cité* (most notably drug dealing)' (Higbee 2007b: 43). Furthermore, the film also features a hip hop soundtrack that Bluher (2001) might identify as in many respects synonymous with *banlieue* cinema (the film was co-written by Madjid Benaroudj, a 'leading figure on the French hip-hop scene' [O'Shaugnessy 2007: 79]).

However, Carrie Tarr suggests that the film also incorporates certain elements that are not usual for *banlieue* cinema: namely, the possibility of intercultural exchange, as signalled by the interactions between Kamel, other Maghrebi-French inhabitants of the *cité*, and Irène (Serpentine Textier), a white school teacher who also lives on the estate; and the possibility of a space of 'escape,' signalled by the park to which Kamel retreats in order to go fishing (Tarr 2005: 180-181). That both are ultimately destroyed – Kamel's family rejects Irène, while Kamel is seemingly shot in the park by the police at the end of the film – suggests that Ameur-Zaïmeche is sceptical about the possibility of integration and/or fulfilment for Maghrebi-French citizens in France. Nonetheless, these motifs do offer up challenging possibilities for the *banlieue* as a site for intercultural exchange, as well as widening the lexicon of images included in the *banlieue* 'genre.'

As we have seen is the case with Ameur-Zaïmeche's latest film, *Dernier maquis* (*Adhen*, France/Algeria, 2008), *Wesh wesh…?* is also preoccupied with mobility and movement in its imposing suburban spaces. Kamel is initially hitchhiking in order to get home, and most of the time we see him travelling around the *cité* on foot, including when accompanying Irène and when fleeing the police. However, towards the film's climax, Kamel goes to a showroom and test-drives a Harley Davidson, which he uses as an escape vehicle for his attack on the policeman that injured his mother during a heavy-handed drugs raid. Suddenly empowered through his ability to negotiate and speed through the film's suburban space with ease, the attack seems something of a fantasy moment in the film: we are not privy to Kamel's negotiations for the motorbike, and while no doubt getting hold of a Harley is possible in this manner, it takes place so quickly and without much visible work, that we are left pondering its reality. As it turns out, Kamel is tracked down by the police and as he runs from them through the park where he goes fishing, two gunshots ring out suggesting that he has been killed. In other words, the 'fantasy' revenge sequence involving the motorbike leads only to more destruction, in the same way that the 'fantasy' or escapist space of the park is similarly not secure enough to protect Kamel from the external forces of the 'real' world.

Martin O'Shaughnessy reads *Wesh wesh...?* as a political film that engages with class more than it does with race or ethnicity: when Kamel is refused a job by a fellow *beur* on account of his lack of legal status, '[t]he hero comments that all bosses are the same and make their money from the sweat of their employees, thus suggesting that class attitudes run deeper than ethnic solidarities' (2007: 76). Ameur-Zaïmeche would seemingly concur with this interpretation, as O'Shaughnessy points out: 'Class struggle is no longer restricted to factories or workplaces. It now takes place in urban space. Nowadays, government policy is to destroy the housing estates even though people have taken years to weave social ties. The aim is to prevent people developing a political consciousness that could lead to an oppositional movement' (O'Shaughnessy 2007: 76). While one might forgive any employer for refusing to take on Kamel or any illegal employee (a practice that itself might lead to accusations of bonded labour and/or contemporary slavery), the distinction between class and race is an important one, especially as it centres upon space as Ameur-Zaïmeche characterises it. Class is signified by the ability to travel through spaces with ease, and class struggle therefore is a battle waged around access to the technologies that enable this ease of movement to take place.

In a certain sense, then, the technological construction of *Wesh wesh...?* also plays a key role in our understanding of it. As has been noted (Higbee 2007b: 43; O'Shaughnessy 2007: 75), the film was shot using a DV camera of the kind commonly used for French news reports. If these cameras allow for greater mobility on the part of the filmmaker, owing to their lightweight nature and their ability to record image and sound in minimal conditions, then they are also a technology that is in many respects invasive. News reports of the *banlieues* that are made with such cameras tend to be characterised by critics as 'impersonal and sensationalised' (Higbee 2007b: 43). By gaining access to these technologies, Ameur-Zaïmeche has turned their invasiveness on its head. Rather than offering a glossy and polished recreation of *banlieue* life, as happens in *La Haine* (*Hate*, Mathieu Kassovitz, Frace, 1995), Ameur-Zaïmeche presents to us a 'raw' film that is 'amateur' in construction (particularly through the use of non-professional actors, including family members). This in turn lends to the film not a sensationalist aesthetic (although Ameur-Zaïmeche does play with some of the iconography of sensationalist reportage by blurring the faces of police officers walking through the *cité*), but an 'authentic' feel. The frenzy of movement that is the film's ending – a frenzy that has been initiated by the invasion of the police into Kamel's family's home – contrasts with the 'slowness' of the rest of the film, a slowness also mirrored in the film's production in that it took several years for Ameur-Zaïmeche to take the project from conception to completion. Those who are not accorded the rights of full citizenship are consigned to a 'slow' existence in which characters are not the masters of the spaces they inhabit, but are to a certain extent engulfed by them (shots of the tower blocks dwarfing the protagonists). Made through the use of DV technology, Ameur-Zaïmeche's film functions as a politicised riposte to the 'sensationalist' images that typically characterise the coverage of these spaces. The technology here allows not for invasiveness but for intimacy, an intimacy that is indeed tied to the pace of the film, in that it allows the characters to exist in their own *time*, if not in a space that they would choose as their own. A 'difficult' film, therefore, *Wesh wesh, qu'est-ce qui se passe?* denies to its characters the ease of movement and image consumption that might otherwise typify popular representations of the *banlieue*.

To return to the subject that is the focus of this book, namely human trafficking, *Wesh wesh...?*'s analysis of class does raise some interesting issues. That we have not seen Kamel's return journey from Algeria to France is undoubtedly in part a budgetary restriction: the film would have cost a lot more had Ameur-Zaïmeche tried to include scenes in Algeria and/or travelling from Algeria to France. But it also reflects upon the impossibility of depicting trafficking as it takes place in the real world. This is not to say that the many films that do depict the 'realities' of the process of human smuggling achieve the impossible. Rather, this is to suggest that filmic representations of a practice that is invisible and therefore otherwise impossible to screen except through recreations, which will *de facto* be stylised as opposed to genuine, are 'unfilmable.' More than this, however, *Wesh wesh...?* raises questions about a Europe (here, France) that cannot in this case offer employment to an otherwise invisible class of people who are not accorded the full rights of citizens. It is not that Kamel or his brother, Mousse (Ahmed Hammoudi), who becomes embroiled in drug dealing as the film develops (hence the police raid on the family home), can find employment even in service sectors that full citizens refuse to accept (bonded labour, sweatshop work, nannying, etc.). With the exception of Kamel's sister, who is a lawyer, these characters are offered nothing in terms of employment or hope for the future. What this brings into relief, therefore, is that a country like France, through its policy of the *double peine*, actively seeks to 'traffic' its citizens outside of the country in order to forego its duty towards these people who are otherwise French in every sense of the word. In other words, the *double peine* involves a forced migration, a state-endorsed human trafficking that has illegal human trafficking as its dark counterpart (and, in the case of Kamel who returns to France, its logical if invisible consequence).

If *Wesh wesh, qu'est-ce qui se passe?* does not present to us a France the economy of which is in some small way underpinned by the contemporary peonage that is often a direct result of human trafficking, it does present to us a France that will not look after its own, but which will actively traffic its citizens out of Fortress Europe if it can find sufficient reasons to do so: Kamel had been arrested for dealing drugs, although given the prospects for Mousse and others, how to get by without engaging in illegal, semi-legal and/or quasi-legal activities seems difficult. The reason for including *Wesh wesh...?* in this study of human trafficking and cinema, therefore, is to suggest that the traffic of humans is not one way. While a policy like the *double peine* has the law on its side, the forced migration of people from their homeland to a country that is only in part their own is problematic. If it is standard practice for a 'conventional' human trafficker to deprive a 'customer' of their passport in order to exact debt bondage from them, to remove a French person's passport is a similarly sinister if state-sanctioned measure taken against someone who should still function within the legal system that has deprived them of legal rights. With Fortress France happy to expel its citizens, a film like *Wesh wesh qu'est-ce qui se passe?* does not so much clarify for us what human trafficking is or means in the contemporary world, but it does allow us to glimpse the complexity of this phenomenon when the traffic of humans has such legalised and problematic iterations. Some people are trafficked to escape their homeland. Some people subject themselves to human trafficking because they want to go home.

Poniente

Since the 1990s, Spanish cinema has begun increasingly to turn its attention to the issue of immigration. A shortlist of the more prominent films that deal with immigration might include *Cartas de Alou* (*Letters from Alou*, Montxo Armendáriz, Spain, 1990), *Bwana* (Imanol Uribe, Spain, 1996), *Saïd* (Llorenç Soler, Spain, 1998), *Flores de otro mundo* (*Flowers from Another World*, Icíar Bollaín, Spain, 1999), *El Traje* (*The Suit*, Alberto Rodríguez, Spain, 2002), and *Ilegal* (Ignacio Vilar, Spain, 2003), although there are many more.

Of these films, few deal with the physical process of trafficking. *Saïd* opens with immigrants scrambling from a boat and away from a police helicopter, while *Letters from Alou* shows us Alou (Mulie Jarju) crossing the Mediterranean in a speedboat, a journey that is initially marked as dangerous when one of Alou's fellow passengers falls overboard and is presumed drowned. However, the same character reappears later unscathed, with both films therefore suggesting (impossibly) that trafficking is not dangerous, despite the fact that the European Council on Refugees and Exiles (ECRE) estimates that up to 10,000 migrants were drowned in the Mediterranean Sea in 2006 alone (quoted in Berger & Winkler 2006). *Bwana* does feature a drowned migrant, but the treacherous passage from North Africa to Spain is eschewed in favour of a melodrama concerning the hysterical reactions of a Madrid-based family as opposed to the experiences of the surviving immigrant, Ombasi (Emilio Buale). In other words, the process of trafficking itself – that is, exactly how and why an immigrant manages to get to Spain – is more or less absent from these films.

Instead, the films often prefer to filter the immigration experience through the lens of the Spaniard. *Bwana* in particular gives Ombasi little to say and we are not given any translation/subtitles for his words when he says it. Instead our attention is directed towards the (largely unsuccessful) efforts of taxi driver Antonio (Andrés Pajares), his wife Dori (María Barranco), and their children, to understand him. *Letters from Alou* does give us subtitles for Alou's voice over, which recounts in epistolary form his experiences in Europe. But the film also sees Alou begin a relationship with Carmen (Eulalia Ramón), and it is in some respects through this interracial relationship and the obstacles in its way (threat of arrest, society's disapproval of the relationship, which must therefore be carried out in a clandestine manner), that we begin to identify with Alou and his situation. Similarly, *Saïd* sees the title character (Noufal Lhafi) begin a relationship with Spaniard Ana (Núria Prims), who becomes the most vocal supporter of Saïd's cause. As Daniela Flesler says, therefore, the films end up 'sanctioning… policing [of immigrants], allowing one obstacle or another to precipitate the end of the romance, and in doing this they unwittingly endorse the belief in its impossibility' (2004: 106). In other words, most films dealing with illegal immigration do not address directly the issue of trafficking and, on the whole, they remain conservative in their attitude towards immigrants by endorsing, even if tacitly, the repatriation of the immigrants/the impossibility of integration.

Chus Gutiérrez's *Poniente* (Spain, 2002) is not necessarily much different from *Bwana*, *Saïd*, and *Alou*, in that the film's main protagonist is Lucía (Cuca Escribano), a teacher from Madrid who inherits and decides to take on her dead father's tomato farm. That is to say, this film is also one told from the point of view of a Spanish character. The title might suggest as much, since 'poniente' can be translated as 'West,' in that the word evokes the setting of the sun, suggesting that the film is told from the Western perspective, although to look at the setting sun is to look West from the East, so there is some ambiguity in the title. The title would also lend itself to the theme of visibility, in that without light from the sun, in darkness, human trafficking remains invisible. And it would also suggest some pessimism on the part of the filmmakers: this is not a new dawn, but the setting of the sun. But on whom? On an old Spain? On bonded labourers? On both? While *Poniente* is, like the other films mentioned above, told from the European, here Spanish, perspective, therefore, the film does differ from those titles in certain key respects.

Firstly, the romance that develops in the film is not between Lucía and one of the illegal immigrants who works on the farm, but between Lucía and Curro (José Coronado), a Spaniard who himself was brought up in Switzerland after his parents emigrated from Spain years before. In other words, 'Gutiérrez is interested in emphasising the link between Spain's own past migratory experiences and the current situations and attitude resulting from present immigration' (Ballesteros 2005: 11). As Gutiérrez herself has said: 'in the end, we are all a cultural mix' (quoted in Santaolalla 2003: 49), although this is an attitude that in and of itself might make the immigrant/ potentially trafficked person one with whom we can identify because somewhere along the line we are all 'homeless' in the contemporary geopolitical climate – an attitude that might ring false when comparing freely mobile Europeans with immigrants trapped in bonded labour.

Secondly, the film takes care to show us the 'miserable and sub-human environments where immigrants are forced to live' (Ballesteros 2005: 11): as much as *Poniente* is a film about Lucía and Curro's relationship, it is also about Lucía's growing realisation that the economic success of her father's Almería farm is based upon the exploitation of illegal workers through a system of contemporary peonage that Bales, Trodd and Williamson see as being directly linked to human trafficking (2009: 17). While Flesler argues that the eventual rift between Curro and Moroccan immigrant and farmhand Adbendi (Farid Fatmi) compounds the impossibility of integration (2004: 107-108), Isolina Ballesteros finds the film 'innovative' in comparison to other Spanish films dealing with this topic because it does not reduce the black/Arab characters to objects of the Spanish female's sexual desire (2006: 175). Ballesteros furthermore argues that the violence that erupts over the presence of the immigrants, by being taken out not on the immigrants but on Curro, emphasises 'shared cultural links, rather than differences' (2006: 176). In other words, *Poniente* not only seeks to make clear the systematic exploitation of trafficked workers, who are held virtual prisoners in Europe on account of their poverty and debts, but it also seeks to make clear the hypocrisy of those who react violently to the presence of such workers, since these workers are in fact the contemporary equivalent of Spanish emigrants of the 1950s and 1960s.

The destruction of the farm and of the immigrants' homes at the end of the film, together with the lynching that Curro receives, is directly based on the El Ejido incident of 2000. In 'Negotiating the Visible,' William Brown argued that this effort to eradicate illegal immigrants from Spain, immigrants who provide a taskforce that in some respects underpins that country's agriculture, paradoxically makes those otherwise invisible members of Spanish society precisely visible. According to the European Foundation for the Improvement of Living and Working Conditions, a body of the European Union working on the planning and design of better living and working conditions in Europe, Almería was, at the turn of the millennium, an economic 'miracle' as a result of its agriculture. However, it is argued that the economic upturn of this region, which had traditionally been among Spain's poorest, was in large part as a result of illegal immigrants, since this illegal taskforce (consisting of about 10,000 people in El Ejido alone) would take on the poorly paid jobs typically refused by Spanish nationals (Quits 2000).

Although filtering through Spanish characters the exploitation of labour that is often a direct consequence of human trafficking, *Poniente* also differs from the other films mentioned above, in that it does not simply deal with the 'problem' of immigrants or immigration, but is prepared to consider not just the motivation for entering Europe illegally, but also the motivation for Europeans (here, Spaniards) to have an ambivalent attitude towards such immigrants. That is, as long as there is silence on the part of the illegal immigrants regarding the poor living conditions and pay that they are forced to endure, then there is a smooth-running business-as-usual acceptance of immigrants. However, when those illegal immigrants demand recognition and better pay by going on strike, as happened in El Ejido in 2000, and as happens in Gutiérrez's film (with Lucía endorsing their actions), then violence on the part of the local residents seems to be the reaction. This violent reaction would seem to compound the sense that debt bondage or bonded labour is even a *desired* underside of contemporary Europe: illegal immigrants are accepted as long as they do not make themselves visible, but they are unjustified in making themselves visible through community-based action because they should not demand more than what they already have. As long as they are happily exploited, everything is fine. For them to complain about their exploitation is to arouse anger. Few Spaniards, *Poniente* and the El Ejido incident seem to suggest, share Lucía's desire simply to see this exploited labour force receive a fair pay as a human right; these immigrants, it would seem, have no rights and are punished for demanding them. If there is a recognisable move to deny these illegal immigrants their human rights (decent housing, fair pay), then this reflects a Spanish and perhaps wider European attitude towards its unrecognised workforce: that they are somehow sub-human.

That *Poniente* is predominantly told from the point of view of Lucía (the film opens with her journey from Madrid to her father's farm in Almería, emphasising her journey as opposed to that of Abdendi and the other immigrants), this does suggest the seeming 'impossibility' of, or at the very least a refusal to, engage with this outcome of human trafficking from the perspective of those who take part in human trafficking – even though, as mentioned, the journey from North Africa to Europe is one fraught with danger and involving multiple fatalities.

Letters from Alou does go some way to countering this by offering us Alou's journey and his perspective on life in Europe through his letters home to his native Senegal. However, *Letters from Alou* is directed by a Spanish director, Montxo Armendáriz, as is *Poniente*, which is directed by Chus Gutiérrez. Armendáriz, as a Catalan, may, like Chus Gutiérrez, as a woman director, have sympathy for the immigrant, not least because both directors might perceive kinship with immigrants through their own 'minority' status within their own country, but in neither case do we have a film about the life of a trafficked person (or illegal immigrant) made by someone who has been through those experiences. Ryan Prout summarises recent Spanish cinema that deals with issues of illegal immigration by comparing it to France:

> Whereas in France there is a generation of *beur* and *verlan* filmmakers who are holding France up to an external light, this step has yet to be taken in Spanish cinema, a fact that reflects (leaving aside Iberia's 800 years as part of Arabia) the relative novelty of the population movement from Africa to Spain (2006: 731).

In other words, the experience of human trafficking and the exploitation of labour that is one of its direct consequences still needs to be told from the perspective of the trafficked person and, if possible, by someone who has undergone those experiences. That way, perhaps Spanish cinema will be able to overcome the Eurocentrism that lies at the heart of these films (Spanish women coming to the rescue of illegal immigrants who are persecuted by the police and exploited by their employers).

The El Ejido incident coincided with the passing of Spain's

Foreign Persons Law, which offered social and legal rights to immigrants and which sought to bring about their integration into Spanish society. Perhaps the last gasp of a crumbling system of exploitative labour within Spain's agricultural south, El Ejido, and the immigrant/trafficked experience more generally, remains at the very least a moment in history, even if one now condemned to the past, that deserves to be considered from the point of view of those who experienced the worst of it most directly.

Spare Parts

Written and directed by Slovenian Damjan Kožole, *Rezervni Deli* (*Spare Parts*, Slovenia, 2003) follows two ordinary blokes who just happen to work as traffickers. It is a film about male bonding and the coming of age, a buddy film featuring the unlikely friendship between Rudi (Aljoša Kovacić), a good looking chap fresh out of school, and Ludvik (Peter Musevski), a middle-aged, cancer-suffering widower. As a backdrop to their relationship, we see the clandestine migrants that Rudi and Ludvik help to traffic, and yet they remain in the shadows, following the underground journey that, as the traffickers believe, is taking them to an endless life of exploitation and abuse in the treacherous dreamland of Europe.

Both men live in Krško, a provincial town in newly emancipated Slovenia, not far from the Croatian border and a few hours' drive from Italy. Krško has seen days of past glory, especially when comrade Tito and his partner Jovanka came to the town in a black Mercedes on 1 December 1974 for the triumphant setting of the cornerstone of the first nuclear power plant in Yugoslavia: footage of this visit is shown as part of the opening credits.[35] The plant is still there, and so is the speedway track, a site for the regional motorcycle Grand Prix with a long glorious history of roaring engines and crowds, mud, and the triumph of man over machine. The film's opening also features sepia-coloured photos of past speedway heroes, including pictures of Ludvik Zajc's own stellar past on a motorbike.

It is at the racetrack where Rudi and Ludvik first meet, in the spectator's area. Rudi has been sent by someone to approach Ludvik for work; the 'job interview' consists of a single question: 'Have you

---

[35] The plant opened in 1983. Co-owned by Croatia and Slovenia, the plant is expected to complete its life cycle in 2023. It currently stores nuclear waste locally (source: Wikipedia).

got a clean driving license?' Having answered 'yes,' Rudi lands the job. The rest of the film shows a string of episodes featuring the two men, at work and at play.

Arguably, there are more scenes that show the pair at work, especially in and around the van that both of them operate, with one of them driving while the other sits idle in the passenger seat. Theirs is a job in transportation, so to speak: they get passengers from near the Croat border, then drive them through Slovenia and drop them near Italy. Most of these gigs take place in the dark, in the small hours of the night, and in locations far from the beaten track; one needs to drive quietly through woods or on muddy farm roads. Distant city lights are occasionally seen down there, far away, usually linked to an anonymous industrial landscape. The passengers come and go in the dark; their scared foreign faces are seen only occasionally when lit by torchlight; a motley group of men and women, young and old, and children, blacks, Chinese, Arabs. They emerge from the woods, often wet and shivering, and, after a short ride, disappear into the woods again; they usually keep quiet except the occasional baby that decides to cry at the most inopportune moments. Rudi and Ludvik do not get very involved with them; they pick them up and drop them off the same way as they would do a load of potatoes. After offloading near the border crossing, it is Rudi's job to wash the back of the van; it often stinks, somebody may have even puked in there. Meanwhile cash changes hands between the passengers and the people who run the operation: Marcello (Matija Vasti), the Italian, and Pigl (Rudi Pozek), the Austrian, both greedy bastards in the eyes of Rudi and Ludvik, who are just hired hands working for lower wages on this side of the border. It costs €1,000 per person. There isn't much talk as all involved speak different languages; only the occasional English expression gets thrown in ('let's go'). With the police lurking around, it sometimes gets tense and they need to duck into the shrubs with the lights off. If anything happens, Rudi is advised to run away, leaving 'the load' behind; if questioned at a later point he is to say that the van was stolen and he has no knowledge of what it may have been used for. He is not hugely thrilled with the job, especially as the hours are long and the environment unsociable. But what can he do? It's a job, after all, and business is business.

Occasionally, there are waiting periods during which the traffickers hang around the same premises where the trafficked hide, in workshops or on remote farms. They sleep covered with their jackets on armchairs surrounded by ashtrays overflowing with cigarette butts, empty fizzy drinks cans and greasy pizza boxes. There isn't much to do except look through tabloids, play cards, smoke, or invent ways to squeeze more cash out of the clandestines (like charging them €50 for delivering a pizza).

The furtive characters that are being trafficked have got no faces or names; they are just shadows that come out of the dark and go back into it. Only occasionally do they turn into individuals, whose ordeal can trigger the sympathy of even a hardened trafficker like Ludvik. A veiled Iranian woman clutches a dead baby; Ludvik helps her to come to terms with the death of the child and to bury it, and he even gives her some money. Then, there is a black family – father, mother, and boy – who suffocate to death in the trunk of the car while hiding from the police in the bushes. A fatso trafficker has taken their last cash for the privilege of stuffing them into the trunk of his sedan ('Fuck, I could get six or seven Chinese in there,' he comments). Their bodies are dumped in shallow water in the woods; burial is not part of the service. 'Shit happens.'

Ludvik wants Rudi to know that showing sympathy to the clandestines will not change their fate; they are doomed anyhow. Even if they help someone here and now, it would not make any difference as they all end up as whores or as 'spare parts' as soon as they cross to the other side. 'What spare parts?' Rudi asks, and Ludvik responds matter-of-factly: 'On the Italian side they drug them, then take away everything – kidneys, lung, heart, anything you can transplant; a kidney is €15,000.' Slovenian traffickers, Ludvik claims, are something like tourist guides compared to the guys to whom the clandestines are transferred on the other side.

Rudi has experienced a momentary weakness when he observes the ordeal of a young Macedonian couple, a boy and a girl of his age, evidently in love. They have run out of money and have been starving; the boy is running a high fever. The girl is being blackmailed by Rudi's 'colleagues,' who will get food and antibiotics for the couple if she will have sex with them. 'Listen, me and my friends – clean and nice people, we will give you €50 each,' the traffickers negotiate. She refuses, but not for long, as she enters the adjacent room of the dilapidated farm where they are based, followed by the men. When she comes back to the semi-delirious boyfriend later on with medicine and food, he pushes her away; evidently he has grasped what is happening. Later on, when the group of refugees are taken into the woods for their border crossing, she cannot stop sobbing.

Rudi has been truly sympathetic to the girl's ordeal, but there isn't much he can do for her – she is just another one of the shadows that they transport. The next morning, while Rudi is still sleeping, the radio reports the death of a Macedonian girl who either perished in an accident or committed suicide while attempting illegally to cross the border with Italy. There is symbolic value to the fact that Rudi is asleep when the report airs. No knowledge of the girl's death will ever reach him; Rudi's choice is oblivion. It may appear as a loss of humanity on his part, but in fact he is simply doing his job. Like the other traffickers, he behaves professionally, follows procedures and business routines. 'Collateral damage' is inevitable, yet he is doing his best to maintain good standards, and the smaller his emotional involvement, the more professional he is likely to be. Commiseration to or sympathy for those who put their lives on the line by getting themselves into the traffic is not on the checklist. While watching a group of clandestines climb into a cistern to hide, Rudi wonders how they could possibly get as far as London like this. Ludvik reacts with disdain: 'Say hallo to the Queen from a retired Slovenian racer!' Ludvik's conscience is clear: he is providing the service these people want.

When not at work, Rudi and Ludvik are at play. Play mostly revolves around drinking marathons that take place usually in the early morning hours, after the night shift, when the van returns to Krško and they have time to themselves. Celebrations are drowned in alcohol; work is followed by beer, *burek*, and kebab. A repetitive and monotonous life, not different from the life of ordinary truck drivers. The bar, near the nuclear power station, seems to be open non-stop. Binge drinking seems to be part of everybody else's routine as well: in the toilets of the local disco Rudi meets a girl who has just puked and who is high on coke. He helps her balance for the next few shaky steps. After a night of casual drunken sex, this girl, Angela (Aleksandra Balmazovic), eventually becomes Rudi's girlfriend.

Rudi's main relationship, however, is with Ludvik. They learn a lot about each other, and they bond during their trips. Balding and with a gold chain around his neck, Ludvik is not a bad guy; he likes farting and is a chain-smoker. He lives on past glories from his racing days at the speedway track, and he mentors Rudi by telling stories about his challenges and achievements – how the bullying that he was exposed to at school drove him to take up racing and to become the first speedway champion in independent Slovenia in 1991. Everybody rooted for him back then. Before that, however, he was also a school champion in rock-and-roll for the whole of Yugoslavia, and indeed won a national competition in Tuzla in 1977. At another time he used to be a test-smoker for a tobacco company; back then he would get three steaks a day just to evaluate the cigarettes. In general, the Yugoslav days seemed better…

Ludvik does not have children and genuinely misses his wife, who died of cancer some time ago. He lives alone and now has cancer himself. The prognosis is not too good, even though he tries to cure himself by drinking a glass of his own urine every morning out of a canister in the fridge. The frequency of cancer is linked to the nuclear plant; everyone seems to know as much, but what can they do about it? There aren't many opportunities around, so both Ludvik and Rudi have to put up with their job as traffickers and living in the shadow of the power plant.

Nice things happen to Rudi who, with some hiccups, finally gets a steady girlfriend (Angela, who turns out to be a nicer person than first impressions suggest). Ludvik still acts like an older brother to him, a role model of sorts, and he gives his blessing to Rudi's relationship, especially as Angela soon announces that she is pregnant. Ludvik's illness gradually deteriorates. A few months later, Angela's pregnancy has advanced, but Ludvik has not lived to witness the birth. Rudi is the only friend who stays at the grave after his funeral, swallowing his tears. He will now be taking over the operation, and so wears a black leather jacket and has a gold chain around his neck. The final scene, almost identical to one of the opening sequences, shows him at the racetrack where he himself is approached by a young man with a clean driving license. Life goes on; new groups of clandestines have arrived and are waiting in the woods to be processed.

Ludvik and Rudi are ordinary working Slovenians who get into the human trafficking business simply because this is what happens to be available for them. Ludvik always knew how to grab opportunities as they came along: biking at the speedway, testing cigarettes. Rudi, similarly, took the job and seems to be happy to stay in trafficking, maybe even to retire in it. In focusing on such mundane, non-enterprising average individuals, Kožole's film gives a rare glimpse into the lives of what seem to be typical small-country small-town East European males. In the years of communism they were getting into weightlifting in droves and, after the end of communism, sumo wrestling became hugely popular, with both sports perceived as nice 'niche' opportunities by people with low confidence and limited prospects. In a similar vein, occupations in smuggling, trafficking and other grey zones are regarded as decent career paths. It all needs to be assessed against the background of restricted opportunity, in a context where underground economies thrive better than the legitimate ones.

Slovenia was the first former Yugoslav republic to be admitted to the European Union in 2004, the year after *Spare Parts'* release. But people like Ludvik are not in the film overjoyed by what some would describe as a triumphant entry into Europe. He is precisely what one calls a 'Yugonostalgic,' even if of the Western-most variety: he misses the paternalistic safety of state socialism and is pissed off by globalisation. He yearns for the lost times of comrade Tito and his communism of 'brotherhood and unity,' when he travelled to nearby countries and was celebrated for his speedway skills. He hates the way things have turned out lately, and he hates the clandestines for wanting to go to Europe: 'Those shits piss me off. Europe. I hope that, as long as I live, Slovenia doesn't fucking join Europe.' He still wears a Polish T-shirt he brought from a visit there, and reminisces about the *Blutwurst* and salami that back in the day he would bring back from Hungary, together with *Becherovka* from Czechoslovakia and *Mozart Kugeln* from Austria. But it is all fucked up now; you can get whatever you want in the shop next door. 'The world is a sewer; it is one big hard shit.'

Joining Europe, of course, means that both protagonists may soon be put out of business: as of 2004 the Croatian border, and no longer the Slovenian one, has become the threshold for the coveted Schengen passage into Europe, and the jobs for people like Rudi and Ludvik may go to those on the other side of this key migratory divide. For the time being, however, the radio in the trafficker's van keeps reporting that 'in the last year 35,000 people have been apprehended and placed in the centre for deporting refugees, and for the first three months of this year there have already been 10,000.' The influx of those lining up to enter the affluent West European economies as 'spare parts' does not seem to be anywhere near exhaustion.

Promised Land

Along with *Alila* (Israel/France, 2003), *Free Zone* (Israel/Belgium/ France/Spain, 2005), and *Hitnatkoot* (*Disengagement*, Germany/ Italy/Israel/France, 2007), *Ha-Aretz Hamuvtachat* (*Promised Land*, Israel/France/UK, 2004) is a recent Amos Gitai film that focuses on the contested realities of contemporary Israel, with a focus, in this instance, on transnational sex traffic. Shot on digital video and then blown up to 35 mm, the camerawork is often shaky and the image grainy. This, the director believes, enhances a certain 'sense of urgency' in the viewers.[36] Shot on location near Cairo, Eilat on the Red Sea, Haifa, and on the outskirts of the Palestinian capital Ramallah, as well as in Tallinn (Estonia), the film tackles the geography of contemporary human traffic while making best use of a transnational female cast from Germany (Hanna Schygulla), France (Anne Parillaud), the UK (Rosamund Pike), and Russia (Diana Bespechny). The plot is straightforward: a group of East European women is trafficked into Egypt and re-sold in the middle of the desert, at which point some are sent off to Ramallah while others end up in a brothel on the shores of the Red Sea, and subsequently in another brothel in Haifa, where they are about to be auctioned off once again when an unforeseen terrorist attack causes havoc and allows some of them to escape. The focus is on the group, but in the course of the film several of the women gain individual characterisation and stand out.

The most memorable (and shocking) sequence in the film is the scene of the modern-day slave market in the Sinai desert. It takes place at daybreak, amidst a wintry barren landscape under

---

[36] Gitai speaking in 'About *Promised Land*: The Making of…' on the French DVD of the film (2006, MK2 edition).

the dramatic fiery skies of morning twilight, all yellow and pink. A group of modern-day Bedouin men wake up the girls, who arrived on camels and spent the previous night near a bonfire, and silently they herd them through difficult terrain to a circle of vans, which sit in the dust with their engines running and their headlights on, illuminating the centre of the circle, the constant engine hum making the scene tense and anxious. Men in black and a leather-clad woman come out of the vans; another woman stays in one of the vans and observes from a distance. The men brutishly begin dragging the girls one by one into the middle of the circle: 'A nu-ka devushki, spokoyno, bystro' (Russian: 'Come on, girls, relax, hurry!'). Who are these types? The girls form a line and are hastily inspected with a torch that travels over their faces and hair. The soundtrack is of disembodied voices that discuss figures in a mixture of English, Russian and Hebrew; the bidding usually starts at 'four' and then rises quickly to 'fife-five-and-a-half.'[37] In one case the bidding goes up to 'six-and-a-half' and 'seven'; one of the girls fetches an 'eight' after her bottom is exposed, causing a squabble between the bidders. Hair colour, skin, and the shape of the belly and breasts can make a difference to the price; T-shirts are pulled up for inspection in the torchlight. The younger girls go for more, but 'experience' is also valued, obedience is praised. Clearly, the girls have been through the pipeline before ending up here; for some this is just the next sell-through event. One is still a virgin; she will go for significantly more, maybe fifteen. It is all sorted out and is over in about ten minutes. The girls are divided into groups and loaded into vans and cars, and the vehicles turn around and leave. The goods are delivered, and the Bedouins can go now – but they stay around the bonfire to warm up some more, discussing the next delivery that is to arrive in a few days' time. It is still twilight, before dawn.

[37] According to Morawska (2007: 102), the reported proceeds for East and South-East European women 'range between US$2,500 and US$7,000.'

The dramatic skies that overlook the pre-historic desert and the endless mountain chains claim an important presence in the film.[38] The mighty beams of light that descend vertically and pierce the morning clouds suggest that a supreme deity may have been presiding over the profoundly heart-rending scene of the slave market, which, not accidentally, takes place in the Biblical 'promised land' of the title. Director Gitai has said in interviews that he intentionally wanted such spiritual references to come through, while both retaining and downplaying the concrete background of Israel, as he subscribed to the universal concerns that are the global felt effects of trafficking in humans.

The women have been shown arriving in the desert the previous night in total silence, broken only by the occasional insect screeching or dog barking. Then one hears steps and voices, Arabic and Russian phrases are recognised, and images gradually emerge from the pitch dark: a bonfire, some men nearby, girls clinging to each other... It is freezing cold; they have always imagined the desert as a white-hot place, but now they see it can be chilly in Sinai. They have come through Cairo, Port Said and Ismailia, led by their Bedouin guides whose faces now appear lit by the moon, which emerges from behind the clouds. One of the men, tall and young, separates one of the girls, nearly a child, from the group and drags her aside by the arm, between the camels. The jittery camera records their silent struggle in a close-up: she is pushed down on the ground while he tears her clothes away; she does not resist but only breathes heavily. The girls in the group do not react; the moon at first lurks over the site of the rape but then dispassionately retracts.

After the sale, the group is broken down into smaller squads assigned to different vehicles. At the back of one of the trucks, the girls are trying to peek from under the canvas: they are driven through some

---

[38] Actress Rosamund Pike reportedly re-read parts of the Old Testament, specifically the book of Amos, while on the shoot.

early morning urban sprawl, amidst low-rise apartment buildings, no trees, empty streets, and ruins on the side of the road. The Palestinian capital of Ramallah is identified on a sign, a place that none of the girls seems to have heard about before. The driver slows down and stops near a checkpoint. Some men come to the back of the truck and, despite slaps and kicks, hide two of the girls under black burkas; then they drag them out, clutching them by the arm and, making sure that all blond hair is well covered, walk them through a gathering of people and across the checkpoint in front of some puzzled children who look on. The truck carries on with the other girls.

It is still early morning when the truck arrives at the resort of Eilat on the Red Sea; the town is still asleep, with towels drying on empty hotel balconies. Four black-clad bouncers come to the vehicles and escort the women with slight pushes and controlling hands; Anne Parillaud, in business-like black attire is in charge, issuing brisk orders to the men. Shot from behind, the girls carry their luggage over a wooden bridge that features an assortment of international flags and which links the shore to the Red Sea Star building, which looks like some sort of floating restaurant.

Once inside, the group is pushed into a dark cave under a staircase; a rapid descent leads them deep into the belly of this aquarium-like structure. Surrounded by handlers who shout interchangeably in Russian, Hebrew, and English ('Igor, get them ready!, Do not let them escape!, Separate them!'), they have to throw their belongings into a storage room, quickly remove their clothes, and line up naked in a corridor, where they are nearly blown over by a pressure hose. It is a scene reminiscent of a mass execution, an episode of mass violence practiced at a distance, the women vulnerably herded into one corner, trying to protect their bodies. It is soon over and towels are thrown at them; then they are rushed through labyrinthine corridors, one after the other. Pushed around by bouncers who clutch their arms and shout 'Kadima, kadima' ('keep going, go forward'), the girls, now wearing only lacy bras and panties, wet and trembling, are pushed down a further flight of stairs and into a large fantasy space, lit by orange lanterns and featuring high chairs, glass aquarium walls, and wavy furniture.[39]

The décor of the restaurant makes for an improbable setting, amplified by the absurd combination of sea creatures, semi-naked girls, and black-clad bouncers. This is the point when 'Madam' appears, the woman who sat silently in the car at the slave market. It is a glamorous Hanna Schygulla, who comes down wearing a turban and scores of bracelets, heavily made up and surrounded by a cloud of cigarette smoke. She immediately dominates, her confidence further enhanced by a violin solo on the soundtrack. Her presence is somehow soothing; she approaches a girl and curls her wet hair around the tips of her fingers, then applies make-up to her face and begins a lengthy monologue.

She is a philosopher, this 'Madam.' Speaking slowly in accented English, she compares the girls to little fishes who have arrived into the 'dark belly of a shark.' But they should not cry – she is like them. Then she tells her story: born in Germany, she fell in love with a Jew and came to Israel. She talks of travel and borders, of eternal voices, of submitting one's fate to a lover – and then to other lovers that come along:

---

[39] The Red Sea Star Underwater Restaurant, Bar and Observatory is a well-known attraction in Eilat. Built in 1996 by architect Sefi Kiryaty, it is reached via a 70-metre long bridge to the shore between the Meridien and Ha'Sela Ha'adom (Red Rock) hotels. Mostly targeting the family market, the establishment's website does not mention that *Promised Land* was shot there; instead they advertise it as one of the most romantic places in the world and a perfect place to propose. Here is an excerpt from the Frommers Guide's description of the place: 'This amazingly designed restaurant is 5m (16 ft.) below the surface of the Red Sea, with thick Plexiglas windows that give you an octopus-eye view of the surrounding fish, corals, and other creatures. The decor is fantasy-oceanesque, with sand floors covered by a layer of clear epoxy; velvet, sea urchin cushions on the chairs; starfish lighting fixtures; and wavy blue underwater light filtering through the subsea pavilion from natural sources by day, and artificial sources by night. It may sound campy, but the details are so well done that the effect is enchanting.'

Life s not just one main road, there may be side-roads… I was curious about exploring… Slowly we have accepted to become an object – a sculpture or a painting… Stop crying. I just want to soothe you, I just want to be nice with you, I need somebody to be nice to… You will be working for me, working, and just think of it as work, work; you do not have to think you are a prostitute, you just have to think you are working. And I will always be nice with you.

Schygulla's presence is caring and reassuring yet at the same time it is strangely commanding and theatrical; it contrasts with the rude business-like demeanour of her employees. She sips a red cocktail out of a tall glass and compares herself to the Queen of Sheba. She pulls off one of her many bracelets to give as a consolation prize to one of the girls. This is the moment when Diana (Diana Bespechni), crying on the Madam's shoulder, comes to the Madam's, and the viewer's, attention: from this moment on, she will become the film's main protagonist. Diana's make-up is given special attention by the Madam, and foundation is applied to cover up the imperfections on her skin; the Madam herself paints Diana's lips red, with her own lipstick which she gets out of a special clutch.

Later on, clients arrive and the girls have to start 'working'; there is a noisy party atmosphere, with drinks and loud music. A new girl, Rose (Pike), who seems to be a guest (but who eventually will end up with the others), is brought down the stairs by a young man. She looks around in disbelief; her paramilitary-style khaki jacket could not present a sharper contrast to the topless girls in the bar. Diana approaches Rose and starts begging:

You are the only person who can help me; I cannot see anyone. We are eight girls here, eight girls. They brought

us here against our wish. We are suffering here, the men
are hitting us very hard, you must listen to me... You will
arrange my escape... Bring money.

When precisely Diana decides she wants out is not clear. But Rose
is not willing to listen: 'There is nothing I can do... This is not my
country, I do not speak the language... Nothing I can do.' She rushes
out in haste, leaving Diana behind.

The very next scene shows the girls on the back of a truck: they
are again being transported to some new destination. Diana, raped
as a punishment for seeking a way out, is thrown into the truck,
next to Rose. How did Rose end up here? One never finds out; the
important thing is that Westerner Rose is now one of them. Now they
are all in the same position, even if their nationalities – one is from
Estonia, the other from the English-speaking West – seem to make
them unequal. They cuddle quietly, packed together in a hopeless
embrace, on the road again, without knowing the destination or what
awaits them there. The camera wanders over close-ups of faces
and hands and belongings, while the truck drives through nighttime
cityscapes, before arriving in some backstreet district, where a red
neon sign reads Promised Land. 'Welcome to Haifa,' someone says.
Then, again, the familiar routine: bouncers, who direct their moves,
rushing them through corridors, down some stairs.

This time there are metal walls all around them: it looks like a
ship. Rose and Diana are thrown in a cabin, where they will cling
to each other for a while, trying to console each other on a large
bed, caressing each other and telling one another that they are
beautiful, like angels. Who knows how long they will be kept here,
in this makeshift confine, or what is to follow? In this moment of
introspection, the narrative is intercut with Diana's intense rapid
flashbacks, which proliferate and overwhelm, and which bring her
story to the fore. There are visions of her life back home in Estonia

(a snowy yard, cats on a fence, a forest in the rain, a granny) and moments of the journey (Diana is naked, being photographed at an agency somewhere in the city; Diana climbing a semi-dark staircase; various moments of her life as a white slave, where she is sold and re-sold), all images permeated with the feeling of poverty and loneliness. There is one flashback that comes to dominate, however, and in it, quite inexplicably, Rose figures as well, wearing a black scarf: Diana is at an Orthodox chapel, wearing a white dress alongside other angelic-looking girls from the church choir, singing praise to Jerusalem and Israel, frankincense and myrrh, peace and justice. It is impossible to tell how long ago this was. The flashbacks intensify, intercut with the image of the two women clinging to each other in bed, amidst replays of their arrival in Promised Land. And then a series of Diana's brisk hallucinatory visions of three-way sex in a red-lighted room, a man with a large belly, fishnet stockings… Hastily, the scene cuts to daylight: Diana is being undressed and handled like an object, shivering in front of several professional-looking buyers, one of them a woman, who asks her to turn around as they look on. The flashbacks seem to have turned into flashforwards now, showing the next round of re-selling into further bondage and slavery.

The angelic singing of the girls in the Estonian church, which has been the background music to all these scenes, comes to an abrupt halt while the sequence of slave trades continues. It turns into the real life diegetic soundtrack of men discussing the new re-sale price of the girls, with a female voice commentary gradually coming to the fore: it is the monotonous voice of 'Madam,' who sounds as though she is reading aloud from an intimate diary, speaking again of submissiveness and how all women are treated like objects…

And then, all of a sudden, everything comes to an unexpected end and to liberation. There has been an explosion on the street! The brothel owner madly rushes down the stairs; police and ambulance sirens are heard. The firemen push the girls out of the building, some semi-clad in whore gear; lights flash all around; clients wander with lowered trousers; a dead body in the middle of the street is taken care of by the paramedics and then taken to the ambulances. Rose is wearing her khaki jacket and thus looks strangely composed even though she is clearly disoriented, while Diana is possessed with uncontrollable joy upon realising that she may be able simply to walk away. And yet she does not seem capable of pulling herself together or of making a move. The bouncers promptly regroup and come for the girls, trying to round them up and herd them together. Diana jumps at the brothel owner who was negotiating her price just minutes earlier, shouting at him in rage, silenced by the noise from a passing train. Joy and despair blend into one as Rose and Diana grab each other and manage to drag themselves away from the burning cars, further and further away, around the corner; Diana mumbling 'vse horosho… ya svobodna!' ('everything is alright… I am free!'), then shouting it aloud as the two run down the busy street, embracing, with the monotonous voice of 'Madam' reciting from Ecclesiastes in the background: 'time to die,' 'time to destroy,' and 'time to build.'

The reception of *Promised Land*, both domestically and internationally, has been reserved at best. Many of the film's critics have found it challenging and excessive, with some claiming that it rings false and leaves too much to guesswork. Similar to other recent films by Gitai, the presence of established and often European female stars (Juliette Binoche and Jeanne Moreau in *Disengagement*, Natalie Portman and Carmen Maura in *Free Zone*) comes across more as an indulgence than a true stipulation of the film's concept. *Promised Land*, however, is in fact coherent and truly engages with making explicit the issues of slavery and invisibility. Yet, it does not come across this way, maybe because of the inclusion of the sci-fi-looking underwater restaurant and 'Madam''s monologue, which makes the film play more like a parable than like a realistic account of a contemporary social problem.

Sex Traffic

Sex Traffic (David Yates, UK/Canada, 2004) is a Canadian-British co-produced television miniseries whose story, when first broadcast, unfolded over two nights. The narrative also extends across the globe, following the story of two Moldovan sisters, Elena (Anamaria Marinca) and Vara (Maria Popistasu), who seek to emigrate to London. Vara holds out romantic hopes for improved opportunities, persuading her sister to join her with promises of higher income work and a chance to provide for her family, especially her young son, Sasha. But, deceived by Vara's boyfriend Lexi (Andre Prisecaru), they are sold into sexual slavery and forced to work in brothels in Belgrade and Sarajevo. Other narratives weave their way in and out of the sisters' story, beginning with that of Callum Tate (Luke Kirby), a young Canadian officer dismissed from his post with IPC, an international police force, after he is found attempting to purchase the 17-year old Anya Petria (Alexandra Fasola), who is killed when she is thrown into the Adriatic by Albanian traffickers evading capture by Italian authorities. The transnational web introduced through the bodies of these trafficked women expands over the course of the film, which reveals IPC, backed by the private defence contractor, the Boston-based Kernwell, to be behind the trafficking ring that claimed Anya, a gesture to the real-life controversy surrounding DynCorp (as mentioned in 'Making Trafficking Visible, Adjusting the Narrative'). NGOs join in this global portrait, both in the figure of the wife of a Kernwell executive, Madeleine Harlsburgh (Wendy Crewson), who has brokered a sizable donation for the trafficked women's charity WFAFM, and in the figure of Daniel Appleton (John Simm), who works for the London-based Speak for Freedom. It is Daniel's investigation combined with a video of IPC officers with trafficked girls that unpacks these trafficking operations and the multiple levels of collusion from local police and businesses, to transnational corporate enterprises IPC and Kernwell.

Seemingly Byzantine in its complexity, the narrative articulates the contradictory restrictions and constraints that arise from the apparent freedoms of transnational movement. Like the 'Smart Films' of the 1990s (Sconce 2006), the winding, multi-sited and multi-character narrative congregates around themes of coincidence. But rather than emphasising flat affect and the paradoxical meaninglessness of seemingly meaningful encounters, the guiding principle here is one of globalisation, and more specifically, economic globalisation. Indeed, as characters cross paths with circuits overlapping and intersecting, the film visualises the new sovereigns of this transnational terrain: corporate and private entities that supplant states and humans in practices of contemporary governance.

Elena and Vara provide the primary points of identification for a story that encompasses more women than whose stories can be told. The film tracks their voyage into slavery, from the boyfriend's promise to the subsequent loss of agency and autonomy signalled by the surrender of their passports, their luggage, and their personal information. The confirmation of their objectification and entry into commodification culminates in a humiliating auction in a club, where Elena and Vara are forced to display their bodies as traffickers debate their relative value. The brutal rape that follows demonstrates yet another part of this demoralising and degrading process. Presenting the routines of trafficking in close-up, the level of painful intimacy attunes the audience to the background activities that carry on throughout the series: auctions take place in back rooms and back alleys, girls are moved in and out of spaces, and missing posters adorn walls and public presentations. These gestures signal the extent of this network and its horrors. Nevertheless, *Sex Traffic* does take care to personalise the suffering where possible, such as in a sequence in an Italian shelter where other women share their stories.

The scope of this economy, both in its capacity to degrade and in its physical reach, functions to ensure the continued acquiescence of the captive women. At a Bosnian brothel, Elena celebrates a secret phone call home, excitedly telling Vara that they will be helped for sure. Monica (Irina Bucescu), listening on, scoffs at their delight: 'Do you think they really want you back?' she asks, dabbing make-up on a cold-sore that represents more of the threats faced in this world, namely disease and loss of income, the latter directly related to continued viability as a worker, as we soon see. Monica's question raises an important issue, because for many of the economic migrants caught in this brutal web, repatriation is not a desirable outcome. This point is supported elsewhere in the film, as an NGO officer refers to the experience of women returned to husbands and brothers who consider them shameful and damaged. Even when returned home, continued survival in the home country can be a real issue for some trafficked women. 'This is the way the world works,' Monica continues, a sentiment that is echoed at the film's end by Vara, who having risen in the trafficking ranks, refuses to return home. There is, according to Vara, no escape from this economy. Her bleak outlook is hardly surprising given what follows the exchange after the secret phone call that Monica interrupts. Entering the house, kicking goods and issuing directives, a trafficker turns to Elena and hints menacingly about the fates of mothers who call the police about their missing daughters. Evidently, the police have been asking around (or warning him) and drawing unwanted attention to his business. But they will do nothing, and there is no way out for Elena – and these hints become violent truth when the trafficker punctuates his statement by shooting Monica, who, ill, has run out of use-value. If this hasn't convinced Elena about her vulnerability and hopelessness, the trafficker assures her compliance by threatening her son, whose name and address he has learned through the paperwork she filled out earlier. In this world, the women as well as their families are disposable.

The traffickers' reach into legitimate corporate circles further stresses the impossibility of escape from this transnational economy. Kernwell, and by extension global capitalism, wields power to control and regulate all subjects. The control begins at the micro-level, in which Kernwell supports IPC, which traffics girls in Bosnia, a gesture to the true case of DynCorp, the private defence contractor recently accused of the same. A man entering the Blue Bar, a centre for trafficking, declares 'welcome to the free market!' – gesturing to the similarities between trafficking and capitalism, while at the same time implicating Kernwell's involvement. But perhaps more dispiriting is the reach that extends governance beyond these individuals. When Madeleine looks into Kernwell, she comes across a website ('World Takeover Organisation') protesting the corporation with the slogan 'America=Kernwell's Bitch.' Invoking protesters of the World Trade Organisation, the internet activist notes that even states (superpower states at that) are subject to the machinations of this internationally operating private entity. Beyond trading in people and holding nations in its thrall, Kernwell also exerts considerable force over NGOs. When Daniel attacks the company and declares their complicity in trafficking, his boss chastises him, pointing out that this action has jeopardised their access to other regions throughout the world. The corporation's interest in donating to WFAFM speaks to both their continued practice of buying influence and good publicity. When Magnus (Len Cariou), a Kernwell executive, praises Madeleine for securing the partnership between the corporation and the NGO, he lauds her ability to 'flirt' her way to success, tacitly placing her within an economy of sexual trade, a gesture that may produce both outrage and hopelessness. Given the range of this network and its influence, is there any escape?

Sex Traffic's more concertedly cynical outlook, one which questions policing as the inherently beneficial management of trafficking, produces a significantly different portrait of the trafficking economy than another miniseries released at around the same time, *Human Trafficking* (Christian Duguay, Canada/USA 2005). While both share a multi-sited sprawling narrative strategy, the American-Canadian co-production nevertheless locates a single, criminal businessman at the centre of transnational trafficking operations. Unlike the Kernwell executives, who are implicated but not necessarily present, Sergei Karpovich (Robert Carlyle) commits acts of violence, takes part in auctions and even murders people. The film provides us with clear heroes, not so much in the trafficked women, whose stories are touched upon, but in the Immigration and Customs agency to which the heroine, Kate Morozov (Mira Sorvino) belongs. In this story policing and security are part of the solution to this criminal transnational economy; they are not institutions that overlap and intersect and participate. Even if immigration alone were posited as heroic, such a protagonist would stand in contract to *Sex Traffic*. Towards the beginning of *Sex Traffic*, Daniel meets with a Kurdish asylum seeker, smuggled into the country in circumstances so dangerous that he lost his family. He finds no comfort or aid from immigration services, and later we learn that he has died in custody. *Human Trafficking*, meanwhile, assures an affiliation between trafficked women and domestic security forces in the figure of Kate, who bonds with the women when recollecting her own molestation at the hands of a favourite uncle. In keeping with the sorts of characterisations expected of a series made for the Lifetime network, the confession also forges a double identity of rescuer and victim, writing out any possibility of complicity with perpetrators. As observed elsewhere in this volume, the miniseries views trafficking purely through the lens of criminality, advancing security and immigration measures as management.

This perspective is not shared by *Sex Traffic*, which views trafficking as one of many overlapping and intersecting circuits motored by economic globalisation.

NGOs take part in this transnational portrait, but the picture is not one to inspire faith. The frustrations and difficulties are made clear beyond the pressure exerted by traffickers at official and unofficial levels. Daniel repeatedly expresses his anger with the limitations that prevent him from intervening. Speak for Freedom, we learn, is limited to covering routes and writing reports to keep their funding. Moreover, his monitoring strategies lead to humiliating arrests, for example when he is found in a brothel speaking to Elena, and to violent beatings, as when he is found videotaping a back-alley auction. Yet even this grim perspective does not dispel the potential value of monitoring: Daniel's report on Kernwell does raise questions and brings unwanted bad publicity on to the corporation, the interest in self-presentation of which is made clear through its hefty donation to WFAFM. Doubts linger, however, given that Daniel's most useful monitoring – done undercover in an immigration centre where he finds more names on the registry than people who attend classes – occurs after his dismissal from the NGO. This thematic oscillation signals a measure of ambivalence regarding the capacity of the NGO, whose authority remains limited, particularly given the dependence on outside bodies for funding and access.

Ambivalence aside, the film's preoccupation with monitoring and its mechanisms introduce another transnational circuitry for this global portrait: audio-visual media and communications technologies. The opening sequence claims a prominent place for video, beginning in that medium, as a young girl looks into a camera, directed by an American voice off screen. This is Anya Petria, who is 17 years old; she and the other girls who follow, state their name, smile, and then blow a kiss to the camera. Stolen by Callum Tate, the video makes numerous appearances throughout the film, whether in the glimpses of Anya, a cinematic interruption punctuating the narrative like a traumatic memory, or through the physical presence of the tape itself, or in its endless replays for various characters including Daniel Appleton, Madeleine, and Madeleine's husband, Tom Harlsburgh (Chris Potter), who is faced with blackmail. The video, treated as visible evidence of crime and collusion, holds considerable value in this economy, both as a coveted item of information and as a key narrative agent; the tape brings about the arrest of some officers, a public apology from Kernwell, and the end of the Harlsburgh marriage. Although the tape fails to bring a truly satisfying conclusion, one that leaves no trafficker untouched, the film asserts the legitimacy of photographic media, an assertion shared by many human rights organisations. Film has the power to reveal abuses and to mobilise shame in perpetrators, forcing them to respond to the accusations they face (Keenan 2004). And even when not working within this idiom, film and photographic media visualise the hidden networks and the lost women. Anya haunts the miniseries in this way as well: her image is projected behind the spokeswoman for WFAFM at a banquet in Boston; her face appears on a missing poster, one of many (including those of Elena and Vara) to adorn a wall in Bosnia; and a photograph of her corpse, along with her effects, sits on a table in Italy. Images help to flesh out the lost world; they provide the connective tissue that illustrates and makes tangible transnational links. This thematic content hints at the broader aims of the miniseries itself, which draws attention to crime through dramatisation and representation.

Despite the possibility for self-aggrandisement, Sex Traffic demonstrates cynicism and ambivalence, even in moments that could usher in a more celebratory stance. Serra Tinic (2009) suggests that such a presentation results from the context of production. Namely, she points to one of the producers, the Canadian Broadcasting Corporation (CBC), a public channel forced by economic contingency to embrace the marketing tactics practiced by its privatised counterparts. Meanwhile, one can also observe the merger of public and private within the British partner, Channel Four, which is commercially funded and publicly owned. Such combinations, Tinic suggests, cultivate sensitivities to the structural constraints imposed by the larger context of global capitalism. Appropriately, then, the series is rife with the expression of restraints, providing an illustration of a global economy that is violently and frustratingly privatised, diminishing the autonomy of both publics and public options.

Ghosts

The title alone evokes the numerous hauntings of *Ghosts* (Nick Broomfield, UK, 2006), inspired by the real-life Morecambe Bay disaster, in which 23 Chinese cockle-pickers lost their lives in what is considered to be one of Britain's worst industrial accidents. Nick Broomfield's film opens with the tragedy before flashing back to follow the lives of undocumented Chinese labourers, reanimating their spirits and giving them presence in the public eye of the cinema. By following the story of Ai Qin (Ai Qin Lin) from Fujian province in China to the UK, where she labours daily until the tragedy at Morecambe Bay, Broomfield invites attention to another phantom presence: the informal labour market that underpins the mainstream economy. An informative title preceding the action confirms as much, referring to the 'three million migrant workers in the UK [who are] the backbone of the food supply system, the construction, hospitality, and health industries.' And yet suggestive as these ghosts are, the title refers to the Chinese slang term for Caucasians. This knowledge, revealed early in the film, performs an important reversal, animating the spectres of exploitation and menace found in the dominant, visible world. Although people smuggling and human trafficking provide clear demons in the shape of snakeheads, whose name alone conjures up otherworldly and sinister threats, the ghosts here refer to a more mundane manifestation. Here we find the demons in the landlords who overcrowd houses, the employment agencies that demand bribes and exact high fees, and the corporations themselves, which rely on this new slave market in order to turn a profit.

Intentionally or not, the title brings to mind the Freudian notion of the uncanny, which seems to drive the film, and which provides a way to reconcile the coexistence and coincidence of apparent opposites, whether these be in relation to the film's topic (undocumented labourers), or its form (a blend of drama and documentary). A result of Freud's venture into aesthetics, the uncanny (*unheimlich*, or, literally, the unhomely) refers to something whose paradoxical nature evokes fear and dread. Freud seizes upon the root word, *Heimlich* ('homely'), which 'is not unambiguous, but belongs to two sets of ideas, which, without being contradictory, are yet very different: on the one hand it means what is familiar and agreeable, and on the other, what is concealed and kept out of sight' (Freud 1917-1919: 224-225). In this way, '*unheimlich* is the name for everything that ought to have remained... secret and hidden but [which] has come to light' (Freud 1917-1919: 224). Doubling is at the heart of the term, which 'develops in the direction of ambivalence, until it finally coincides with its opposite' (Freud 1917-1919: 226). The uncanny, in concept and etymology, engages therefore the complex combination of legitimate and illegitimate, of native and foreign that sustains the European businesses dependent on illegal migrant workers. Moreover, the uncanny, like the film, destabilises the source of menace: is it the strange element of the foreign labourers who pose a threat to the homeland, or the truth of the home operations, which obscure the genuine risk faced by the foreign workers?

Ghostly encounters on screen yield intellectual uncertainty and transform preconceived notions into their opposite. In a quiet moment, Ai Qin looks out of the window, gazing upon children playing in the road. An eyeline match is achieved in a single frame, as the camera captures both Ai Qin at the window and the image of the children reflected in the glass. Although she is part of the unseen world of the undocumented workers, she holds the more tangible presence in the composition, while the boys exist only in reflection, an elusive presence that reifies the slang term 'ghosts.' Other conceptual pairings draw attention to the contradictions that coincide. While Ai Qin is at work, the police storm the house and roust the Chinese immigrants inside, taking them away and threatening to bring in the immigration authorities. The sense of assault on the workers is amplified upon returning to the house, when they not only find it empty, but also vandalised, with rubbish bins overturned and slogans spray-painted on the door. There is no security or protection, as menace comes from both official and criminal actions. Furthering the irony is a visit to the supermarket after a day of collecting and binding spring onions. As mentioned in 'Foreign Exchange,' Ai Qin and Xiao Li (Zhe Wei) wonder if these are the same onions they prepared, and marvel at the price (58p), which places these onions, the fruits of their labour, beyond their budget. The economy that demands their participation simultaneously alienates them.

Ai Qin's voyage maintains the paradoxical doublings. The travel sequence depicting the six-month journey from China to Britain superimposes scenes from the lengthy and multi-conveyance trek on to a map. Although the strategy is familiar cinematic shorthand for the journey, the gesture places unseen migrants on the map and identifies their ongoing presence within official realms, no matter how faint the imprint. In addition, the technique of the overlay blurs the boundaries already destabilised by transnational phenomena such as neoliberalism, global capitalism and migration. This combination both foreshadows and recalls the arresting image of the Morecambe Bay disaster sequence, wherein the workers struggle to drive their van over the advancing sea. The image vividly fuses the themes of labour, travel, and danger, indicating that questions of border security are misplaced; it is not the state, but the migrant facing the greatest risks in this territory.

Most striking, perhaps, is the way Ai Qin's voyage is one that combines movement and restriction. Her journey originates with a discussion that underscores her lack of choice. Shortly after a title informs us that rural labourers in China, like Ai Qin, earn approximately £30 per month. We witness a dinner-table conversation, in which

Ai Qin considers leaving Fujian so that she may make the money necessary to provide for her son and to send him to school. The language is entirely one of need and requirement, as Ai Qin notes to her mother: 'I have to leave to make a living.' Later, she also asks: 'Do you really think I want to leave?' Her father confirms the necessity, suggesting that financially speaking, she has 'no choice.' A discourse of reluctance and the absence of options sit uneasily with any presumption of freedom associated with movement. Over the course of Ai Qin's journey we become witness to her progressive lack of autonomy visualised through the transition from travel by van and foot to her placement inside cargo containers. In each case, she is utterly dependent on the people guiding her, most drastically so when she is enclosed in a crate, lit only by flashlight. The arrival sequence does little to defuse the conditions of restraint as the handheld camera, staying close to Ai Qin, refuses the comfort of an establishing shot. Keeping in constant motion as it maintains obscured vision, the camera mimics Ai Qin's disorientation and vulnerability. Every effort to leave is thwarted, as Mr Lin (Zhan Yu), the gangmaster, pressures her to accompany him. 'I want to go by myself,' she protests, and asks, 'I've paid my money, why should I come with you?' Whether or not she is still bound by debt, she appears to be bound by dependence on one who can negotiate this foreign world, albeit for a price: £25 per week for the housing and £250 for the false work papers. Every step she takes into the free market increases both debt and dependence.

Merging documentary and dramatisation enhances the uncanny effect, not only in terms of Freud's claim that such an effect 'is often and easily produced when the distinction between imagination and reality is effaced' (Freud 1917-1919: 244), but also in its capacity to render spectacular the observations of the everyday. The strategies Broomfield employs are familiar to the filmmaker who most often works in the documentary mode. Long takes, a hand-held camera in social space and video contribute to the formal register of realism, while non-actors and improvised dialogue function to grant greater authenticity. The documentary element of these formal decisions peaks in the moving reunion scene at the end of the film: Ai Qin Lin, formerly a cockle-picker and now an actress, plays Ai Qin (i.e. herself) returning home to China, but both the character and the actress are doing so for the first time in a long time. The camera follows Ai Qin into the airport where she is greeted by her real family: her mother and her father as well as her son, Bebe (who, in this scene, plays Ai Qin's son Bebe). However, for the most part, the documentary serves to highlight the more mundane elements of labour. For the filming of the work sequences, whether in the poultry processing plant, the orchards or the fields, Broomfield opted to film days of work there. The shooting strategy mimics the observational documentary, allowing for the inclusion of the non-cinematic moments of staring, awkward silences, and even boredom, all of which are part of the day's work. The liminal moments, those that are most familiar and yet most hidden from the cinematic spectacle, break through in this observational mode, which equally calls attention to the labour that is disarticulated from the end product in the supermarkets.

One could note that the film replicates and performs the economy on display through its casting of undocumented workers. Ai Qin Lin was an undocumented worker at the time of the filming, a condition that has since changed. The men playing her housemates had also at some point been undocumented workers (some, perhaps, still illegal). And even South African and Lithuanian migrants joined the film as extras. However, Broomfield's economy may differ slightly. First, he seeks to render visible the invisible, thus reversing the impulse of a mainstream economy that seeks to conceal its reliance on the undocumented worker. Second, his project for increased visibility functions in the service of an advocacy economy. Titles at the end of the film inform the audiences that in the Morecambe Bay disaster, 23 Chinese people died, and that their families are still struggling to pay off their transport debts. Despite the relatively low amount of the consolidated debt, £500,000, the British government refuses to help. A final title explains that a foundation has been established in order to aid the families in the repayment of debt, and directs the audience to a website for donations. The case for why one ought to donate has been established by the film thus far: these are the labourers who are exploited, abused, and endangered, but they are also the 'backbone' of Britain's industries. If there is a debt to be paid, the titles seem to suggest, it belongs to Britain, and to all those who benefit from the labour we have seen.

It's a Free World...

The title ends not with a declarative full stop, but an ellipsis, introducing aporia and ambivalence into the discourse of freedom. There is, on the one hand, the vernacular suggestion of a voice trailing off, leaving room for more to say on the subject. On the other hand, there is the accepted linguistic indication of omission. From the start, *It's a Free World...* (Ken Loach, UK/Italy/Germany/Spain/Poland, 2007) positions itself to doubt the supposed freedom that comes with these new flows of people and money, represented in Britain's migrant workforce, casual labour embraced by a free market economy. The production notes seize upon the term 'flexible labour' as a 'loaded euphemism' that masks the restrictions faced by those without contracts. '"Flexibility" means a workforce that can be hired, fired, mistreated and underpaid with impunity,' they read (Production Notes, n.d.). Such irony is the purpose of this film, which addresses economic deregulation and its agents: the 'recruitment agencies, the use of outsourcing, lengthy subcontracting chains – [that] all obscure and facilitate forced labour, trafficked labour, and illegal migrants.' The liberation of people and money in a global economy constrains many involved: this free market system appears to be predicated on slave labour.

For the reader of this volume, such a message is familiar by now: the intersections between economic globalisation and human trafficking surface in many of the films referenced. However, *It's a Free World...* stages a significant intervention by way of its explicit interest in the system's middlemen, namely the recruitment agencies and low-level employers of casual labourers, illegal and legal. This choice dodges the Manichaean dualities of various trafficking films that present the audience with noble victims, crusading policemen, and ardent charity workers on the one hand, and wicked snakeheads, Albanian rapists, and moustache-twirling corporate executives on the other. Loach maps out a murkier territory, refusing neat categorisations, which, like national borders, have become increasingly permeable in an era characterised by globalisation. This web of economic relations is amorphous and complex, and, more importantly, offers nuance that engages sympathies in morally unsettling circumstances.

It's a Free World... tells the story of Angie (Kierston Wareing), who, just fired from her job for her vigorous protest against a manager's sexual harassment, joins forces with her friend Rose (Juliet Ellis) as they set up their own recruitment agency. Operating on the margins from the start, they set up shop in their shared flat, postponing paperwork and VAT in hopeful anticipation of future income. Angie is the model of pluck and ambition as she carves out a niche for herself in a market that demands flexible labour. She is the modern entrepreneur in the truest etymological sense: she stands in between, to take and exchange goods, in this case, temporal labour for money. Burdened by challenges to overcome, Angie suggests the origins of a success story, even as these difficulties equally hint at her own bounded circumstances. Sexual discrimination is made clear at the outset. And over the course of the film we learn of her copious debt to credit card companies and her own fight to keep jobs – she's held over thirty in her life, she tells her father, and in each one was 'dumped and screwed.' Indeed, her life story points to circumstances of abuse, debt bondage and inconsistent ('flexible') labour that do not so much excuse the actions she takes as enrich our understanding of economic relations. The fact that she also struggles to regain custody of her son amplifies the restrictions and regulations she experiences in this world that is ostensibly free.

What one is free to do, apparently, is to exploit others. As the story progresses, Loach shows how financial pressure leads not only to the exploitation of casual short term labour, but also to the practice of hiring illegal workers, whose recourse to fair treatment and wages is even more limited than that of desperate legal migrants. Angie's exchanges with Tony (David Doyle), a manager at a shirt factory, illuminate the issue. Trying to secure work for her men, she speaks to Tony, who complains about these 'new Poles' who are aggravating him with their complaints and demands. 'The old ones kept their heads down, kept quiet,' he says, while these new ones 'got a bit of paper [so] they fucking think they own the joint.' This comparison suggests that legality brings problems to companies seeking a profit. The hint becomes explicit in their second meeting. Learning that Angie's financial situation is 'tight,' Tony suggests that she follow the lead of a friend of his in Kent. He, too, runs a recruitment agency, where he uses a scanner to ensure the illegality of his employees. As long as they have a fake passport, that's all that matters. With this force, one can afford to pay below the minimum wage and maximise revenue. Angie balks, not so much for the morality, but for the risk that such criminal activities bring in the form of fines and incarceration. Tony allays her fears by recounting the case of Crown prosecution against 'one of the biggest gangmasters in the country,' one who employed hundreds of illegal workers. This man was given a warning letter. 'It's a joke,' he says. Moreover, even the risk of detection is minimal. 'He got caught because he was too greedy and too stupid. You have more chance of winning the lottery than getting caught.' These conditions, it appears, are not illegal, or more likely they are of insufficient concern to the state. The struggle for financial security combined with corporate demand and state laxity direct her into this economic territory that encourages the use of trafficked labour.

Partaking in this economy heightens the risk of violence and abuse for all participants from all sides. Trading in people makes Angie callous and cavalier. She invites Polish men to a party at her place one evening, turning them into casual entertainment, using them as she once refused to be used. Later in the film, she reports to the police a caravan park housing illegal asylum seekers so as to open the space for her own workers. When her father criticises her, Angie becomes irate. 'Don't anyone see what I'm doing?' she questions indignantly. 'I set up my own business… Work my fucking arse off.' She is, after all, doing what is expected in this environment: what she can to avoid poverty and dependence. Her father (played by retired dockworker and union activist Colin Coughlin) questions her means, however, and asks after the widespread implications of her actions. Although his first complaints express anger with the new labour population of new Britain, subject to new member states of the European Union – he speaks angrily of the Romanians with whom his grandson will one day compete – his overall grievance turns to labour injustice on a broader scale. He points out her contribution to a labour market where people, including one day her son, compete for starvation wages. When she answers that she, unlike others, is 'giving them a chance,' he again questions the nature of the option she provides. States and corporations are better sources for this provision, but instead they outsource this obligation to people like Angie. The only people benefiting are 'bosses and governments.' 'No one else is smiling,' he tells her. Angie disagrees. 'Consumers are laughing,' she observes, furthering the film's claim that exploitation is found in this quest for profit. This laughter, after all, comes at the expense of those paid under the minimum wage, at the expense of those who lack job protection.

Such abuse begets abuse. Angie points out the stable employment circumstances her father enjoyed, circumstances that she has not shared. 'Dumped and screwed,' she now holds the position that 'all the world can go to hell.' It is fitting, then, that the following shot has Angie arriving at one of the work sites, only to be confronted by locked gates. She needs to meet with Derek (Frank Gilhooley), who owes her money. However, he cannot pay her. The people at the top have left without paying him and now both are at risk. Derek's face bears the marks of a savage beating and he tells her he is still in danger. Meanwhile, Angie's inability to pay puts her in a dangerous situation, subject to assault and threats (at one point, her son is kidnapped). The absence of any solid authority, the need for financial security, and the system that has consumers, bosses and governments laughing, leaves a massive population vulnerable to violence even as it assures their continued compliance.

The formal qualities of the film speak to this entangled state of affairs. Loach's modus operandi of British social realism allows for melodramatic qualities even as it plays down overly theatrical closure. Loose ends carry through the film as various people come in and out of the frame to point out the varieties of people who populate this new working class – from managers to recruiters to migrants legal and illegal. Not only are they entangled in each other's worlds, but they are also enmeshed in a system that lacks any apparent escape. The film begins and ends in Eastern European recruitment centres, one in Poland, whose citizens can legally work in Britain, and the last in Kiev, whose citizens would be without papers in the UK. Here, the elliptical composition articulates the suggestions of the ellipsis: there is a connection between the exploitation labour in this free market economy. This free world relies on an economy of desperation that assures bondage, by debt or circumstance, and which, for most involved, leads to brutal experiences. And even more sadly, this system can diminish sympathy and solidarity, inviting the exploited to become exploiters.

Import/Export

Ulrich Seidl's *Import/Export* (Austria/France/Germany, 2007) tells the parallel stories of Olga (Ekateryna Rak) and travelling salesmen Michael (Michael Thomas) and Pauli (Paul Hofmann). Employed as a nurse in her native Ukraine (in Enakievo; see Pridnig 2007), Olga travels to Austria in the hope of finding a better life and finds herself working as a hospital domestic. Olga's journey is motivated financially: she does not have enough money to make ends meet in the Ukraine, and after trying her hand at online pornography (cavorting in front of a webcam for paying customers), she goes to Austria, where she is insulted over and again by her new compatriots. Pauli, meanwhile, is an unemployed security guard who travels with his stepfather, Michael, to Slovakia (Košice) and to the Ukraine (Uzhgorod) similarly in search of making more money. Michael buys and sells vending and fruit machines, and tries to live like a king in the impoverished east of Europe, drinking and hiring prostitutes, one of whom we see Michael verbally abuse as he makes her fellate him. While Olga ends with some small token of solidarity with her new co-workers (laughing at a joke around a table at work), Pauli ends up leaving Michael in order to hike his way either home or further east after being rejected for a job as a market worker in the Ukraine.

Seidl's film has courted controversy not least for its graphic presentation of prostitution, both in its cyber and flesh and blood forms. In particular, the scene where Michael, with Pauli watching, makes a prostitute crawl around and bark like a dog, describe herself as a 'stupid fucking cunt' in a language that she does not understand, and fellate him while Pauli watches, is graphic and difficult to endure. Furthermore, the fact that Seidl employed a real-life Ukrainian prostitute who did not speak German for this role has also led to accusations of exploitation, as discussed earlier in this volume. Seidl says in interview that the terms of what the prostitute would and would not allow were arranged in advance (Wheatley 2008: 49), but there remains the fact that this is still a film that pays a prostitute in order to degrade her, regardless of whether or not the film is also a 'comment' upon such practices.

Import/Export has as two of its core concerns the questions of mobility and employment in the contemporary age. The jobs that Olga takes on in Austria – as a nanny, a cleaner, and finally as a hospital domestic – all seem to reflect on the institutionalised exploitation that allows Europeans (here, Austrians) not to have to take on these lower-grade jobs themselves. Nannying/domestic labour is in particular overlooked as a form of bonded labour, which itself is a common consequence of human trafficking (Bales, Trodd & Williamson 2009: 162): Olga here is humiliated by the family with which she stays, the mother also intruding upon Olga's supposedly private space and rifling through her belongings in a way that recalls the confiscation of passports and other important documents that also routinely happens as a result of human trafficking in an effort to create a situation of bondage.

Olga's employment at the hospital, which features a geriatric ward, the infirm inpatients of which howl and cry as if in a state of dementia, also begs questions about freedom and bondage in the contemporary era. Seidl himself has said that in such wards old people are 'isolated, alone, simply left to die' (Wheatley 2008: 49). In other words, once humans have outlived their use-value to society, they, too, can often be kept prisoner in anaemic spaces (sterile, white-walled hospital wards) in which they are treated as sub-human. Olga, herself abused by the majority of her colleagues at the hospital, identifies with these inpatients as humans, in particular one elderly gentleman (Erich Finsches), for whom she begins to smuggle chocolate into the hospital. Although this humanitarian gesture is signalled as leading to the old man's death (chocolate is forbidden him for health reasons), *Import/Export* would suggest that it is better to die a human being than to live in a state of sub-humanity, but that the reduction of humans to this sub-human status is also an inevitable upshot of a world predicated upon the necessities of earning money in order to make ends meet. Useless in the eyes of society, the elderly and the infirm are not literally killed off, but they are isolated and deprived of their humanity in such a way that the disparity between the rich West and those that are 'useless' and/or perceived as their slaves or servants also becomes glaringly obvious.

As mentioned, Olga also finds herself working temporarily as a cyber sex worker before abandoning the Ukraine for Western Europe. In this sequence, she is forced to accept orders from an unseen and aggressive male who is watching her online and who seems obsessed with getting a clear view of her anus (nowhere is this confirmed, but the voice of the man sounds like Michael, and it might be this moment alone that unites the two otherwise separate if thematically similar halves of the film's narrative). If there is extreme mobility for some in this age of the internet and instant telecommunications, this does not seem the case for Olga: the male harassing her from the other end of the webcam is able to see her, but Olga cannot see him back, entrapped as she is in the small nondescript room in which she works, as well as on the computer monitor's window through which the man presumably observes her. There arises a further imbalance, therefore, in that the freedom of movement that supposedly occurs in an era of European integration, globalised capital and interactive information technology is in fact simply a means for aggressive exploitation by the wealthy Westerner of the poorer Eastern 'other,' here gendered as feminine and reduced to a sexual object. Olga, like the prostitute that Michael (and Pauli) engages, is merely a piece of 'meat,' the equivalent of an animal, whose function is simply to pleasure the richer man, reduced to such labour precisely because of a system of bondage that arises from the disproportional nature of the distribution of material wealth. What interactivity the internet is supposed to herald is in fact a 'virtual' violation.

As for Michael and Pauli, their travels east to a certain extent see them liberated from the lower rungs of society in Austria, becoming instead lords of the manor in the Ukraine and the other grey and anonymous-seeming locations that they visit – including a Romani settlement. If webcams are presumed to be commonplace for Europeans, then there is an absence of such leisure technology in the spaces that they visit, as signalled by the 'lo-fi' characteristics of the videogames and vending machines that they set up there: these are hardly state-of-the-art Wii installations that they are carting around, but instead last decade's hits, which now have a prolonged if somewhat exploitative second life in areas more deprived than those of their dealers. Quite how Michael and Pauli make much money with these machines is not clear, but to a certain extent their material wealth in comparison to those who inhabit the places they visit is marked, not least on account of their sizeable drinks and hotel tab.

At one point as they head east, Michael and Pauli, presumably without enough money for a hotel at this point, sleep in the van that they use to cart around their old machines. It is a van entirely reminiscent of the kind used by real people smugglers and those depicted in films, Damjan Kožole's *Rezervni deli* (*Spare Parts*, Slovenia, 2003) in particular. Although they do not have several immigrants claustrophobically packed into the back of their van as do Ludvik (Peter Musevski) and Rudi (Aljosa Kovacić) in Kožole's film, there is a sense in which Michael and Pauli – in some ways a duo that is a darker version of Ludvik and Rudi – are smuggling themselves into the Ukraine, not in the hope of getting some semblance of a life together as is the case for Olga, but in order to exploit those whom they have come to conquer. This is not human trafficking per se, but it does reflect indirectly on the world of trafficking: Michael and Pauli's business of trading near-obsolete technology in an exploitative manner mirrors the would-be 'obsolescence' of those who are trafficked in such similar vehicles. Except that Michael and Pauli are going to the Ukraine to get rich – i.e. they are an inversion of the Western European's (hypocritical) prejudice against Easterners, whom they perceive as coming into 'Fortress Europe' in order to 'steal' jobs and money from those that deserve them, when this is of course not quite the case.

Before leaving Michael and beginning his hike along the open road, Pauli tries to get a job at a market in an unnamed Ukrainian town. Like Olga, he does not speak the language in this new nation and immediately, like Olga, he tries to sell himself on account of his body: Pauli lifts weights and shows his muscle to the local stall holders in the absence of any verbal means of communication. Olga is similarly not credited as a thinking human being, but exists solely as a body to be abused by men over the internet or in person when in Austria. However, what for Pauli is an unsuccessful attempt at gaining some employment is for Olga 'successful,' albeit with undesirable and presumably undesired consequences (humiliation). The comparison, however, is complex: without a *lingua franca*, *Import/Export* would seem to suggest that the reduction of humans to mere bodies is an inevitable upshot of exchange and interchange. Furthermore, if he is walking at the end of the film, Pauli is still mobile, even if his experiences have taught him to feel disgust for the exploitative practices of the older generation as characterised by Michael. In effect, Pauli remains a tourist while Olga has travelled out of necessity and is therefore not an opportunist but a victim of circumstance. Pauli walks through a relatively hospitable Ukraine characterised by the open road, while earlier in the film Olga has walked through a snow-filled and grey Ukraine populated by gigantic smoking chimneys. But there is also hope for Olga: while Pauli dances on his own on a Ukrainian nightclub dance floor, Olga at least has dance partners in the hospital, and is the object of the seemingly well-intentioned affection of fellow domestic Andi (Georg Friedrich).

In some respects, then, *Import/Export* highlights the similarities of experience across borders: both Olga and Pauli are trying to find a way to gain self-respect through finding a regular and sufficiently well paid job. However, rather than suggest that the bonded labour of the illegal immigrant becomes demeaned in the face of presumed kinship on the part of the Western European who, as mentioned in 'Negotiating the Visible,' might also feel bonded to their work, the film highlights important differences between the two – namely that Pauli's travels involve greater levels of freedom than do Olga's.

I shall end this consideration of *Import/Export* by looking at Seidl's aesthetic approach to the film. The film features various handheld tracking shots, as per when we follow Olga through the Ukrainian snowscape. These suggest the slow nature of moving through space when unaided by technology and, by being handheld rather than shot on literal tracks, they also suggest the *work* that movement entails. Fitting as this is for a film about struggling to cross spaces, the film is more predominantly characterised by a relatively immobile camera: still frames with the characters in middle or long shot. This also grounds the characters in the space that they occupy, as opposed to having them stand out against it. The long takes, often painful to watch (especially in the scenes of a graphic sexual nature and with the geriatrics in the hospital), also ground *Import/Export* in a 'real time' that adds to the documentary feel of the film. These also further the sense of entrapment that the characters feel in places and situations that they cannot just turn away from and which become unbearable because of their *duration*. This, it may be argued, more clearly reflects the experiences of the characters, who themselves must – and pleasingly do – *endure*. If *Import/Export* is in many respects a bleak comment on the human condition in contemporary Europe, then it is also one that finds some human warmth in its cold, grey climate.

Love on Delivery and Ticket to Paradise

Fra Thailand til Thy (*Love on Delivery*, Janus Metz, Denmark, 2008) and *Fra Thy til Thailand* (*Ticket to Paradise*, Janus Metz, 2008) are two Danish television documentaries that have entered the global film festival circuit, screening in such venues as SXSW in Austin, Texas, the International Documentary Festival in Amsterdam, and the Thessaloniki Documentary Film Festival. The films outline the intersection of migration, culture, commerce, and emotion in their exploration of an apparent proliferation of international marriages in a remote fishing community in North Jutland, where 575 Thai women live with their Danish husbands.

Love on Delivery begins with Sommai, who only fifteen years earlier was the sole Thai woman in her region of Denmark. Since then, she has engineered multiple marriages between lonely Danes and Thai women looking for a way to support their families back home. Over the course of the film, we meet four couples, Sommai and Niels, Kae and Kjeld, Basit and Frank, and Mong and John; however, it is the story of Kae and Kjeld's potential union that provides the driving narrative. After the expected introductory informative titles and striking landscape footage of wide-open spaces, there is a close-up of Sommai making a phone call. The ring tones provide the first diegetic sounds before the conversation begins: Sommai is buying a plane ticket for her niece Kae, who is coming to Denmark for three months. In that time, she hopes to find a husband. Although the sequence provides necessary exposition, the juxtaposition of depopulated wide-shots with close-up faces hints at the contradictions of the union, while the conversation gestures to the numerous features of globalisation at the heart of the film. There are communications and transportation technologies, which convey voices and people across these vast territories, and in this case marriage is also one of these technologies.

From the start, marriage is presented as a commercial transaction as Sommai, and her husband Niels write Kae's advertisement. While it could be tempting to read this as a simple lonely-hearts advert, the narrative positioning suggests otherwise as interviews reveal more about the couple on screen. The couple met in Pattaya, one of Thailand's sex cities, where Niels was, by his own admission, a 'sex tourist,' and where Sommai was a prostitute. Connecting the writing of this advert to the history of the couple forges an association between sex work, marriage and a global industry predicated on the movement of people. At the same time, the gentle exchange between the couple on screen hints at genuine affection between the two, and opens a space for emotion in the transaction. This is, however, of secondary importance, as Sommai tells her husband towards the end of the film. Indeed, the word she uses is 'tolerance,' as she hopes that the wives come to tolerate their husbands, but the demand to provide for their families back home overrides such possibly petty emotional concerns.

Traces of sex trade pervade the films, implicitly and explicitly. One sequence introduces the Thai cultural events that have popped up in the region. Observational camerawork finds the women excitedly preparing for a night's activities. No doubt part of their delight stems from the sense of community such events offer this new diaspora. At the same time, such evenings function as a meeting space, a site of marriage brokering. It is at one of these events that Sommai first showed John a photograph of Mong. John remembers this photographic encounter as one of love at first sight. 'She's my wife,' he recalls immediately upon viewing the image. Mong responds more cynically to John's story: 'He didn't even know me. How could he say that?' The objectification in the encounter becomes clear, and the observational sequence of the cultural event serves to bolster this interpretation. Made up and clad in skimpy clothes, the women dance with each other in ways that suggest both the pleasures of the disco and a knowing performance of their sexual appeal. The subsequent cuts to the men, standing on the edges and looking on appreciatively, enhance this sense of display. In this regard, the following cut to a steak sizzling on the grill seems overkill in its indication of a meat market. This is about the hungry gaze and the context of consumption. And yet, in keeping with a film that introduces affect into these exchanges, the camera steps back to reveal a backyard barbeque, where husbands and wives gather in friendly and benign domesticity. Whatever objectifying processes exist, the participants also form a warm community with a sense of engagement.

Ticket to Paradise, the sequel that picks up five months after the conclusion of *Love on Delivery*, more explicitly pursues the economic underpinnings of the emotional covenant. This film, primarily set in Thailand, tells three stories: that of Kae and Kjeld, now married but awaiting Kae's visa; that of Basit, who has returned to secure custody of her son, Samlee, whom she wishes to bring back to Denmark; and that of Saeng, a new character whose fate assures the connection between the sex trade and arranged marriages. Wishing to marry a foreigner, she meets with Sommai, only to learn that at 23 years of age, she is still too young to immigrate to Denmark. With the option of marriage unavailable, Saeng moves to Pattaya to become a prostitute. There she will not only be able to provide for her family, including her young son, but she may, like Sommai, meet a foreigner to marry.

By highlighting the training and information exchange necessary in producing happy domesticity, both films place marriage within a labour economy. *Ticket to Paradise* features women learning Danish in a building labelled 'Thai Integration Centre,' an apparently formal acknowledgment of the informal marriage economy. Here Kae discusses her case with an instructor, or guidance counsellor, as they tackle the possibility that she will not get the visa: if this happens, she should be prepared. *Love on Delivery* also presents training on a more casual level. Women convene to discuss the problems they encounter, such as the challenges of sexual intercourse with Danish men, who are larger than their Thai counterparts. Sommai, however, provides more explicit instruction and management of the potential unions. She teaches Kae Danish phrases, including 'Good morning,' 'Good night,' 'Does it taste good?' and 'I have a headache,' the latter two indicating the type of domestic work expected of Kae: cooking and company. Sommai explains that a kiss is required with each good morning and good night, and repeatedly tells Kae not to be 'shy' and that she is expected to give hugs and kisses. Indeed, this admonishment not to be shy carries through this scene and into the next, where Saeng's friend tells her not to be shy in matters of fellatio and intercourse.

Marital expectations are only one dimension of this labour. When the women discuss their reasons for the move, they refer to their plans of working in Denmark. Again, the domestic arrangement is placed within a larger economic context. They do not simply sell their bodies in exchange for caretaking by their husband; the women use this marriage arrangement as an opportunity to find a job in order to provide for their families in Thailand. 'I would like a job so I could send money home,' explains Kae. Mong, Kae's sister, observes this larger goal on her commute to the fish processing plant where she works. Sitting on the bus, she speaks of her Aunt Sommai, who 'sent money home to our family.' She continues: 'I thought of coming to Denmark for a long time until Aunt Sommai got me here. I was sure that my life would be so much better.' As Mong speaks, she is visible both in her bus seat and in the window's reflection, an expression of both her possible ambivalence regarding this better life, and of her doubled position: she lives in Denmark to provide for her family in Thailand. *Ticket to Paradise* illustrates the fruits of this labour, presenting the different houses that Sommai's financing has purchased. These new model homes stand in contrast to the shacks that are also a part of the small village.

Labour and commodification are not the only aspects making marriage part of the exchange economy. Both films address the financial negotiations in the orchestration of a union. Kae's advert introduces the possibility of transaction in its objectification of her availability, not to mention in the presentation of her physical dimensions. This notion of a transaction follows through in Kjeld's response to the advert, which highlights his ability to provide. His letter begins with a statement about his steady job and follows with the information that he owns a car, a six-year old Golf station wagon. His interests take a decidedly secondary position in the introduction. Financial discussions play a constant role in the negotiations of the union, most notably at a family dinner where Kae, accompanied by her sister and brother-in-law John, meets Kjeld's parents. Here the conversation turns to the subject of the bonding practice and the financial guarantees needed in visa acquisitions. In order to procure a resident visa for Kae, Kjeld needs to provide a guarantee of DKK54,000 (€7,200). The money, John explains, is tied up for seven years so 'they're stuck together… if she leaves him, he'll lose the money and she'll be sent home.' The affianced here are possibly better described as 'enfinanced.' She does not need to pay back the cash, but she is bounded by an obligation to this initial outlay. As if to reassure Kjeld of additional rewards for his investment, John explains that there are tax benefits for Danish men with Thai wives, and, moreover, that these women are not high maintenance. On the contrary, they are quite industrious.

Children provide another component of the emotional exchange economy. In both *Love on Delivery* and *Ticket to Paradise*, care for one's children is predicated on the success of the marriage. In *Love on Delivery* Sommai tells Kae to 'be nice, and maybe he will bring

your son over. Do what he wants in bed.' And at the beginning of
Ticket to Paradise, Kae and Kjeld speak of the deal they struck in
this arranged marriage, namely, as Kjeld notes, 'the deal we made
was that I would provide for her son.' Basit's story more explicitly
lays out the nature of this provision as *Ticket to Paradise* follows the
processes of securing custody and bringing Samlee to Denmark.
The pain and circumstances of the separation were laid out in the
earlier film, where she recalled his cries as she left him behind
in the airport, and in her recollection of her divorce from her Thai
husband. Despite her husband's brutal abuse, Thai law granted
him immediate custody, which she fights with the help of her Danish
husband, Frank. The fight is primarily financial, as she must pay off
both legal counsel and her ex-husband. As she haggles over the
price, her husband Frank looks on in a mixture of bemusement and
disappointment; although this is part of their agreement, he does
not appear happy to be sharing his wife. The management of these
emotional bonds is not simply financial but bureaucratic. *Love on
Delivery* sets the stakes of Basit's mission, as Frank explains: 'we
have two years to bring the child over, otherwise the authorities
say there is no affinity.'[40] This information, possibly more than any
other in the film, reveals the bureaucratic and financial institutions
that oversee terrains otherwise perceived as governed by affect –
marriage and motherhood.

The agency of these women entering an uneasy, but otherwise
free alliance may seem to be in conflict with the basic definition of
human trafficking as modern day slavery. Associations are further
diminished as director Janus Metz avoids the more gruelling and
brutal stories, neglecting the abusive, captive marriages this scenario
spurs. And the cases of Thai and Somali prostitutes in Denmark are
only hinted at, as when the women complain that Danish men tend
to presume they are for sale. At the same time, these films present

[40] It is not clear if he refers to Thai or Danish authorities.

us with an exchange economy involved in the practice of moving bodies, wherein parties are bonded and where questions of domestic labour and financial dealings sit at the fore. While the transactions carry an affective, and indeed, affectionate dimension, they are intimately tied to the operations that underpin a trafficking economy. These films complicate the terrain in important ways, not only as near-feminist texts that argue for the labour of domesticity, but as texts that open a place for agency in contemporary phenomena of trafficking and migration. These are not stories of innocents abducted and enslaved, whose only relief comes from repatriation. These are more difficult stories, of the bodily negotiations that take place on a global landscape, where one barters self for economic security. As Siddharth Kara (2009) observes, the risk of sex trafficking in Thailand is tied to cultural obligations of parental caretaking, where women can be sold into prostitution to provide for their families. On the other side of this coin one finds the arranged marriage. That genuine affection can also bloom in these arrangements does not dispel the dangers, nor does it dismiss the root causes of poverty and global disparity. The presence of this emotion serves to remind us of how love is very much bound up in financial and bureaucratic transactions.

The Silence of Lorna

Le Silence de Lorna (*The Silence of Lorna*, Jean-Pierre and Luc Dardenne, Belgium/France/Italy/Germany, 2008) is not the first film by Jean-Pierre and Luc Dardenne to feature human trafficking. In fact, their earlier film, *La Promesse* (*The Promise*, Belgium/France/Luxembourg, 1996), perhaps deals much more directly with human trafficking, in that it tells the story of Igor (Jérémie Renier), a young boy who promises to a dying illegal immigrant, Amidou (Rasmane Ouedraogo), that he will look after his widow, Assita (Assita Ouedraogo), once he is gone. Having made this promise, Igor faces a moral dilemma, in that his father, Roger (Olivier Gourmet), keeps immigrants in bonded labour and in terrible living conditions in Seraing, Belgium, which is the town from which the Dardenne brothers also hail. It is not in Roger's interests to keep Assita in any favourable conditions at all, and so Igor must choose between obeying his father and doing what he feels is right.

The Silence of Lorna, meanwhile, tells the story of Lorna (Arta Dobroshi), an Albanian immigrant living in Liège (a city not far from Seraing). Lorna is married to heroin addict Claudy (Jérémie Renier), their marriage having been arranged by Lorna's 'boss' and local taxi driver Fabio (Fabrizio Rongione), who subsequently 'controls' Lorna since she is indebted to him for her newly-acquired right to be in Europe. Fabio wants Lorna to kill Claudy with an overdose in order that she might then marry and 'make European' a rich Russian would-be immigrant, Andreï (Anton Yakovlev). Money received for this second marriage would help Lorna to start up a café with fellow Albanian and migrant worker Sokol (Alban Ukaj). Lorna, who likes and/or feels sorry for her husband, would rather get a divorce from Claudy than have to kill him, but Fabio unilaterally goes ahead with the plan and kills Claudy through the afore-mentioned overdose. Lorna therefore sabotages Fabio's plans for her to marry Andreï by telling the Russian that she is pregnant with Claudy's child. Fabio (now with Sokol on his side) forces Lorna to go to an abortion clinic, only to find that she is not pregnant at all. Fabio subsequently sends Lorna back to Albania with his right-hand man, Spirou (Morgan Marinne). En route, Lorna attacks and renders Spirou unconscious, before running into the woods where she hides in an abandoned hut. She talks to what she believes is her unborn child.

If Robert Philip Kolker believes that the Dardennes' films are 'anti-family anti-melodramas in which disenfranchised, marginal characters wander – sometimes hurtle – through the streets on painful passages of minute self-discovery' (2009: xi), then *The Silence of Lorna* does not so easily fit this category. Given the complicated intrigue of this film, particularly in comparison to the Dardenne brothers' other works of fiction, *The Silence of Lorna* rather sits squarely within and not against the melodrama genre – or at the very least as part of what Martin O'Shaughnessy would call a cinema of 'melodramatic politics' (2007: 133-159). Furthermore, the 'hurtling' that Kolker describes has been at least in part replaced here by static shots, captured in 35mm as opposed to the brothers' typical 16mm productions. As the brothers themselves explain: 'we… decided that this time around, the camera would not be constantly moving, would be less descriptive and would be limited to recording images. Because of its weight the 35mm was best suited for us' (Sobel 2008: 2).

By featuring fewer shots that involve following a character at close range, normally just behind them, and by featuring less 'confusing' or 'frenzied' camerawork more generally, the film also has less of the 'haptic' quality that has been attributed to the other fiction films of the Dardenne brothers (see Mai 2007). Instead, the film feels more conventional, the focus being on the actions of the protagonists in centre frame, a strategy that in turn lends to the film the quality of a more conventional narrative, hence the above description of *Lorna* as being more 'generically' melodramatic, a notion perhaps reaffirmed by Geoff Andrew when he says that the film can be regarded as 'a thriller, a love story, a political drama and a moral fable' (2008:35).

That said, *The Silence of Lorna* is not 'easy' viewing and it does retain key elements that are typical of the Dardennes. For a start the film does, like many of their others, centre upon a moral dilemma involving murder: whether Lorna should be complicit or not in Claudy's killing (for more on this in their other fiction films, see Cooper 2007; O'Shaughnessy 2007: 108-115). Furthermore, as Wouter Hessels says of other Dardennes films, this moral dilemma is also about betrayal (2004: 243): can Lorna here betray the trust that Claudy places in her, not least in his desire for her to help him recover from his drug addiction? In other words, Lorna, like Igor in *The Promise*, accepts a responsibility that for her will outweigh the debt – or bondage – that she feels for Fabio and fellow Albanian Sokol. It is not that Lorna breaks her 'silence' and testifies against Fabio, even though she does not have to live in fear of discovery since her marriage to Claudy has afforded her legal rights in Belgium. But, by believing that she is carrying Claudy's child, Lorna does seem to manifest her desire to keep Claudy 'alive.' Unlike Amidou in *The Promise*, whom Roger buries in the foundations of the house that he is building thanks precisely to the bonded labour of the illegal immigrants that he exploits, Claudy will not be 'buried' and forgotten. *The Promise* sees Igor endeavour to look after Assita and her child: what he endeavours to preserve is some sense of family continuity among the immigrant population, in spite of his own blood ties to Roger. *The Silence of Lorna*, meanwhile, sees Lorna try to preserve the memory not of an immigrant who might be forgotten but of Belgian national Claudy who, by being her husband, is ironically a member of a newly created 'family.' If the Dardennes' films are generally about how 'dysfunctional and incomplete families can no longer deal' with the contemporary world (O'Shaughnessy 2007: 149), then family does not exist at all in *Lorna* except in this most makeshift form. In other words, as befits O'Shaughnessy's analysis of the fiction films of the Dardenne brothers, communities are fabricated not as a result of ethnic or familial/blood kinship (Sokol in fact is happy to betray Lorna and to take Fabio's money), but out of some sort of *ethical* kinship.

This 'ethical kinship' is also what I would term 'anti-capitalist' in structure. *The Silence of Lorna* does, in a way that is true to the filmmakers' artistic debt to Robert Bresson (Kolker 2009: xi), focus on the exchange of money as a key motivator for (temporary and precarious) human relations. This financial kinship does, as we can see in this film when Fabio and Sokol try to dispense of Claudy and Lorna once they have outlived their use-value with regard to their money-making enterprises, create an alienating and violent society. The quest for profit, particularly through the exploitation of the bodies of others (Claudy and Lorna are simply 'meat' to those trying to use them for profit), means that humans forget to consider each other precisely as human beings: people become, after Kevin Bales (2004), 'disposable.' What is interesting about *Lorna* from the perspective of human trafficking is that the traffickers embody precisely this attitude of regarding people as disposable, while the trafficked and the 'innocent' Belgian (played here as in *The Promise* by Dardenne regular Renier) can develop some sense of kinship, albeit short-lived, because they come to develop emotional rather than financial ties. The irony is, and perhaps this can be deemed a shortcoming of the film, that mail-order brides like Lorna might typically find that it is their husband who keeps them in a state of bondage, while here this power-struggle is transferred on to middleman Fabio.

As a taxi driver by day, Fabio is also associated with ease of movement (for profit) and the dehumanising effect that rapid mobility can have on people. It is as if Fabio's speed around Liège means that, much like Sokol who also travels to make money, it is money and not people that join together the places that he visits and which allows him to make sense of the world. Ironically enough, just before he is killed, Claudy buys Lorna a bicycle that he also rides. While this arguably gives to Claudy some long-awaited freedom of movement, this freedom is short-lived. In some respects, we might even argue that Fabio, in keeping Claudy dependent on drugs and in killing him, actively seeks to *deny* to Claudy, and by extension to Lorna, the ease of movement that he enjoys. In this way, rather than dumping Spirou from Fabio's car and driving to safety at the end of the film (an action that might have seemed the 'logical' thing to do), Lorna instead runs away on foot. This rejection of rapid and depersonalising transport allows Lorna to retain her humanity.

Another feature of *The Silence of Lorna* that will be familiar to viewers of the Dardennes' other films is the use of space. Set in Liège as opposed to Seraing, the film depicts Belgium more as a 'space' than as a 'place' or 'nation,' mainly because of the amalgam of peoples living there (see Mosley 2002: 164). That is, between Fabio, Claudy, Lorna, Sokol, Andreï and Spirou, Liège comes across less as a place with a coherent or unified identity, and more as simply a space where diverse peoples conglomerate. Mosley ties this to the decline of industry and agriculture, as well as to the importation of immigrant workers more generally in the Sambre-Meuse region, in which Liège is located (2002: 163-164). But instead of suggesting that this 'disappearance' of Belgian identity has as its cause the influx of other people, trafficked or not, into the region, *The Silence of Lorna* suggests that the fundamental problem is the combination of industrial decline combined with the need to make money at the expense of others. The film does not make any gross generalisations along the lines of 'Belgian good; immigrants bad,' but rather suggests that the necessities of profit perhaps inevitably put people in situations where moral dilemmas must arise. Much as we can admire Lorna – and Igor before her – for making the 'right' choice, *Lorna* (and *The Promise*) do not seek too didactically to make clear any moral message. Lorna is, after all, on her own at the end (and Igor in *The Promise* has moments when he rues the day he made his promise to Amidou).

When Lorna first inspects the café that she wishes to buy with Sokol, she can only peer through boarded windows to get a sense of the space that might become her own. R.D. Crano (2009) has written about how there are often spaces in the Dardennes' films from which their protagonists are excluded, and we get a sense here in which Lorna is excluded from the space of the café and the legitimate business that owning it might signify. Although Lorna does have legal rights in Belgium, there is a sense in which the trafficked 'mail order' bride is still excluded, even if Belgium, as per Mosley's argument above, has no coherent or easily recognisable identity. This is true even when it comes to language in Belgium, even if Liège is situated in French-speaking Wallonia, and even if Lorna speaks some French in the film. Connected to Lorna's physical exclusion from the 'legitimate' workspace that would be her café, then, is Lorna's silence, her inability, perhaps her choice not to converse fully with those around her. This makes of Lorna what O'Shaughnessy (2007: 142) might term a 'text of muteness.' Without a voice in society, Lorna is unheard in a manner similar to the way in which trafficked humans are often invisible. However, given the cynicism and dehumanising attitudes of those who do have voices, it seems that the Dardennes attribute honour and dignity to Lorna's silence, a dignity expressed not in words, but in the actions of her 'ethical kinship' with Claudy, and in her beliefs, as manifested by her belief that she is going to have Claudy's child.

The film ends with Lorna in a hut in the woods – a standard trope from fairy tales. Perhaps *The Silence of Lorna* does involve Lorna's retreat from reality and into a world of fantasy, which is the only way (together with her outburst of violence aimed at Spirou) that she can deal with the reality of her 'sub-human' and 'disposable' status. However, the Dardennes also manage to confer on to Lorna, even if through cinematic conventions that are not normally within their repertoire (tropes from melodrama, etc., underlining perhaps the film's fantastic core), a humanity that sees her 'fantasy' emerge as significantly more 'human' than the 'humans as meat' attitude of those around her.

Taken

Directed by Pierre Morel and co-written by Luc Besson, *Taken* (France, 2008) is yet another in EuropaCorp's prodigious roster of film outputs. Although attention has been given to Besson's work as a director (Hayward 1998; Hayward & Powrie 2006), relatively little has been made of his work as a producer. Elsewhere William Brown (2007) has suggested that Besson's work through EuropaCorp is ambivalent in that, contrary to accusations that Besson is the 'death' of French cinema (Deplasse 2003), the commercial success of his bigger budget films allows him to produce 'smaller' features that are more in keeping with France's 'prestige' cinema, an idea taken up and elaborated upon by Isabelle Vanderschelden in a recent article (2008). (For more on Besson as producer, see also Maule 2006.) Furthermore, EuropaCorp's constant output of action films also sees Besson, as the company's figurehead, 'take' audiences away from Hollywood products proper and towards European (here, French) versions thereof, in this way diverting profits from the USA and back into the French film industry. I shall return to this notion of 'audience abduction' later.

Taken is a breezy action flick featuring Liam Neeson as Bryan, an ex-military security guard whose preoccupation with his (violent) work has led to the breakdown of his family. When his daughter Kim (Maggie Grace) decides to travel to Europe for a vacation, Bryan is immensely sceptical, fearing that something terrible will happen to her. However, in spite of his efforts to prevent her from going, Kim eventually heads to Paris with Bryan's blessing, thanks in part to some negotiation with Bryan's ex-wife Lenore (Famke Janssen). However, no sooner is Kim in Paris than she is abducted by some Albanians, who are going to sell her into slavery. Alerted to Kim's abduction thanks to a last gasp telephone call, Bryan arrives in Paris and more or less kills everyone that stands between him and his daughter. At one point, Bryan even shoots an old French colleague (Olivier Rabourdin) and threatens the colleague's family when the French police try to prevent Bryan from carrying out his violent revenge (because the police are of course complicit in the people smuggling). Bryan finds Kim, her virginity preserved on account of the high price that she would have fetched from an Arab dignitary and prospective buyer, and takes her home, his role as *pater familias* restored. Bryan then introduces Kim to Sheerah (Holly Valance), a pop star whom Bryan earlier happened to save from a psychotic fan, and who will give Kim singing lessons.

Read ideologically, *Taken* is juvenile stuff: Bryan's violent lifestyle might have torn his family apart, but that is not his fault, and his (typically American?) paranoia about constantly being under attack is in fact justified when Kim is 'taken' moments after arrival in Paris, having been targeted for abduction right at the airport. In other words, xenophobia and gung ho violence are necessary and to be encouraged in a world where arriving even in somewhere as 'developed' as Paris, let alone the Eastern Europe (specifically Slovakia) mythologised in, say, *Hostel* (Eli Roth, USA, 2005), results in immediate human trafficking.

That said, the 'violence solves all problems' moral of the tale is complicated by the fact that this is a French film projecting such values on to an American character who is in turn played by an Irish lead. Albanians and Arabs may lazily be cast here as the villains of the piece, but how much this film is an American or a French fantasy about being able to carry out senseless acts of violence against Eastern Europeans and Middle Easterners is open to debate. In other words, the film is highly xenophobic and racist at times, but is it revealing to us the xenophobia and racism of the makers or their imagined versions of the protagonists and audiences? Either way, the overwhelming commercial success of the film suggests that it touched something of a nerve with those audiences: grossing nearly US$145 million in the USA and almost US$77 million in other territories, *Taken* was a box office phenomenon of 2008-2009 (*Box Office Mojo* 2009). In some respects, this is a testimony to Besson's canniness as a producer who can put together streamlined 90-minute productions that have maximum appeal among what are presumably predominantly young male audiences. But it also signals some truths about the international film industry that are perhaps unwanted: namely that no one can go broke making puerile and violent films that are vapid and superficial.

Furthermore, it suggests that while many of the films considered in this book struggle to enjoy an extended or significant commercial career, those that make light of serious topics, such as *Taken* with human trafficking, demean that topic by removing from it any of the complexities that naturally are involved. In making a film that features human trafficking, Besson evidently has his finger on the pulse of society and has chosen a timely topic for his film, as the rise of publications and indeed films and documentaries dealing with this issue makes clear. (This is not the first time that Besson has produced a film dealing with this issue: EuropaCorp's first *Transporter* film (Corey Yuen, France/USA, 2002) also deals indirectly with human trafficking, as does *Danny the Dog* (*Unleashed*, Louis Leterrier, France/USA/UK, 2005).) However, one cannot necessarily defend Besson for raising awareness of an issue by making nods to it in his film: yes, thousands of viewers may now know that human trafficking exists as a result of watching *Taken*, but if the issue has only been dealt with in a racist/xenophobic and pro-violent manner, then this can do no good whatsoever (even if this or any film's ability to do 'harm' to viewers is equally open to debate). Certain issues require mature responses, and to package them as flashy, easily consumable and not-to-be-pondered-over-in-any-meaningful-way runs counter to this, even if there is always the possibility of reading the film 'against the grain' (i.e. finding subtlety in a film that otherwise seems to lack it), and even if a 'slow' film that takes time to explore the complexity of an issue runs the risk of alienating audiences and receiving poor returns because it is not easy to consume.

We enter into the territory here of moral debates concerning cinema, which must in turn draw upon hypothetical arguments concerning the effects that films have on audiences. However, even if a film like *Taken* has neither positive nor 'detrimental' effects on an audience, by tackling at least in part an issue that, in its wider manifestation of human slavery, affects many millions of people worldwide, then one can feel inclined to make accusations towards Besson of irresponsibility and the exploitation for profit of a topic that merits serious consideration.

In an era of globalised capital, in which Besson has created his own production company and therefore is a free agent who can make whatever films he and his collaborators want, Besson can ignore accusations of irresponsibility, not least if the profits from *Taken* directly or indirectly allow other filmmakers to produce three 'smaller' but 'more mature' films about human trafficking (though this has yet to be the case). In an age when any audience member is free not only to watch but also to demand 'mindless' entertainment, not least because this same audience member may feel that he has enough on his plate the rest of the time, one might similarly say that we are powerless to demand more from films and filmmakers, and that by and large there is only preaching to the converted: serious audiences will find the serious films, which emerge as simply a niche market on an entirely capitalised globe. However, I would contend that one can and should challenge filmmakers to take more seriously any issues that their films deal with. Not in the sense of disseminating contact information for those affected, donating money to charities, or diverting profits toward the production of more 'serious' films, although these are laudable in and of themselves. I mean in the sense of making a film that maturely deals with an important issue, human trafficking, and in such a way that it inspires a mature response: not 'I don't want to think about it,' nor 'I'll think about it tomorrow,' but 'I'll think about this now.' Utopian as this will sound in an era when immature films dominate the market, and in the face of a film industry that, bereft of trust between professionals to believe that everyone will up their game and make mature films, such that more often than not audiences watch 'grown up' films (rather than leaving maturity to the mature niche), immature films should still be critiqued, and a concerned public should lobby filmmakers to do a better job at conveying important considerations of crucial moral concerns rather than idly make profit out of them.

If human trafficking and contemporary slavery make clear a growing 'class' distinction between those who have money and those who do not (people endangering their own lives through trafficking as a result of poverty), then, as has been discussed elsewhere in this book, it is money that affords more powerful technology and which in turn affords greater mobility across borders that to many others remain closed. Besson and Morel's film may well 'abduct' American audiences by drawing them into a French (version of a Hollywood) film. But the film itself is indicative of a globalised system of capital in which imbalances of prosperity remain deeply problematic. If you will, *Taken* travels around the world and greedily exploits mass markets, its ease and speed of travel, together with the speed and ease of its images, meaning that it misses out on, overlooks, and even dehumanises the people both in it and who see it. It is an inhumane cinema both in form and content, and, as a material product in the real world, it is designed not to 'talk' to people but to yield maximum profit from the people it meets, regardless of whether they are complicit in this relationship or not. Compare this to the 'small' and 'slow' film that attempts to deal with human trafficking in a human way: it must travel slowly, often 'on foot,' and, like a human engaged in trafficking, it may even have to cross borders illegally and eke out an existence through alternative economies (such as piracy). And it must work for the longest time (its whole life) and very hard to achieve this. *Taken* can reply by saying that it works hard, too, as if the labour required to make a success of *Taken* created kinship between that and the 'mature' trafficking film. But this is not the case; while *Taken* no doubt shows the perfection of a streamlined and inane cinematic craft (Besson and Morel are 'good' at what they do), the film still revels in its millions. Meanwhile, there is an undergrowth of films out there that are made for a relative pittance, and which slog their guts out for practically nil return. It is not a question of choice in that 'anyone' could choose to make *Taken* if they wanted to (and are somehow foolish not to). No, Besson's skills are quite unique and he has every right to use them. But nor is it a question of *Taken* fulfilling a role that otherwise 'needs' to be filled ('if it weren't *Taken*, it would be a different action film'). Films don't *need* to make millions of dollars in profit; or if they do, they should perhaps just be inane rather than hang on the tailcoats of a serious issue; to do so potentially impedes the mobility of that issue seriously to make it into the wider public domain. While there are at least 27 million humans living under slavery today, a number greater than at any other time in recorded human history, then something does need to be done about this. Raising awareness of the issue through the production of films that deal with it maturely is one such way of achieving education, which can lead to action, which can lead to change. Doing so in an immature manner (*Taken*) is exploitative and pointless, even if the profits from blockbusters are understood as financially propping up and/or enabling a cinema of political engagement/an art cinema. For in the same way that the overlooked, invisible, and disposable peoples of the world service the comfort and ease of mobility of Europeans (when we consider trafficking from the European perspective), so in fact might smaller and overlooked films service the big-budget film industry in its best-known manifestations. Grassroots, humanist and politically engaged filmmakers don't owe their jobs to Luc Besson, in the same way that a domestic worker does not 'owe' their bonded labour to the person employing them (even if this is the myth peddled to them). In fact, the relationship is the other way round: luxury is owed to those without it. It is time for grassroots filmmakers who make relevant, human, and politically engaged films, especially those that deal with human trafficking, to take the power back. Besson, hopefully, will acknowledge their value and importance, and let them do so.

Traffic Jam: Film, Activism, and Human Trafficking

Leshu Torchin

The story begins anecdotally. As we discussed the literature on human trafficking, Dina Iordanova commented on the complete absence of films in the scholarship. Despite an overall commitment to making the crime of modern-day slavery known, and despite the commitment to mobilising for change – whether in developing efficient policies for managing this global crisis, or in pushing readers into action – there was near to nothing that addressed this popular medium. This absence merited comment given the use of film in drawing attention and encouraging responses to human trafficking.

The scholarship on human trafficking adopts varied methodological approaches to accomplish similar and twinned goals: to develop a better understanding of this unseen enterprise in order more efficiently to intervene in this practice. Some argue for greater testing of legal definitions (Di Nicola 2007); others seek to understand contemporary slavery in terms of its historical roots (Bales 2004; Picarelli 2007) and there are those who seek economic analyses of the business, as well as the financial incentives for participation (Kara 2009; Kyle & Koslowski 2001). Much of this work seeks to understand root causes for human traffic, exploring the roles of poverty, globalisation, gender, war, and ethnicity in the production of groups vulnerable to trafficking. Many dedicate themselves to broadening initial conceptions, finding the exploitative and coercive measures in all sectors: manufacturing, agricultural, and service, and not simply in sexual slavery and prostitution. Human rights and labour rights come to the fore in many of the studies (Bales 2004; Hudson 2007; Kara 2009; Lindquist & Piper 2007; Kempadoo et al 2005), as scholars seek frameworks better capable of addressing asymmetries in wealth and opportunity, and redressing the abuses of those forced to work in untenable circumstances in any industry. These approaches frequently question anti-trafficking strategies of strict border enforcement, suggesting that immigration laws fail to protect the vulnerable publics, and, in fact, risk disempowering and further endangering the victims of trafficking. No matter what approach, or position, all these studies share a demand for greater analytical attention and improved policy approaches.

And yet, amidst this commitment to uncovering the veiled and vast operations of trafficking, and to making them the subject of public knowledge, there is little mention of film and popular culture. There are passing references, to be sure. Kara (2009), for instance, argues for the need for greater understanding despite media attention already granted. More notably, Rutvica Andrijasevic (2007) analyses the anti-trafficking campaigns and the ways in which these construct highly gendered notions of European citizenship. However, apart from this instance, and the casual comments on media misrepresentation and the central role of media in publicising the abuses, films and popular culture go unmentioned. Studies of governmental and non-governmental organisations and their use of media in various anti-human trafficking initiatives are few. The hidden character of human trafficking, due to the cover of illicit enterprise or to vast and mysterious global movements, motors the methodological perseverance for visibility, and yet the instruments for providing visibility go without analysis.

Fortunately, this is a growing field, with forthcoming publications positioned to intervene in the absence. This scholarship outlines the depiction of trafficking, and observes the anxieties and concerns reflected in the representation. However, there is also a need to examine the work that bridges policy and media. Specifically, we need to open a discussion on the use of film and video in anti-trafficking campaigns, taking up questions of what they look like (how do these items represent the concerns) and how they are used (what is the context of distribution and exhibition in which these items travel).

The use of media in activist programmes is nothing new, particularly in relation to the subject of slavery. Throughout the 19th century, the abolitionist movements in Britain and the United States relied on the performance and publication of slave narratives, which made visible their lives and abuses, and which sought to foster compassion in audiences made witness to the suffering. At the turn of the 20th century, the popularity in white slavery spiked, indulging titillation and edification through social problem films. Enthusiastic (if salacious) reviewers recommended viewing for purposes of social reform. On the moral value of *Traffic in Souls* (George Loane Tucker, USA, 1913), George Blaidsell wrote:

> It is a big subject – one that has been given grave consideration by many thoughtful men and women. These divide naturally into two groups – one favouring battling with the evil, or, as the more advanced would phrase it, the evils of the evil in the old time secret way; the other would come into the open and fight a condition as ancient as the beginnings of history with modern weapons – and the chide of these publicity. To those who hold the latter of these opinions, *Traffic in Souls* will be warmly welcomed (1913: 849).

According to Janet Staiger, 'F' of the New York *Dramatic Mirror* found the film to provide a 'good lesson' that was suitable even for young people, while *The Outlook* wondered if the film might not become 'requisite viewing in the schools' (1995: 143-144). Ulterior motives notwithstanding, specifically those ulterior motives associated with the governance of young women along with their newfound mobility and sexuality, film offered means of visualising a concern and educating (and arousing) a larger audience. Technologies of publicity aided in making these dangers public.

Today, media are widely used by governmental and non-governmental organisations in the publicising and attempted implementation of initiatives. With the intention of instigating future discussions on the subject, the following sections identify a few of these programmes and describe their efforts.

Bought and Sold (Global Survival Network and WITNESS, 1997)

The Global Survival Network (GSN) was initially investigating the illegal trade in wildlife, specifically the trafficking of tiger bones and skins, when their contact, a member of the Russian mafia, offered to sell them women as well. The organisation contacted civil rights attorney Gillian Caldwell, and sought assistance with local NGOs and government agencies. Finding apathy and an overall disinclination for involvement, GSN took up the cause in a most unconventional way: they set up a dummy corporation that specialised in foreign escorts and models. 'There were business cards, brochures, a telephone and a fax line to give the operation a look of authenticity,' explains Executive Director Steven Galster. 'Under the guise of this company, GSN successfully gained entry to the shadowy operations of international trafficking networks in Russia and beyond' (Galster 1997).

Although this strategy lent insight into the operations of this clandestine economy, the GSN, with the help of Caldwell, went further: they secretly filmed the meetings that revealed not only the protections afforded by Russian organised crime, but also the alleged complicity of the Russian Ministry of Foreign Affairs, which, as Caldwell explains, 'was falsifying passports to get under-age girls out of the country.' Caldwell supplemented this footage with interviews with trafficked women, NGO representatives, and social science scholars, in order to make a larger film that articulated both the horrors and the political ramifications of this new slavery.

The resulting 42-minute documentary, *Bought & Sold: An Investigative Documentary about the International Trade in Women*, became a centrepiece in a campaign designed to capitalise on the outrage it provoked and to galvanise support for broader anti-trafficking campaigns, fighting forced labour in sexual, agricultural and domestic sectors. The film's hidden camera, drawing on a visual language of surveillance – such as the security camera – supplied the visual truth claims that bolstered the evidence of trade. Meanwhile the testimonies of the women provided an unavoidably emotional component, making claims for the compassion of the audience. The film did not circulate alone; it was accompanied by a written report published in multiple languages to facilitate worldwide distribution and use in a multinational advocacy campaign. The additional materials illuminated key issues and provided talking points to help frame discussion of the issue and produce recommendations for decision makers.

The film travelled through multiple circuits to reach a variety of audiences. Footage from *Bought & Sold* was featured on many national news broadcasts, including BBC, CNN, and ABC. The documentary has been distributed with a manual to over 2,000 organisations and 'is used as a training tool by the US Department of State, Department of Justice, the INS, and Embassy and Consular officials worldwide.' In 1998, MiraMed, an anti-trafficking coalition based in Russia, used the film in multiple ways, showing the film to young women at risk from trafficking, NGOs, educators and parents. Each audience necessitated a different approach. The girls watched in discussion groups. NGOs received a wealth of materials including a synopsis of 'The Trafficking of NIS Women Abroad' – an international conference held by the GSN in 1997, a copy of 'The Rights of Russian Woman – Laws and Practices' (Women's Information Database and Westminster Foundation for Democracy**)**,

NIS-US Women's Consortium membership information, and a copy of grant applications for the Soros Open Society Institute. According to MiraMed's report, 'NGO participants watched the film, then took part in a roundtable discussion of the contents of the film and their own experiences with girls from their communities. This was followed by a facilitated session on looking for solutions.' Educator screenings also coalesced around problem solving as teachers and administrators engaged in round-table discussions on how to disseminate this information in their districts. Parents also watched in groups, and, according to the report, participated. 'Some meetings included several mothers with daughters who had been trafficked overseas. They came mainly to share their experiences and to encourage resistance' (Engel 2002: 8-10). Even within this limited example, one can see how the film became a tool for NGO capacity building and public information campaigns on a local grassroots level.

The WITNESS report finds results well beyond these community campaigns. The organisation notes the particular effects of the footage used in a 1998 ABC-TV special on trafficking between the Ukraine and Israel. As explained on the WITNESS website, after airing

[then] US Secretary of State Madeleine Albright added trafficking to the agenda in her meeting with Israeli Prime Minister Netanyahu and laid the groundwork for a bilateral relationship to address the issue. Affected by the same ABC special and a *New York Times* front-page story, [then] President Bill Clinton issued an Executive Order allocating US$10 million to fight violence against women, with a special emphasis on trafficking.

In 2000, the United Nations and US Congress both passed legislation on trafficking: the United Nations Protocol on Trafficking and the Trafficking Victims Protections act, respectively. Clearly, one cannot credit a single film or campaign for all the changes, but it would appear that this film and the varying uses of footage went a long way to publicising the issue and galvanising support for a cause. Strategic exhibition and distribution educated audiences, illustrating the crime and promoting means of prevention and protection. The film served as a powerful tool for advocating policy, and, indeed, served as an effective starting point for WITNESS, an American-based NGO that educates its partners in the use of video in activist campaigns. The instruction includes far more than technical training as the organisation addresses tactics of distribution and exhibition as well as audience targeting.

For more information, visit: www.witness.org.

Holly (Guy Moshe, US/France/Israel/Cambodia, 2007)

In 2002 Guy Jacobson launched the Redlight Children Campaign (RCC) in order to protect young children caught up in the global sex trade. While the campaign supports existing modes of intervention, namely the rescue of victims and the prosecution of perpetrators, the mission focuses on diminishing demand. A daunting task, to be sure, but the campaign works on a policy and public level, seeking to close legal loopholes and implement new laws as they create an 'informed and educated public.' Grassroots outreach and mass media utilisation provide the central means of raising awareness and of promoting support for new legislation and increased enforcement, which the RCC sees as necessary for deterrence.

The K-11 project has emerged from this mission to lead the awareness campaign. Comprising two documentaries, *Children for Sale* (*The Virgin Harvest*, Adi Ezroni and Charles Kiselyak, USA, 2009) and *The K-11 Journey* (Daniel Kedem and Charles Kiselyak, USA/France/Israel, 2007), and a feature length narrative film, *Holly*, Jacobson sees the project as a means of inspiring involvement and advocating practical action. The feature film appears to function as the centrepiece for the campaign, most readily distributed and most easily publicised given the presence of internationally recognised talent such as Udo Kier, Virginie Ledoyen, Ron Livingston, and Chris Penn. Although the film has experienced only a relatively limited commercial release, it has also received substantial attention in the media, with interviews and short pieces running on radio and television (CNN and ABC-TV news) and in print (*Glamour*, *The New York Times*, and *The Los Angeles Times*). These short news items do not simply promote the film, but also mention the campaign and its programmes. The outreach potential builds even before the film has been screened.

The film itself also provides opportunities for coalition building. *Holly* tells the story of Patrick (Livingston), a jaded American living in Phnom Penh, where he meets a 12-year old Vietnamese girl, Holly (Thuy Nguyen), who is sold into prostitution. Her plight shakes him from his fog and launches him on a bid to save her. The narrative positions him as a stand-in for the viewers, who, upon their own encounter with the film should become equally inspired. And fortunately the film moves beyond the more individualistic approach to show the work of Somaly Mam's NGO, *Agir Pour les Femmes en Situation Précaire* (AFESIP) – or Acting for Women in Distressing Circumstances. Thus, the film does more than invite the simple and highly gendered and racialised fantasy of rescue by a First World white man, but also provides a story of community effort and the mobilisation of Cambodian women.

The exhibition set-up serves to channel sentiment into forms of action, or at least to further information gathering. The DVD for the feature offers documentaries for its special features including pieces on the K-11 project and an excerpt from *Children for Sale*. Prior to the film's commercial release *Holly* was screened at the United Nations Headquarters in New York as well as at the US State Department in Washington DC 'in order to establish a political presence' for the campaign. Since then, the RCC has cultivated partnerships with NGOs and corporations alike in order to organise screenings accompanied by series of speaker events featuring experts on trafficking, filmmakers, government officials, and activists. These meetings become opportunities to promote activist organisations and to engage audiences in an action plan. The website offers information to those who wish to 'spread the word.' There a visitor can sign up for more information, volunteer, send a donation, contact a state representative, or organise screenings for schools, corporations, and organisations. They explain:

> We are interested in strengthening your organisation and we welcome the opportunity to incorporate the screening as part of your fundraising efforts, as a platform for publicity and media for your organisation and as an opportunity to bring in new members or keep in touch with existing ones.

To this end, the RCC provides guidance for setting up a screening, recommending setting up Q&A sessions with the filmmakers and advising a reception for guests. The film is a component of a larger, ready-made event that functions to promote causes and organisations, to raise funds, and to recruit volunteers of all kinds, including pro bono legal aid, and corporate sponsors.

For more information please visit:

http://www.priorityfilms.com

http://www.redlightchildren.org/

Public Service Announcements

In recent years, the United Nations Office on Drugs and Crime (UNODC) and the United Nations Global Initiative to Fight Human Trafficking (UNGIFT) have sought to use audio and visual media in their programmes. While they have benefited from the publicity around screenings for feature films such as *Holly*, they often rely on non-theatrical video, namely, Public Service Announcements (PSAs). These are short, non-commercial films, often running the length of a standard advert, or 30-60-90 seconds, intended to promote a message for the public good. Although traditionally used for television and as a motivational tool in meetings, the short video has migrated to the internet. In fact, the online resource for PSAs indicates that the UNODC has an active presence not only on YouTube, but also Flickr, Twitter, and Facebook, and the videos are found on other anti-human trafficking sites, such as MTV-EXIT (End Exploitation and Trafficking). The spots function to promote awareness to general audiences, to warn those vulnerable to trafficking, and to advance specific action plans for those able to act.

The most common type of PSA seeks to educate a broader public, alerting them to the concerns of the organisation. UNGIFT produced *Open Your Eyes to Human Trafficking* (2008) for the Vienna Forum to Fight Human Trafficking. In the video (which runs either 30 or 60 seconds), a man walks through a marketplace, unaware of the evidence of trafficking: a boy dragged off, a girl eyed by a seedy tourist. The camera calls attention to the details in order to open our eyes.

Other spots, such as the UNODC-produced PSAs *Better Future* (2002) and *Work Abroad* (2001), are aimed at potential victims. *Better Future* tells three stories in three languages as three different people embrace with optimism a work opportunity – the chance to learn a trade and to provide for one's family. The hope is quashed as a young boy toils in the fields, a young man finds himself in a dark and dangerous factory, and a young woman is a domestic worker, and all are subject to brutal violence. For some the travel is overseas, for others, more localised – but for all, there lurks threat in the promise. *Work Abroad* offers a similar caution, while focusing on sex work. Here, the images belie the words on screen. 'Housing will be provided,' it states over a scene of a Spartan shelter featuring a woman crying on a cot. 'No work permit required,' we are told, as a passport is surrendered and destroyed. 'Meet new interesting people,' promises the text, as a small girl lies immobile on a table, meaty hands reaching out from off screen to stroke her face and move downwards. She turns her face towards us, eyes rolled up in disgust and desperation. The spot carries on in this vein, with an 'excellent salary' represented through drug work and a pimp shoving a girl against a wall, demanding what little money she has made. 'Interested?' the textual interrogator asks the girl on the table, her face screwed up in a rictus of pain and misery. Both videos conclude with the information that over 700,000 people are trafficked every year for the purposes of sexual exploitation and forced labour. These videos lend themselves to global distribution through replacement of the titles or substitution of voice over, as in the case of *Tráfico para trabalho forçado* (UNODC), the Portuguese version of *Better Future*. Meanwhile, the images continue to relay the brutal realities of trafficking.

PSAs can also serve to empower both trafficked people and bystanders, alerting them to means of taking action. *Cleaning Woman* (UNODC, 2003) and *Telephone* (UNODC, 2003) draw attention to plans for a hotline and a number to call. *Telephone* shows three victims of trafficking coming across the phone number: one from a flyer, one handed the number from a mysterious source, and another by watching television and who then writes the number on her arm. Each woman makes something of a bold escape, running to find a telephone where they dial the number. 'There is a way out,' the title promises, suggesting that there is possibility for escape. The short performs its own efficacy as it promotes a message, illustrating both the ready transmission of information and success in implementation. While *Telephone* speaks to the victims of enforced labour, *Cleaning Woman* tells the story of the bystander who spots a victim and passes on the necessary information. 'You can help,' this spot concludes, alerting the viewer to the possibility of action. According to the UNODC, the filmmakers worked closely with local partners in the distribution of the spot to add a telephone number where victims are able to receive assistance and support.

Some PSAs may contribute to deterrence in their address. *Terre des Hommes Germany* (a national branch of the International Federation), in collaboration with the Federal Ministry for Family Affairs, Senior Citizens, Women and Youth, produced *Witness* (TDHG, 2006) a spot intended for television and in-flight viewing on planes en route to sex tourism destinations. The video is aimed at the bystander, travellers who are sure to encounter the sexual exploitation of children and who are encouraged to intervene. Like *Open Your Eyes*, *Witness* alerts the viewer to signs of abuse and trafficking. Beginning at the ostensible point of no return, when an older man leads a child into his hotel room, the video launches a backwards chronology that illustrates the many opportunities for intervention: at the bar, on the beach, etc. Each sequence shows a bystander to demonstrate how much takes place in sight of those who can act. The spot seeks to hail the viewer into responsibility, to become empowered to act on behalf of the child. Indeed, the entire piece is told in the vocative, beginning with the direct address of 'you' and the imperative of its motto, 'Please Disturb!' There is admittedly little information provided on how one may intervene; unlike *Cleaning Woman*, there is no hotline or official recourse, which leaves the spot as empowering solely through moral justification and suspicion. However, this spot, aired in-flight, may harbour an alternative function as a warning to predators. They will be monitored, by this group, and by the tourists in the cabin.

For more information please visit:

http://www.unodc.org/unodc/en/human-trafficking/index.html

http://www.ungift.org/

http://www.terredeshommes.org

http://www.child-hood.com/

Film Festivals: Invitation to Witness

In recent years, film festivals have gained momentum as sites for advancing political agendas and promoting anti-human trafficking initiatives. Human rights film festivals such as the Human Rights Watch International Film Festival (New York and London) and the One World Festival (Prague) regularly programme films on the subject of trafficking. Even broader film festivals have taken the opportunity to present on the cause. In 2007, the Jackson Hole Film Festival hosted a forum sponsored by the Humpty Dumpty Institute and the UNODC on the subject of global crime and the role of film and media in raising awareness. The event included a screening of *Human Trafficking* (Christian Duguay, USA/Canada, 2005) and a panel including representatives of the UNODC, UN Goodwill Ambassador and actor Julia Ormond, activist and former victim of trafficking Shakira Parveen, and film producers (www.jacksonhole.bside.com).

However, a more recent phenomenon involves dedicated anti-trafficking film festivals, which highlight the issue of modern slavery whilst fundraising and community building. Most often these projects are sponsored by and developed though partnerships between organisations, which have adopted film and celebrity to attract audiences, and which rely on a shared political affinity to foster communities of concern and to build activist publics from general audiences. This section includes a list of recent examples.

Anti-Human Trafficking Film Festival (Taiwan)

Organised by the Garden of Hope Foundation, and receiving sponsorship from MTV-EXIT, this film festival has run for two years (2007 and 2008) with the goal of raising 'social awareness of the worsening problem of human trafficking.' Support also comes from the American Institute in Taiwan, the Taiwan Foundation for Democracy, and the Human Rights Research Centre at the College of Law,

National Taiwan University. The screenings are free, but frequently accompanied by 'expert discussions' where audiences may learn more about the problem and about the action others are taking. In 2007, the line-up included five films made by both professionals and amateurs and which focused on women and children, 'underscoring the dreadful fact that global transportation has benefited the crime of human trafficking.' The following year, the agenda appears to have broadened to include the abuse of undocumented migrants in labour sectors beyond sex work.

Of Inhuman Bondage (Kolkata/Calcutta, India)

Taking place in 2009 at the Indian Council of Cultural Relations, Of Inhuman Bondage was a two-day film festival organised around Women's Day through a partnership between NGO Apne Aap Women Worldwide and the American Centre. The event was part of a larger general education programme of workshops, films, and discussion panels held by the consulate in Calcutta and throughout the northeast regions. Celebrities such as dancer Gita Chandran and actor Jaya Seal Ghosh were in attendance. The programme line-up boasted five films, beginning with *Kaal* by Bengali director Bappaditya Banerjee. *Mondo Meyer Upakhyan/A Tale of a Naughty Girl* (Buddhadev Dasgupta, India, 2002), the story of a Lati (Samata Das), a girl whose mother is a prostitute in rural India, and whose story is contrasted with three prostitutes in Calcutta, was also featured, as was the Bollywood film, *Chameli* (Sudhir Mishra, India, 2003), which focuses on a chance encounter with a prostitute named Chameli (Kareena Kapoo) in Bombay's red light district. In addition to the screenings, the festival provided channels for action in the form of petitions for trafficking legislation.

Unchosen: Bristol Film Festival against Human Trafficking

Unchosen, a Bristol-based festival, ran in 2008 with the aim of raising awareness and funds. The festival took place over the course of a week, with screenings accompanied by speaker events, performances, and the distribution of literature. Each night featured a single film and guest. The line-up included: *Ghosts* (Nick Broomfield, UK, 2006); *Sex Traffic* (David Yates, UK/Canada, 2004); *It's a Free World...* (Ken Loach, UK, 2007); *Holly*; *Our Big Fair Trade Adventure* (Ricardo Pollack, UK, 2007), a documentary covering a mission to source a fairtrade school uniform; and *Amazing Grace* (Michael Apted, UK/USA, 2006), a film about William Wilberforce (Ioan Gruffudd) and the 18th century campaign against the slave trade. Covering a diversity of subjects in trafficking, from the historical slave trade to sexual slavery to the place of trafficked people in the formal economy, the programme lends itself to educational purposes. While *Ghosts* and *It's a Free World...* illustrate the local benefits and exploitation, *Our Big Fair Trade Adventure* reveals the distant abuses implicated in free trade policy. Thanks to the sponsors (which included Pathé International, Christian Aid, Century Films, Lafayette Films, Priority Films, Momentum Pictures, Hot:Haus, Hope, and the Bible Society), the entire proceeds from ticket sales could go directly to the charities Daughters Day Centre in Phnom Penh, Morecambe Bay Victims Fund, and Stop the Traffik.

Website: http://unchosen.org.uk/

To be continued

Having only touched the surface of this rich territory, this chapter refuses a set conclusion. Potential case studies accumulate as films become central to multiple campaigns. Nick Broomfield's *Ghosts* is tied to the Morecambe Bay Victims Fund, with the film's website providing a source of information and donation options (http://www. ghosts.uk.com/index.html). The UNODC offers multiple suggestions for using *Human Trafficking*, which they themselves also used to open the UN Vienna Forum to Fight Human Trafficking in February 2008. A recent press release suggests that they will provide the DVD – available in nine languages – to those wishing to organise screenings (albeit with the proviso that the event includes the participation of a US State Department official).

The United States Agency for International Aid Trafficking in Persons Project (USAID) has been particularly active in producing and distributing films. Although also working to advance US foreign policy, this independent agency provides humanitarian and economic assistance, working with NGOs to assist in regional development. In 2007, USAID and the International Organisation for Migration (IOM), an intergovernmental agency dedicated to promoting 'humane and orderly migration' helped to create *Boz Ki*. The film, which focuses on the experiences of Tajik migrant labourers in Russia, premiered at the XIV Film Festival in Minsk, Belarus, before being deployed in a public information campaign throughout Tajikistan. It is hoped that the screenings and discussion sessions will help those travelling abroad to protect themselves from traffickers. More recently, USAID partnered with MTV-EXIT on *Intersection* (produced by JM Animation, Korea, 2009). This anime illustrates the chain of trafficking and its players as a means of warning and educating audiences. Thai and English versions aired on MTV's Southeast Asia channels, and in June it was announced that popular actors Zhang Hanyu, Yuan Quan and Su You Peng had contributed to a Chinese-language version that aired on MTV-China. As with other films by MTV-EXIT, *Intersection* is used on the ground to animate discussions on the subject, and has been made available online, open to download by broadcasters and activists (http://www.usaid. gov and http://www.mtvexit.org/).

When organisations do not actively engage in production or distribution or forge partnerships with filmmakers, they nonetheless recognise the value of film in outreach. Many programmes publish lists of films and contact information for producers. These include such groups as the Foreign Policy Association (http://children.foreignpolicyblogs.com/human-trafficking-and-slavery-related-movies-and-documentaries/) and Vital Voices (http://www.vitalvoices.org/).

This is, as stated above, only the most cursory look at a field that proliferates under scrutiny. Campaigns repeatedly rely on film and video to attract attention as well as to educate and excite publics to action. This is not a matter for easy celebration, as some of the earlier examples may have intimated. Indeed, if anything, this is an invitation to carry out more sustained analysis of each case and its facets. Critical work is required in the following areas:

Representation

This heading yields three basic areas of genre, content, and medium. First, what genres and modes are deployed? The ontological claims of a documentary can aid in the report functions of film use, making a case for decision-makers who prefer not to acknowledge the affective dimensions of the political and ethical claims embedded in a film. Meanwhile, one may also ask what different emotional responses are encouraged in each genre: does the melodrama produce a substantially different engagement from the action film? How exactly is one to understand the function and representational strategies of the public service announcement?

This question of strategy engages questions of content as well as form. What are the discursive frameworks used in presenting the information? How are trafficking and its violations represented? Whose voices do we hear? In what ways do they articulate the missions of the organisation? Do these expressions risk smuggling in racist, sexist, or xenophobic sentiment? Films like *Holly* may be too reliant on a model of First World saviours and Third World victims, for instance, while using *Human Trafficking* not only requires the agreement of the US State Department, but also produces a story that sees US security and immigration measures as paramount in addressing trafficking. And while *Intersection* admirably uses multiple languages in the story of Asian trafficking, the English-language version offers a victim with a European accent whilst traffickers speak with East Asian accents. Assessing the ways in which a story is told will be helpful in understanding the uses of media in advocating policy.

Further contributing to questions of genre, form, content, and thus representation is that of the medium. The registers of film and video can produce differing claims upon the real. The latter format is often associated with surveillance and amateur footage, which can confer a semblance of innocence or non-interference. Although the non-professional usage can yield images challenging to interpret, the footage can also invite a more forgiving and generous stance: video can work to present itself not as art (not always), but as record. An important addition to this consideration of medium is the internet, which combines technologies of representation, exhibition, and distribution. We may not only ask how these images travel, and how they encourage response, but also how they overcome the limitations of their presentation. These are small screens, often embedded in other small screens, which compete for attention with the life world immediately beyond the frame. At the same time, the presumptions and possibilities of interactivity may sustain attention and interest, leading to engagement with action plans on- and offline. These concerns tie in with the next sets of questions covered.

Production

Under what conditions were these films produced? Are these pieces developed and commissioned by organisations? Or are these commercially or independently made films taken up in an activist venture? At times, the production circumstances determine representational strategy, as the hidden cameras of *Bought & Sold* convey a truth revealed as they illustrate the processes of trafficking. Indeed, who are the players in production and in usage? These aspects have bearing on the potential uses of a film.

Exhibition and Distribution

Who is using the film? Where and under what circumstances are these films screened? In what ways do these circumstances promote response? The ways a film can be used are many and varied. There are fundraisers. There are screenings with panel discussions and Q&As. There are in-flight PSAs and even websites that provide short films and spots. In what ways do the strategies around exhibition make the films effective in the fight against trafficking? Do they attract volunteers and sponsors? Do they serve to warn potential victims?

Audiences

As indicated above this is a key question that can determine representational and exhibition strategies. For whom are the films made and directed? Potential victims? Bystanders hailed as activists? Policy makers? Or even perpetrators (warned, or shamed)?

These questions, like the examples provided, merely touch upon all that is to be done and asked. What is certain, however, is that there is a necessary field of scholarship that requires attention.

Bibliography

Agamben, Giorgio (1998) *Homo Sacer: Sovereign Power and Bare Life*. Trans. Daniel Heller-Roazen. Stanford: Stanford University Press.

Anderson, Perry (1984) 'Modernity and Revolution,' *New Left Review*, 1:144, pp. 96-113.

Andrijasevic, Rutvica (2007) 'Beautiful Dead Bodies: Gender, Migration, and Representation in Anti-Trafficking Campaigns,' *Feminist Review*, 86, pp. 24-44.

Anon. (1913) 'Park Theatre Shut On Court Order,' *New York Times*. 27 December.

Anon. (2000) *Protocol to Prevent, Suppress and Punish Trafficking in Persons, Especially Women and Children*, *United Nations*. Online. Available HTTP: http://untreaty.un.org/English/TreatyEvent2003/Texts/treaty2E.pdf (2 October 2009).

Anon. (2002) 'Status of Observance of Ukrainian Migrant Workers' Rights in the Receiving Countries,' *Ukrainian Parliament Commissioner for Human Rights*. Online. Available HTTP: http://www.ombudsman.kiev.ua/S_Report1/gl2_3.htm (2 October 2009).

Anon. (2007) 'Exported and Exposed: Abuses against Sri Lankan Domestic Workers in Saudi Arabia, Kuwait, Lebanon, and United Arab Emirates,' *Human Rights Watch*, 19:16 (November). Online. Available HTTP: http://www.hrw.org/en/reports/2007/11/13/exported-and-exposed-1 (2 October 2009).

Anon. (N.D.) 'About *H-2 Worker*,' *Life and Debt*. Online. Available HTTP: http://www.lifeanddebt.org/h2worker/ (2 October 2009).

Anon. (N.D.) 'H-2A Certification,' *United States Department of Labor*. Online. Available HTTP: http://www.foreignlaborcert.doleta.gov/h-2a.cfm (2 October 2009).

Anon. (N.D.) '*It's a Free World...* (2007): Production Notes,' *Sixteen Films*. Online. Available HTTP: http://www.sixteenfilms.co.uk/films/production_notes/its_a_free_world/ (2 October 2009).

Anon. (N.D.) 'Krško Nuclear Power Plant,' *Wikipedia*. Online. Available HTTP: http://en.wikipedia.org/wiki/Krško_Nuclear_Power_Plant (16 November 2009).

Anon. (N.D.) 'Red Sea Star Underwater Restaurant, Bar and Observatory,' *Frommers.com*. Online. Available HTTP: http://www.frommers.com/destinations/eilat/D40205.html (2 October 2009).

Anon. (N.D.) 'Red Sea Star.' Online. Available HTTP: http://www.redseastar. com/ (2 October 2009).

Anon. (N.D.) Taken (2009) – International Box Office Results, *Box Office Mojo*. Online. Available HTTP: http://www.boxofficemojo.com/ movies/?page=intl&id=taken.htm (30 May 2009).

Anon. (N.D.) 'Sri Lanka Bureau of Foreign Employment,' *Sri Lanka Bureau of Foreign Employment*. Online. Available HTTP: http://www.slbfe.lk/ article.php?article=23 (14 October 2009).

Appadurai, Arjun (1996) *Modernity at Large: Cultural Dimensions of Globalization*. Minneapolis: University of Minnesota Press.

Andrew, Geoff (2008) 'Emotional rescue,' *Sight & Sound*, 18:12 (December), pp. 34-35.

Anzaldúa, Gloria (1987) *Borderlands/La Frontera: The New Mestiza*. San Francisco: Aunt Lute Books.

Arendt, Hannah (1963) *Eichmann in Jerusalem: A Report on the Banality of Evil*. New York: Viking.

Augé, Marc (1995) *Non-places: Introduction to an Anthropology of Supermodernity*. Trans. John Howe. London: Verso.

Bales, Kevin (2004) *Disposable People: New Slavery in the Global Economy*. Berkeley: University of California Press.

Bales, Kevin, Zoe Trodd, and Alex Kent Williamson (2009) *Modern Slavery: The Secret World of 27 Million People*. Oxford: Oneworld.

Ballesteros, Isolina (2005) 'Embracing the other: the feminisation of Spanish "immigration cinema,"' *Studies in Hispanic Cinemas*, 2:1, pp. 3-14.

—— (2006) 'Foreign and racial masculinities in contemporary Spanish film,' *Studies in Hispanic Cinemas*, 3:3, pp. 169-185.

Bauman, Zygmunt (1998) *Globalisation: The Human Consequences*. Cambridge: The Polity Press.

Bardan, Alice Mihaela (2007) '"Enter Freely, and of Your Own Will": Cinematic Representations of Post-Socialist Transnational Journeys,' Katarzyna Marciniak, Anikó Imre, and Áine O'Healy (eds.) *Transnational Feminism in Film and Media*. New York: Palgrave Macmillan, pp 93-108.

Bennett, Bruce and Imogen Tyler (2007) 'Screening Unlivable Lives: The New Cinema of Borders,' Katarzyna Marciniak, Anikó Imre, and Áine O'Healy (eds.), *Transnational Feminism in Film and Media*. New York: Palgrave Macillan, pp 21- 37

Berger, Verena and Daniel Winkler. '*Clandestino*: The Cinema of Irregular Migration and the Question of Space: France, Italy and Spain,' paper presented at *Migrant and Diasporic Cinema in Contemporary Europe*, Lincoln College, University of Oxford, 6-8 July 2006. Formerly available online.

Bergfelder, Tim (2005) 'National, Transnational or Supranational Cinema? Rethinking European Film Studies,' *Media, Culture & Society*, 27, pp. 315-331.

Berghahn, Daniela and Claudia Sternberg (eds.) (2010) *Cinema in Motion: Migrant and Diasporic Film in Contemporary Europe*. London: Wallflower Press.

Bhabha, Jacqueline (2005) 'Trafficking, Smuggling and Human Rights,' *Migration Information Source*, March. Online. Available HTTP:http://www.migrationinformation.org/Feature/display.cfm?ID=294 (2 October 2009).

Biemann, Ursula (2007) 'Videographies of Navigating Geobodies,' Katarzyna Marciniak, Anikó Imre, and Áine O'Healy (eds.) *Transnational Feminism in Film and Media*. New York: Palgrave Macillan, pp 129-147.

—— (ed.) (2000) *Been there and back to nowhere: Gender in transnational spaces. Postproduction documents 1988-2000*. Berlin: B Books.

Blaidsell, George (1913) '*Traffic in Souls*,' *Motion Picture World*, 18:8 (22 November), p. 849.

Bluher, Dominique (2001) 'Hip-Hop Cinema in France,' *Camera Obscura*, 46 (16:4), pp. 77-97.

Brown, William (2007) 'Sabotage or espionage? Transvergence in the works of Luc Besson,' *Studies in French Cinema*, 7:2, pp. 93-106.

—— (2009) 'Not Flagwaving but Flagdrowning, or Postcards from Post-Britain,' Robert Murphy (ed.) *The British Cinema Book (3rd Edition)*, London: BFI, pp. 408-416.

Brysk, Alison (2002) *Globalization and Human Rights*. Berkeley: University of California Press.

Bukatman, Scott (1993) *Terminal Identity: The Virtual Subject in Post-Modern Science Fiction*, Durham, NC: Duke University Press.

Caruth, Cathy (1996) *Unclaimed Experience: Trauma, Narrative and History*, Baltimore, MD: The Johns Hopkins University Press.

Chang, Kimberly and L.H. Ling (2000) 'Globalization and its Intimate Other: Filipina Domestic Workers in Hong Kong,' Marianne H. Marchand and Anne S. Runyan (eds), *Gender and Global Restructuring: Sightings, Sites and Resistances*. New York: Routledge.

Cooper, Sarah (2007) 'Mortal Ethics: Reading Levinas with the Dardenne Brothers,' *Film-Philosophy*, 11:2 (August), pp. 66-87.

Crano, R.D. (2009) '"Occupy with Counting": Furtive Urbanism in the Films of Jean-Pierre and Luc Dardenne,' *Film-Philosophy*, 13:1 (April), pp. 1-15.

David, Caroline (2009) *Frontières invisibles - Invisible Borders*. Companion to the exhibition at *Lille3000*. Antwerp: Stichting Konstboek.

De Certeau, Michel (1984) *The Practice of Everyday Life*. Trans. Steven
Rendall. Berkeley: University of California Press.

Deleuze, Gilles (1992) 'Postscript on the Societies of Control,' *October*, 59
(Winter), pp. 3-7.

Deplasse, Hervé (2003) 'Besson a tué… mon cinéma,' *Brazil: le cinéma sans
concession[s]*. Online. Available HTTP: http://www.banditscompany.
com/Bessontxt.html (2 October 2009).

Di Nicola, Andrea (2007) 'Researching into Human Trafficking: Issues and
Problems,' in Lee, Maggy (ed.), *Human Trafficking*. Portland: Willan
Publishing, pp.49-73.

Glenny, Misha (2008) *McMafia: A Journey through the Global Criminal
Underworld*. New York: Alfred A. Knopf.

Elsaesser, Thomas (2006) 'Space, Place and Identity in European Cinema of
the 1990s,' *Third Text*, 20:6, pp. 647-658.

Felman, Shoshanna and Dori Laub (1991) *Testimony: Crises of Witnessing in
Literature, Psychoanalysis and History*, New York and London: Routledge.

Ferreira, Carolin Overhoff (2006) 'Fortress Europe in the Film Foreign Land.'
Third Text. 20:6, pp. 733-743.

Flesler, Daniela (2004) 'New racism, intercultural romance, and the immigration
question in contemporary Spanish cinema.' *Studies in Hispanic
Cinemas*, 1:2, pp. 103-118.

Foster, Kevin (2006) 'Migrants, Asylum Seekers and British Identity,' *Third Text*,
20:6, pp 683-691.

Freud, Sigmund (1917-1919) 'The "Uncanny"' in *The Standard Edition of the
Complete Psychological Worlds of Sigmund Freud, Volume* XVII,
trans. J. Strachey. London: The Hogarth Press.

Friedlander, Saul (ed.) (1992) *Probing the Limits of Representation: Nazism
and the 'Final Solution'*. Cambridge, MA and London: Harvard
UniversityPress.

Gibson, Sarah (2006) 'Border Politics and Hospitable Spaces in Stephen
Frears's *Dirty Pretty Things*,' *Third Text*, 20:6, pp 693-701.

Goodey, Jo (2003) 'Migration, Crime and Victimhood,' *Punishment & Society*,
5:4, pp. 415-431.

Grieveson, Lee (1997) 'Policing the Cinema: *Traffic in Souls at Ellis Island*,
1913,' *Screen* 38:2 (Summer), pp 149- 171.

Hansen, Miriam (1991) *Babel and Babylon: Spectatorship in American Silent
Film*, Cambridge, Mass.: Harvard University Press.

Hardt, Michael and Antonio Negri (2000) *Empire*. Cambridge, Mass.: Harvard
University Press.

Hargreaves, Alec G. (2000) 'Resuscitating the father: New cinematic representations of the Maghrebi minority in France,' *Contemporary French and Francophone Studies*, 4:2, pp. 343-351.

Hashamova. Yana (2007) 'Trafficking in the Balkans: Screening Imaginary and Real Trauma,' Talk at the University of Illinois at Urbana-Champaign, USA, 21 September.

Hayward, Susan (1998) *Luc Besson*. Manchester: Manchester University Press.

Hayward, Susan and Phil Powrie (eds.) (2006) *The Films of Luc Besson: Master of Spectacle*. Manchester/New York: Manchester University Press.

Hessels, Wouter (2004) '*Rosetta*,' Ernest Mathijs (ed.) *The Cinema of the Low Countries*. London: Wallflower, pp. 239-247.

Higbee, Will (2007a) 'Locating the Postcolonial in Transnational Cinema: The Place of Algerian Émigré Directors in Contemporary French Film,' *Modern & Contemporary France*, 15:1, pp. 51-64.

—— (2007b) 'Re-Presenting the Urban Periphery: Maghrebi-French Filmmaking and the *Banlieue* Film,' *Cineaste* 33:1 (Winter), pp. 38-43.

Horton, Andrew James (2006) 'Tirana: Year Zero,' Dina Iordanova (ed.) *Cinema of the Balkans*. London: Wallflower Press.

Hudson, Barbara (2007) 'The rights of Strangers: Policies, Theories, Philosophies,' Maggy Lee (ed.) *Human Trafficking*. Portland: Willan Publishing, pp. 210-232.

Hughes, Donna M. (2001) 'The "Natasha" Trade: Transnational Sex Trafficking,' *National Institute of Justice Journal*, January, pp. 8-15.

Imre, Anikó (2009) Identity Games: Globalization and the Transformation of Media Cultures in New Europe. Cambridge and London: MIT Press.

Iordanova, Dina (2001a) 'Displaced? Shifting Politics of Place and Itinerary in International Cinema,' *Senses of Cinema*, May. Online. Available HTTP: http://archive.sensesofcinema.com/contents/01/14/displaced.html (2 October 2009).

—— (2001b) 'Villains and Victims,' Dina Iordanova (ed.), *Cinema of Flames: Balkan Film, Culture and the Media*. London: BFI, pp. 175-197.

—— (2008) 'Mimicry and Plagiarism: Reconciling Real and Metaphoric Gypsies,' *Third Text*, 22:3 (May), pp. 305-310.

Jameson, Fredric (2003) 'The End of Temporality,' *Critical Inquiry*, 29 (Summer), pp. 695-717.

Kara, Siddharth (2009) *Trafficking: Inside the Business of Modern Slavery*. New York: Columbia University Press.

Kasabova, Kapka (2008) *Ulitsa bez ime: Detstvo i drugi premezhdiya v Bulgaria*. Sofia: Ciela.

Kelly, Liz (2005) '"You Can Find Anything You Want": A Critical Reflection on Research on Trafficking in Persons within and into Europe,'

Frank Laczko and Elzbieta Gozdziak (eds.), *Data and Research on Human Trafficking: A Global Survey*. Offprint of the Special Issue of *International Migration* 43:1/2, pp. 235-265.

—— (2007) 'A Conducive Context: Trafficking of Persons in Central Asia,' Maggy Lee (ed.) *Human Trafficking*. Portland: Willan Publishing, pp. 73- 92.

Kempadoo, Kemala (ed.) (2005) *Sex Trafficking and Prostitution Reconsidered: New Perspectives on Migration, Sex Work, and Human Rights*. London and Boulder: Paradigm Publishers.

Kolker, Robert Philip (2009) *The Altering Eye: Contemporary International Cinema*, Cambridge: Openbook Publishers.

Koslowski, Rey (2001) 'Economic Globalization, Human Smuggling, and Global Governance,' David Kyle and Rey Koslowski (eds) *Global Human Smuggling: Comparative Perspectives*. Baltimore and London: Johns Hopkins University Press.

Kyle, David and Rey Koslowski (eds.) (2001) *Global Human Smuggling: Comparative Perspectives*. Baltimore and London: Johns Hopkins University Press.

Laczko, Frank and Elzbieta Gozdziak (eds.) (2005) *Data and Research on Human Trafficking: A Global Survey*. Offprint of the Special Issue of *International Migration* 43:1/2.

Lazaridis, Gabriella (2001) 'Trafficking and Prostitution: The Growing Exploitation of Migrant Women in Greece,' *European Journal of Women's Studies*, 8:1, pp. 67-102.

Lee, Maggie (ed.) (2007) *Human Trafficking*. Portland: Willan Publishing.

Lindquist, Johan and Nicola Piper (2007) 'From HIV Prevention to Counter-Trafficking: Discursive Shifts and Institutional Continuities in South-East Asia,' Maggie Lee (ed.) *Human Trafficking*. Willan Publishing, pp. 138-158.

Lindsey, Shelley Stamp (1997) '"Oil Upon the Flames of Vice": The Battle over White Slave Films in New York City.' *Film History*, 9, pp. 351-364.

Long, Kat (2008) 'Prostitution and White Slave Films: Moral Dangers in the Most Popular Genre of Early Cinema,' *American History Suite101.com*, 24 January. Online. Available HTTP: http://americanhistory.suite101.com/article.cfm/prostitution_and_white_slave_films (2 October 2009).

Loshitzky Yosefa (2006) 'Journeys of Hope to Fortress Europe,' *Third Text* 20:6, pp. 745-754.

—— (2010) *Screening Strangers: Migration and Diaspora in Contemporary European Cinema*. Bloomington: Indiana University Press.

Lu, Sheldon (2000) 'Soap Opera in China: The Transnational Politics of

Visuality, Sexuality, and Masculinity,' *Cinema Journal* 40:1 (Fall), pp. 25-48.

Maher, Kristen Hill (2002) 'Who Has a Right to Rights? Citizenship's Exclusions in an Age of Migration,' Alison Brysk (ed.) *Globalization and Human Rights*. Berkeley and Los Angeles: University of California Press, pp. 19-43.

Mai, Joseph (2007) 'Corps-Caméra: The Evocation of Touch in the Dardennes' *La Promesse* (1996),' *L'Esprit Créateur*, 47:3 (Fall), pp. 133-144.

Malarek, Victor (2004) *The Natashas: Inside the New Global Sex Trade*. New York: Arcade.

Marciniak, Katarzyna (2006) Alienhood: Citizenship, Exile and the Logic ofDifference. Minneapolis: University of Minnesota Press

Marciniak, Katarzyna, Anikó Imre, and Áine O'Healy (eds.) (2007) *Transnational Feminism in Film and Media*. New York: Palgrave Macillan.

Maule, Rosanna (2006) '*Du côté d'Europa*, via Asia: the 'post-Hollywood' Besson,' Susan Hayward and Phil Powrie (eds.) *The Films of Luc Besson: Master of Spectacle*. Manchester & New York: Manchester University Press, pp. 23-41.

Mazierska, Ewa, and Laura Rascaroli (2006) *Crossing New Europe: Postmodern Travel and the European Road Movie*. London and New York: Wallflower Press.

Menon, Sunita (2007) 'Sri Lanka sets minimum wage for workers,' *Gulfnews. com*, 8 October. Online. Available HTTP: http://archive.gulfnews.com/ indepth/labour/Pay_and_conditions/10159057.html (2 October 2009).

Morawska, Ewa (2007) 'Trafficking into and from Eastern Europe,' Maggy Lee (ed.) *Human Trafficking*. Portland: Willan Publishing, pp. 92-116.

Morrison, John, with Beth Crosland (2000) '*The Trafficking and Smuggling of Refugees: The End Game in European Asylum Policy*,' Pre-publication edition of a report commissioned by the UNHCR's Policy Research Unit, Centre for Documentation and Research, July. Online. Available HTTP: http://library.gayhomeland.org/0047/EN/EN_traffick.pdf (2 October 2009).

Mosley, Philip (2002) 'Anxiety, Memory and Place in Belgian Cinema,' *Yale French Studies*, 102, pp. 160-175.

Nora, Pierre (1996) 'Between Memory and History: Les Lieux de Mémoire,' in Pierre Nora and Lawrence D. Kritzman (eds.), *Realms of Memory: Rethinking the French Past. Vol. 1: Conflicts and Divisions*. New York and Chichester: Columbia University Press, pp. 1-20.

O'Healy, Áine (2007) 'Border Traffic: Reimagining the Voyage to Italy,' Katarzyna Marciniak, Anikó Imre, and Áine O'Healy (eds.) *Transnational Feminism in Film and Media*. New York: Palgrave

Macillan, pp. 37-53.

O'Shaughnessy, Martin (2007) *The New Face of Political Cinema: Commitment in French Film since 1995*. London: Berghahn.

Panagalangan, Raul C. (2002) 'Sweatshops and International Labor Standards: Globalizing Markets, Localizing Norms,' in Alison Brysk (ed), *Globalization and Human Rights*. Berkeley and Los Angeles: University of California Press, pp. 98-114.

Pekerman, Serazer (2009) 'Representation of Former USSR Identity in Turkish Cinema,' Paper presented at *Post-Communist Visual Culture and Cinema*, 20 March, University of St Andrews.

Picarelli, John T. (2007) 'Historical Approaches to the Trade in Human Beings,' Maggy Lee (ed.) *Human Trafficking*. Portland: Willan Publishing, pp. 26-49.

Ponzanesi, Sandra (2005) 'Outlandish Cinema: Screening the Other in Italy,' Sandra Ponzanesi and Daniela Merolla (eds.) *Migrant Cartographies: New Cultural and Literary Spaces in Post-Colonial Europe*. Lanham, MD: Lexington Books, pp. 267-281.

Prout, Ryan (2006) 'Integrated Systems of External Vigilance: Fortress Europe in Recent Spanish Film,' *Third Text*, 20:6 (November), pp. 723-731.

Pridnig, Klaus (N.D.) 'Shooting Diary,' *Import/Export: Official Website*, 2006-2007. Online. Available HTTP: http://importexport.ulrichseidl.com/en/shooting_diary.php (2 October 2009).

Quits, Teresa Torns (2000) 'First strike by immigrants follows racist riots in El Ejido,' *EIROnline*, 28 April. Online. Available HTTP: (http://www.eurofound.europa.eu/eiro/2000/04/feature/es0004184f.htm) (2 October 2009).

Ruggiero, Vincenzo (1997) 'Trafficking in Human Beings: Slaves in Contemporary Europe,' *International Journal of the Sociology of Law*, 25, pp. 231-244.

Santaolalla, Isabel (1999) 'Close Encounters: Racial Otherness in Imanol Uribe's *Bwana*,' *Bulletin of Hispanic Studies*, 76, pp. 111-122.

—— (2000) 'Ethnic and Racial Configurations in Contemporary Spanish Culture,' Jo Labanyi (ed.) *Constructing Identity in Contemporary Spain: Theoretical Debates and Cultural Practice*. Oxford: Oxford University Press, pp. 55-71.

—— (2003) 'The Representation of Ethnicity and "Race" in Contemporary Spanish Cinema,' *Cineaste: Contemporary Spanish Cinema Supplement*, Winter, pp. 44-49.

Salt, John (2000) 'Trafficking and Human Smuggling: A European Perspective,' *International Migration*, Special Issue 2000/1, pp. 31-56.

Sconce, Jeffrey (2006) 'Smart Cinema,' Linda Ruth Williams and Michael
Hammond (eds) *Contemporary American Cinema*. Open University
Press, pp. 429-439.

Seneviratne, Kalinga (N.D.) 'The Plight of Sri Lankan Women.' *Third World
Network*. Online. Available HTTP: http://www.twnside.org.sg/title/
plight-cn.htm (2 October 2009).

Sivanandan, A. (2001) 'Poverty is the new Black,' *Race & Class*, 43:2, pp. 1-5.

Shelley, Louise (2007) 'Human Trafficking as a Form of Transnational Crime,'
Maggy Lee (ed.) *Human Trafficking*. Portland: Willan Publishing, pp.
116-138.

Shohat, Ella and Robert Stam (1994) *Unthinking Eurocentrism: Multiculturalism
and the Media*. London: Routledge.

Shostak, Natalia (2004) 'Through Networks and Ordeal Narratives, or Making
Meaning of One's Displacement: Recent Labour Migration from
Western Ukraine,' *Spaces of Identity*, 4:3. Online. Available HTTP:
http://www.univie.ac.at/spacesofidentity/_Vol_4_3/_HTML/Shostak.
html (2 October 2009).

Smith, Anthony D. (1992) 'National identity and the idea of European unity,'
International Affairs, 68:1, pp. 55-76.

Sobchack, Vivian (1984) 'Inscribing Ethical Space: 10 Propositions on Death,
Representation, and Documentary,' *Quarterly Review of Film
Studies*, 9:4 (Fall), pp. 283-300.

Sobel, William (2008) 'An Interview with Jean-Pierre and Luc Dardenne,' *The
Silence of Lorna* Press Kit, pp. 2-3. Online. Available HTTP: http://
www.festival-cannes.fr/assets/Image/Direct/025619.pdf (2 October
2009).

Staiger, Janet (1995) *Bad Women: Regulating Sexuality in Early American
Cinema*. Minneapolis: University of Minnesota Press.

Tarr, Carrie (2005) *Reframing Difference: Beur and Banlieue Filmmaking in
France*. Manchester/New York: Manchester University Press.

—— (ed.) (2007) 'Maghrebi-French Filmmaking Supplement,' *Cineaste*, 33:1
(Winter), pp. 32-51.

Taylor, Ian, and Ruth Jamieson (1999) 'Sex trafficking and the mainstream of
market culture: Challenges to organised crime analysis,' *Crime, Law &
Social Change*, 32, pp. 257-278.

Tinic, Serra (2009) 'Between the Public and the Private: Television Drama and
Global Partnerships in the Neo-Network Era' in *Television Studies after
TV: Understanding television in the post-broadcast era*, ed. Graeme
Turner and Jinna Tay, London: Routledge, pp. 65-74.

Vanderschelden, Isabelle (2008) 'Luc Besson's ambition: EuropaCorp as a

European major for the 21st century,' *Studies in European Cinema*, 5:2, pp. 91-104.

Walker, Janet (1997) 'The Traumatic Paradox: Documentary Films, Historic Fictions, and Cataclysmic Past Events,' *Signs*, 22: 4 (Summer), pp. 803-825.

Wheatley, Catherine (2008) 'Europa Europa,' *Sight & Sound*, 18:10 (October), pp. 46-49.

Žižek, Slavoj (1997) 'Multiculturalism, Or, the Cultural Logic of Multinational Capitalism,' *New Left Review*, 1:225, pp. 28-51.

Filmography

40 Quadratmeter Deutschland (*40 Squre Metres of Germany*, Tevfik Baser, Turkey/West Germany, 1986)

A Decent Factory (Thomas Balmès, France/Finland/UK/Australia/Denmark, 2004)

Andjeo čuvar (*Guardian Angel*, Goran Paskalvejić, Yugoslavia, 1987)

Alila (Amos Gitai, Israel/France, 2003)

Amazing Grace (Michael Apted, UK/USA, 2006)

Apo tin akri tis polis (*On the Edge of the City*, Constantine Giannaris, Greece, 1998)

Ap' to hioni (*From the Snow*, Sotiris Goritsas, Greece, 1993)

Asfalt Tango (*Asphalt Tango*, Nae Caranfil, Romania, 1999)

Auf der anderen Seite (*The Edge of Heaven*, Fatih Akin, Germany/Turkey/Italy, 2007)

Balalayka (Ali Ozgenturk, Turkey, 2000)

Better Future (UNODC PSA, 2002)

Bila jednom jedna zemlja (*Underground*, Emir Kusturica, France/Yugoslavia/Germany, 1995)

Birthday Girl (Jez Butterworth, UK, 2001)

Bled Number One (Rabah Ameur-Zaïmeche, Algeria/France, 2006)

Bolse vita (*Bolshe Vita*, Ibolja Fekete, Hungary, 1996)

Bought and Sold (Global Survival Network and WITNESS, 1997)

Boz Ki (USAID and IOM, 2007)

Bwana (Imanol Uribe, Spain, 1996)

Candestins (*Stowaway*, Denis Chouinard and Nicholas Wadimoff, Switzerland/Canada/France/Belgium, 1997)

Caregivers (Libia Castro and Olafur Olafsson, Holland, 2008)

Cartas de Alou (*Letters from Alou,* Montxo Armendáriz, Spain, 1990)

Children for Sale (*The Virgin Harvest*, Adi Ezroni and Charles Kiselyak, USA, 2009)

Cleaning Woman (UNODC, 2003)

Cobra Verde (Werner Herzog, Germany/Ghana, 1987)

Code Inconnu: Récit incomplet de divers voyages (*Code Unknown: Incomplete Tales of Several Journeys*, Michael Haneke, France/Germany/Romania, 2000)

Dallas Pashamende (*Dallas Among Us*, Robert Adrjan Pejo, Germany/Hungary/Romania, 2004)

Danny the Dog (*Unleashed*, Louis Leterrier, France/USA/UK, 2005)

Darwin's Nightmare (Hubert Sauper, Austria/Belgium/France/Finland/Sweden, 2004)

Dernier maquis (*Adhen,* Rabah Ameur-Zaïmeche, France/Algeria, 2008)

Den hvide slavehandel (*The White Slave Trade*, Alfred Cohn, Denmark, 1910)

Den hvide slavehandels sidste offer (*The White Slave Trade's Last Victim*, August Blom, Denmark, 1911)

Det andet Europa (*The Other Europe*, Poul-Erik Heilbuth, Denmark, 2006)

Die Helfer und the Frauen (*The Peacekeepers and the Women*, Karin Jurschick Germany, 2003)

Dirty Pretty Things (Stephen Frears UK, 2002)

Dom za vešanje (*Time of the Gypsies*, Emir Kusturica, UK, Italy, Yugoslavia, 1988)

Dunav most (*Danube Bridge*, Ivan Andonov, Bulgaria, 1999)

Elvjs e Merilijn/Elvis and Marilyn, Armando Manni, Italy, 1998.

El Traje (*The Suit*, Alberto Rodríguez, Spain, 2002)

Evropa preko plota (*Europe Next Door*, Želimir Žilnik, Serbia/Montenegro, 2005)

Flores de otro mundo (*Flowers from Another World*, Icíar Bollaín, Spain, 1999)

Free Zone (Amos Gitai, Israel/Belgium/France/Spain, 2005)

Gemide (*On Board*, Serdar Akar, Turkey, 1998)

Ghosts (Nick Broomfield, UK, 2006)

Gomorra (Matteo Garrone, Italy, 2008)

Gölge Oyunu (*Shadow Play,* Yavuz Turgul, Turkey, 1992)

Gori Vatra (*Fuse*, Pier Zalica, Bosnia/Herzegovina, 2003)

H-2 Worker (Stephanie Black, USA, 1990)

Ha-Aretz Hamuvtachat (*Promised Land*, Amos Gitai, Israel/France/UK, 2004)

Harragas (Merzak Allouache, Algeria/France, 2009)

Heremakono (*Waiting for Happiness*, Abderrahmane Sissako, France/ Mauritania, 2002)

Hitnatkoot (*Disengagement*, Amos Gitai, Germany/Italy/Israel/France, 2007)

Holly (Guy Moshe, US/France/Israel/Cambodia, 2007)

Hostel (Eli Roth, USA, 2005)

Human Trafficking (Christian Duguay, US/Canada, 2005)

Hyôryû-gai (*City of Lost Souls*, Miike Takashi, Japan, 2001)

Ilegal (Ignacio Vilar, Spain, 2003)

Import/Export (Ulrich Seidl, Austria, 2007)

In This World, Michael Winterbottom, UK, 2002.

Intersection (JM Animation, Korea, 2009)

It's a Free World... (Ken Loach, UK/Italy/Germany/Spain/Poland, 2007)

Kaal (Bappaditya Banerjee, India, undated)

Kud plovi ovaj brod (*Wanderlust*, Želimir Žilnik, FRY/Slovienia/Hungary, 1999)

La faute à Voltaire (*Blame it on Voltaire,* Abdel Kechiche, France, 2000)

La fuente amarilla (*The Yellow Fountain*, Miguel Santesmases, Spain/France, 1999)

La Haine (*Hate*, Matthieu Kassovitz, France, 1995)

Lamerica (Gianni Amelio, Italy/France/Germany, 1994)

La Promesse (*The Promise,* Jean-Pierre and Luc Dardenne, Belgium/France/
    Luxembourg, 1996)

La Sconosciuta (*The Unknown*, Guiseppe Tornatore, Italy, 2006)

Last Resort (Pawel Pawlikowski, UK, 2000)

La vie nouvelle (*A New Life*, Philippe Grandrieux, France, 2002)

Le Silence de Lorna (*The Silence of Lorna*, Jean-Pierre and Luc Dardenne,
    Belgium/France/Italy/Germany, 2008)

Lethal Weapon 4 (Richard Donner, USA, 1998)

Leydi Zi (*Lady Zee*, Georgi Dyulgerov, Bulgaria, 2005)

Life and Debt (Stephanie Black, USA, 2001)

Lilja 4ever (*Lilya 4-ever,* Lukas Moodysson, Sweden/Denmark, 2002)

Los novios búlgaros (*Bulgarian Lovers*, Eloy de la Iglesia, Spain, 2003)

Mardi Gras: Made in China (David Redmon, US, 2006)

Maria (Calin Peter Netzer, Romania, 2003)

Maria Full of Grace (Joshua Marston, USA/Columbia, 2004)

Massa'ot James Be'eretz Hakodesh (*James' Journey to Jerusalem*, Ra'anan
    Alexandrowicz, Israel, 2003)

Metropolis (Fritz Lang, Germany, 1927)

Mondo Meyer Upakhan (*A Tale of a Naughty Girl,* Buddhadev Dasgupta, India, 2003)

Montenegro (Dusan Makavejev, Sweden/UK, 1981)

Nata pa hënë (*Moonless Night*, Artan Minarolli, Albania, 2004)

Occidente (*West*, Corso Salani, Italy 2000)

Ola einai dromos (*It's a Long Road*, Pantelis Voulgaris, Greece, 1998)

Omiros (*Hostage*, Constantine Giannaris Greece, 2005)

Open Your Eyes to Human Trafficking (UNGIFT, 2008)

Otan erthei i mama gia ta Hristougenna (*When Mother Comes Home for
    Christmas*, Greece/India/Germany, Nilita Vachani, 1996)

Otobüs (*The Bus*, Tunç Okan, Turkey/Switzerland, 1976)

Our Big Fair Trade Adventure (Ricardo Pollack, UK, 2007)

Parees (*Pals*, Sotiris Goritsas, Greece, 2007)

Patul conjugal (*Conjugal Bed*, Mircea Daneliuc, Romania, 1993)

Phoolan Devi (*Bandit Queen*, Shekhar Kapur, India, 1994)

Poniente (Chus Gutiérrez, Spain, 2002)

Portami Via (*Take Me Away*, Gianluca Maria Tavarelli, Italy, 1994)

Pretty Woman (Garry Marshall, USA, 1990)

Pummarò (Michele Placido, Italy, 1990)

Quando sei nato non puoi più nasconderti (*Once You're Born You Can No Longer
    Hide,* Marco Tullio Giordana, Italy/France/UK, 2005)

Reise der Hoffnung (*Journey of Hope*, Xavier Koller, Switzerland/Turkey/UK, 1990)

Rezervni Deli (*Spare Parts*, Damjan Kožole, Slovenia, 2003)

Rus Gelin (*Russian Bride*, Zeki Alasya, Turkey, 2003)

Saïd (Llorenç Soler, Spain, 1998)

Schengen (*The Castle*, Xavier Arenos, Spain, 2007)

Sex Traffic (David Yates, UK/Canada, 2004)

Shooting Dogs (Michael Caton-Jones, UK/Germany, 2005)

Showgirls (Paul Verhoeven, USA, 1995)

Skupljaci perja (*I Even Met Happy Gypsies*, Aleksandar Petrović, Yugoslavia, 1967)

Sleep Dealers (Alex Rivera, Mexico/USA, 2008)

Sonbahar (*Autumn*, Özcan Alper, Turkey, 2008)

The Sopranos (David Chase, USA, 2000-2007)

Striptease (Andrew Bergman, USA, 1996)

Sürü (*The Herd*, Zeki Ökten, Turkey, 1979)

Sweet Sixteen (Ken Loach, UK/Germany/Spain, 2002)

Taken (Pierre Morel, France, 2008)

Tamanrasset (Merzak Allouache, France, 2008)

Telephone (UNODC, 2003)

Terra Estrangeira (*Foreign Land*, Walter Salles and Daniela Thomas, Brazil, 1996)

The Beach (Danny Boyle, USA/UK, 1999)

The Constant Gardener (Fernando Meirelles, UK/Germany, 2005)

The Good Woman of Bangkok (Dennis O'Rourke, Australia/UK, 1991)

The Inside of White Slave Traffic (Frank Beal, USA, 1913)

The K-11 Journey (Daniel Kedem and Charles Kiselyak, USA/France/Israel, 2007)

The Last King of Scotland (Kevin Macdonald, UK, 2006)

The Searchers (John Ford, USA, 1956)

The Transporter (Corey Yuen, France/USA, 2002)

The Transporter 2 (Louis Leterrier, France/USA, 2005)

The Transporter 3 (Olivier Megaton, France/USA, 2008)

Tirana, année zero (*Tirana Year Zero*, Fatmir Koci, Albania, 2001)

Traffic in Souls (George Loane Tucker, USA, 1913)

True North (Steve Hudson, Germany/Ireland/UK, 2006)

Tvrdjava Evropa (*Fortress Europe*, Želimir Žilnik, Slovenia, 2001)

Un'altra vita (*Another Life*, Carlo Mazzacurati, Italy, 1992)

Vers le Sud (*Heading South*, Laurent Cantet, France/Canada, 2005)

Vesna va veloce (Carlo Mazzacurati, Italy, 1996)

Welcome (Philippe Lioret, France, 2009)

Wesh wesh, qu'est-ce qui se passe? (Rabah Ameur-Zaïmeche, France, 2001)

Why Braceros? (Wilding-Butler/Council of California Growers, USA, c1959)

Why Cybraceros? (Alex Rivera, USA, 1997)

Work Abroad (UNODC, 2001)

Yol/The Way (Serif Gören/Yilmaz Güney, Switzerland, 1982)

Index

Africa   25, 35, 65, 87, 88, 90-1, 93,
95 97, 142, 148, 153, 184; African
cinema   93.
Adhen (Rabah Ameur-Zaïmeche)
41-2, 143.
Agamben, Giorgio   41.
Albania   57, 61, 84-6, 88, 91, 97,
100, 103 n18, 108, 172, 187, 204-
7, 211-2; Albanian cinema   100,
108; traffickers and trafficking
rings   57, 97, 172, 187.
Andrijasevic, Rutvica   115 n25, 219.
Appadurai, Arjun   49, 52, 55,
134; ethnoscape   52-82, 134;
financescape   52, 55-6, 64, 79;
ideoscape   52; 'labourscape'   55,
73-6, 81; mediascape; 52, 55-6,
81; technoscape   52, 55-6, 79,
81, 134.
Arendt, Hannah   94.
Arranged marriages   2, 39, 197, 199,
202-3, 204; mail-order brides   2,
39, 60-2, 207, 209.
Asphalt Tango (Nae Caranfil)   98,
108.
Augé, Marc   11, 27-30, 83, 89-92;
Non-Place   11, 27-30, 40, 44,
83, 87-94.

Bales, Kevin   4, 43, 73, 150, 207.
Banlieue   28, 142-7.
Bauman, Zygmunt   29
Besson, Luc   40, 42, 45, 47, 211-7.
Beur Cinema   42-5, 120, 142-7.
Bhabha, Jacqueline   101-2.
Birthday Girl (Jez Butterworth)   61-2.

Bosnia Herzegovina   91, 92, 94, 99,
112, 174-5, 178.
British Broadcasting Corporation
(BBC)
Bulgaria   56, 84, 85, 89, 100, 103
n18, 106; Bulgarian cinema   85,
103 n18.
Bus, The (Tunç Okan)   15, 93, 96,
109, 118-25.
Bwana (Imanol Uribe)   35, 42, 148-9.

Capitalism   17-8, 21, 38-9, 64; 'anti-
capitalism'   207; global capitalism
11, 63, 79, 175, 179, 182, 214;
post-capitalism   38.
Certeau, Michel de   30.
Children   2, 83 n10, 94, 96, 105-6,
111, 126-33, 135, 139, 149, 156,
160, 166, 181, 201, 224-6, 229,
231.
Chinese Immigration Act, The (1894)
51.
China   10, 24, 46, 56, 66-7, 69-72,
77-8, 96-7, 156, 180-5, 233;
snakeheads   57; traffickers and
trafficking rings   57 n2, 97.
Citizenship   22, 30, 54-6, 67, 108
n22, 145-7, 190, 219.
Cold War   5, 16; 'Iron Curtain' (new)
26.
Colonialism   19-22, 38, 44-5, 77;
imperial project   7; slavery   26,
31, 73.
Communism   89, 161.
Croatia   90, 155, 161.
Cuba   28, 89.

Debt bondage 2, 16-7, 22, 65-8, 71, 73-7, 83, 151-2, 183-5, 187, 190.

Deleuze, Gilles 21-3, 31.

Disposable people 4, 18, 103, 216.

Dirty Pretty Things (Stephen Frears) 12, 42, 45, 53, 113.

DynCorp 99 n16, 172, 175.

Economic: disparity of means 16-7, 20, 86, 102-6; globalisation 11, 49, 52, 55-6, 58, 64, 75-9, 82, 100, 103, 134, 173, 177, 186-8, 199, 200, 203; market 10, 24-6, 64-5, 75-9, 91, 100, 103, 112, 150-1, 175, 178, 183, 186-90, 191, 214-5; migrants 16-7, 60-1, 63-5, 102-3, 141, 174; root causes of trafficking 16-7, 63-5, 69-73, 75, 102-6, 150-1, 218.

Elsaesser, Thomas 26.

Elvis and Marilyn (Armando Manni) 100, 105, 107.

Empire (Michael Hardt and Antonio Negri, 2000) 18, 27.

Eurocentrism 7, 20, 22-7, 28, 42, 153.

European corporations 79

European Union (EU) 1, 11, 16-7, 27, 43, 52, 56, 61, 90 n13, 98, 151, 161, 189.

Female (see Women)

Finland 78-9.

France 13, 28, 41-3, 58, 86, 98, 142-7, 153, 211; *Beur* 42-3, 120, 142, 153; Calais 88, 94; French cinema 40-2, 58, 107, 142-7, 211-7.

Freud, Sigmund 180-3.

'Fortress Europe' 26, 88, 195.

Free trade zones 10, 76.

Gangmasters (see Traffickers)

Gaza 87

Gender: depictions of women 77, 193, 225; disparity 12; gendered films 56; imaginaries 51, 62, 90, 104, 218-9; sexism 72; tropes 56.

Genre 13, 45, 47, 48, 51, 90, 143, 234-5; melodrama 20, 46, 50, 56, 148, 190, 210, 234; mockumentary 9, 80; road movie 25; Western 58.

Ghosts (Nick Broomfield) 6, 9, 10, 24, 41, 65-7, 93, 114 n24, 180-5, 232-3.

Glenny, Misha 87.

Globalisation 6, 10, 16, 29, 49, 50-1, 52-6, 65, 67, 69, 77, 125, 161, 173, 197, 218; economic 16, 64-5, 77, 82, 103, 134, 173, 177, 186-7; flows 52, 56, 69, 82; anxieties about 49, 52, 55-6, 82.

Godard, Jean-Luc 47.

Georgia

Greece 13, 96, 113-4, 134-41; Greek cinema 84-5; domestics in 107, 140.

'Grey economy' 104, 114, 161.

Guardian Angel (Goran Paskaljevic) 5, 87-8, 96, 106, 109, 111, 126-33.

Hannerz, Ulf 23, 125.

Hierarchies 23, 88, 103; class 90; race 90; gender 90; ethnicity 90; economic 17.

Hughes, Donna M. 2.

Human Trafficking (Christian Duguay)
57-60, 96, 98, 104-5, 113, 176,
230, 233, 235.
Hungary   84, 90, 106, 161.

Ilegal (Ignacio Vilar)   42, 148.
Immigration/Immigrants: asylum
seekers   20, 81, 104, 176, 189;
economic migrants   27, 66, 75,
80, 86, 93, 109; illegal   2, 17-8,
23, 26-7, 30, 32, 35-7, 46-9, 54,
58, 63, 67-9, 77, 86, 90 n13, 118-
21, 124-5, 142, 148-54, 181-2,
194, 196, 204, 206, 208; legal
37, 41-2, 47, 50-1, 54, 65, 97-8,
104, 199, 204, 208; policy   54-9,
65, 71-2, 149, 154, 176-7, 219,
235; Undocumented   65-8, 180-
5.
Immobility   37, 39-41.
Import/Export (Ulrich Seidl)   6, 40-
1, 80-1, 92, 104, 106, 109, 113,
191-6.
International Monetary Fund (IMF)
75, 76, 103.
In This World (Michael Winterbottom)
12, 43, 86, 88.
Israel   13, 88, 91, 163-71, 223;
Beer Sheba   87; Israeli cinema
163-71; Sinai   87, 92, 163, 165;
The Red Sea   98, 163, 166-7;
traffickers   97.
Italy   1, 28, 54, 85-6, 88, 90, 96,
99-100, 113, 126-31, 155-8, 172-
3, 178; Italian cinema   42, 105;
traffickers   97; Trieste   88, 90.
It's a Free World… (Ken Loach)   6,
65, 67-9, 78, 101, 107, 186-90,
232.

Jameson, Fredric   19, 35-7, 47-8.
James' Journey to Jerusalem
(Ra'anan Alexandrowicz)   65-6,
88.
Journey of Hope (Xavier Koller)
106.

Kafka, Franz   91.
Kara, Siddharth   1-2, 53, 64, 94,
103, 111-4, 203, 219.
Kempadoo, Kemala   49, 54, 64-5.
Korea   89, 96.
Kurdistan   88, 109.
Kusturica, Emir   33-4, 88, 126.

Labour: export   64-5, 73-5, 79-80,
100, 134-7, 199-203; involuntary
2, 4, 7, 12, 16-38, 43, 45, 53-6,
63, 66-7, 74, 76-82, 96, 105, 144,
146, 150-4, 186, 188, 192-4, 196,
204, 206, 217, 222, 208; migrant
61, 63, 66-8, 75, 80, 95, 101-9,
186-90, 192-4, 231, 233; roaming
6, 103; undocumented   65, 67-8,
180-5, 231.
Lagerfeld, Karl   107.
Lamerica (Gianni Amelio)   85, 88,
100.
Last Resort (Pawel Pawlikowski)   9,
12, 40-1, 42, 80-1, 88-9, 105.
Lee, Maggie   3, 144 n24.
Letters from Alou (Montxo
Armendáriz)   24, 42, 148, 153.
'Lieux de Mémoire' (Pierre Nora)
91-3.
Lilya 4-ever (Lukas Moodysson)   12,
43, 59, 63, 86, 101, 105, 106,
108, 112.
Lithuania   184; traffickers   97.
Loshitsky, Yosefa   iv, 53, 115 n25.

Love on Delivery/Ticket to Paradise
(Janus Metz) 6, 60, 197-203.

Macedonia 88, 158.
Mail-order brides (see Arranged
marriages)
Malarek, Victor 69-70, 87, 97, 110
n23.
Mann Act, the/the White-Slave Traffic
Act (1910) 51.
Maps 86.
Mauritania 93.
Mazierska, Ewa and Laura Rascaroli
25, 115 n25.
Mediterranean 90, 94, 100, 148.
Middle East 74 n7, 87, 119, 137,
212; Cairo 87, 163, 165; Egypt
87, 163.
Moldova 87, 91, 106, 112, 172.
Montenegro 91, 99.
Morawska, Ewa 97, 164 n37.
Multiculturalism 54, 61.
Myth of bondage 30, 33, 35, 100,
217.

Newfoundland 93.
Nigerian traffickers 97
Nomadism 25-6, 30-2.
Nora, Pierre (see 'Lieux de Mémoire')
North Africa 90-1, 142, 148, 152-3;
North African traffickers 97.

O'Healy, Áine 105, 107, 115 n25.
On Board (Serdar Akar) 85.
Once You're Born You Can No Longer
Hide (Marco Tullio Giordana) 28,
42, 94, 100.
Organisation for Security and
Cooperation in Europe, The
(OSCE) 1.

Organised crime 3, 11, 49, 58, 60,
77, 87, 97, 102 n17, 104, 230;
Sister Ping 97; Russian Mafia
221.

Passport 61, 98, 106, 108, 123,
188, 221; surrender of 66, 74,
147, 173, 192, 228.
Poland 32, 101, 190; Polish
traffickers 97.
Poniente (Chus Gutiérrez) 6, 42,
46-7, 107, 148-54.
Pornography; 9; internet 81, 191.
Postcolonialism 19-22, 43-5, 91.
Poverty and Migration 6, 20, 27,
64, 69, 71-3, 113, 129, 151,
170, 189, 203, 215, 218; Albania
85-6; Bhabha's definition of
trafficking 102-3; position of
vulnerability 2, 102, 105.
Promise, The (Jean-Pierre and Luc
Dardenne) 24, 42, 204, 206-7,
209.
Promised Land (Amos Gitai) 6, 59,
62, 92, 98, 104, 109, 163-71.
Prostitution 9, 19, 27, 31, 38, 49,
58-60, 63, 69, 81-2, 84, 89, 92,
96, 98, 106-7, 123, 128, 191,
198-9, 202-3, 231; 'Natashas'
2, 70, 87, 110 n23; sex-trafficking
2-3, 38-9, 50, 53-4, 59, 78, 106
n21, 112-3, 218, 225.
Prout, Ryan 26, 153.
Pummarò (Michele Placido) 28,
42.

Recruitment agency 50, 67, 74,
135, 186-90.
Repatriation 54, 58, 60, 99, 127,
132, 149, 174, 203.

Rights: abuses of human 17-8,
27, 64, 102, 103, 152; abuses
of labour 71, 78, 103, 218;
activists of human 8, 115; class
of 72; discourses of political
71-2, 76; economic 55, 71-2,
75-6, 103, 145-7; human 2, 7-8,
11, 12, 72, 75, 99, 103, 154, 178,
218, 230; Human Rights Watch
74, 137, 230; International Bill of
Human 71.
Roma 96, 109, 126-33, 194; hamlet
87; Roma/Gypsy traffickers
96-7
Romania 56, 60, 85, 86, 89, 100,
129 n30; Romanian cinema 89,
98, 106; Romanian migrants
60, 86, 108, 189; Romanian
traffickers 97.
Royal Academy (UK) 29.
Russia 63, 81, 83, 89, 97, 108, 163-
6, 204, 233; Moscow 29, 87;
Russian traffickers 57, 97, 105
n19, 221-2; Russian protagonists
61-2, 84-5, 106.
Rwanda 25.

Schengen Agreement 90, 106, 161.
Serbia 90, 106; Belgrade 88, 172.
Sex Traffic (David Yates) 6, 59, 63,
108, 172-9, 232.
Sex Trafficking 59-60, 62-4, 106,
107, 111-2, 114, 163, 203; films
63, 66, 79; Natashas 2, 70, 87,
110 n23; prostitution 2-3, 38-9,
50, 53-4, 59, 78, 106 n21, 112-3,
218, 225.
Silence of Lorna, The (Jean-Pierre
and Luc Dardenne) 6, 43, 45,
61-2, 98, 204-10.

Slavery: Anti-Slavery International 1,
4; institutionalised 18, 33, 44, 68,
73; modern 2-5, 11, 21-39, 43-5,
47-9, 52-6, 59-60, 63, 68, 71-3,
77-9, 83, 87, 92, 102, 105, 112,
128, 132, 135-6, 139, 141, 144,
170, 171, 172, 180, 186, 193, 202,
211, 214-6, 218, 220, 222, 230;
old versus new 55-6, 75, 232;
problems of 'slavery' 16-8; slave
trade 17-8, 26, 29, 47-8, 95, 99
n16, 232; slave market 10, 98,
163, 165, 167; white 50-1, 56,
126, 170, 220.
Slovakia 191, 212; Dubi 92.
Slovenia 13, 88, 90, 155-62; Krško
92, 155, 159.
Shohat, Ella and Robert Stam (see
Unthinking Eurocentrism) 22.
Soviet Union 6, 12, 16, 85, 112.
Snakeheads (see China)
Spain 13, 35, 42, 46, 65, 91, 148-54.
Spare Parts (Damjan Kožole) 6, 90,
92, 113, 155-62, 194.
Sweden 42, 63, 118, 120, 121-3, 125;
Swedish migrants 50-1.
Switzerland 13, 42, 88, 99, 120, 130
n31, 150.

Taken (Pierre Morel) 6, 40, 57-8, 59,
104, 105, 107, 211-7.
Tarr, Carrie iv, 42, 115 n25, 143.
Technology: computer 16, 31; 'the
Cybracero' 80; internet; 80,
194-5, 227, 235; internet and
pornography 81, 191, 193;
in restricting movement 80;
telecommunications 24, 39,
50, 177, 197-8; technologisation
of society 33-4, 36, 50, 52,

55, 82, 144-5, 194-5, 196, 215;
technological age 24, 36, 221.
Thailand 25, 112, 197-203.
Time of the Gypsies (Emir Kusturica)
88, 96, 126.
Tourism 25, 38, 39, 57, 59, 76,
77, 158, 195, 198, 227, 229;
economic interactions 77
Trade Protections 76.
Traffic in Souls (George Loane) 50,
81, 220.
Trafficking: anti-trafficking NGOs
and initiatives 1, 5, 49, 60,
114-5, 219, 222; body farming/
Organs 2, 53, 54, 79, 113;
children 2, 71, 83 n10, 94,
96, 106, 111, 113, 126-33, 156,
157, 160, 165, 224-5, 229, 231;
criminality 3, 18, 49, 54, 56-64,
65, 81-2, 96-7, 101, 128-9, 176,
182, 188; definition 1-3, 43, 53,
59, 82, 102, 107, 136, 202, 218;
film festivals 13, 115, 230-2;
policy 29, 54, 57-60, 65, 68, 72,
82, 102-3, 110, 114-5, 144, 146,
218-21, 224, 232-3, 235; women
2-4, 8, 12, 38-40, 51, 57-63, 66,
69, 74 n7, 76-9, 81, 83-5, 89, 94-
8, 105, 108, 110, 112, 114 n24,
115 n25, 122, 134, 136-7, 140,
153, 156, 163-6, 170, 172-6, 178,
197-203, 220-3, 225, 229, 231.
Trafficking tropes: abduction 2,
50, 51, 53, 57-8, 105, 211-2;
auction 58, 163, 173, 176-7;
fallen woman 85; non-spaces
11, 28-30, 40, 44, 83, 87-92;
organised crime 3, 11, 49, 55,
60-1, 72, 77, 87, 90, 97, 104,
221, 230; rape 59-60, 62, 66, 74,

78, 82, 165, 169, 173; surrender
of passport 66, 74, 147, 173,
192, 228.
Traffickers 8, 12, 17, 20, 22, 27,
59, 90, 94-5, 99-100, 104, 108
n22, 114 n24, 122, 123, 128,
131-2, 147, 155-62, 172-8, 207,
233, 235; gangmasters 100,
183, 188; pimps and slave-
holders 17, 22, 59, 68, 95, 96,
110 n23, 126, 228; recruitment
agencies 50, 67, 74, 135, 186-
90; women 95-6, 98, 103.
Trafficking Vehicles: bus 93, 98,
108, 118-25, 136, 140, 200; boat
35, 69-70, 94, 100, 148; freight
container 93, 183.
Transporter, The (Corey Yuen) 24,
40, 213.
True North (Steve Hudson) 65,
69-73, 104
Turkey 83, 87, 88, 91, 96, 109;
Istanbul 83, 89, 92, 107, 115;
Turkish cinema 85, 120; Turkish
traffickers 97.

Uganda 25
Ukraine 81, 87, 91, 101, 106,
112-3, 114 n24, 191-6, 223;
sex trafficking 87; slavery (old
vs new) 55-6, 75; Ukrainian
traffickers 97; Ukrainian
prostitutes 81, 191.
Unions and Unionisation 72, 76,
189.
United Kingdom 13, 57, 83 n10,
97, 180-5, 186-90.; British
cinema 62, 172, 190;Dover 69,
94; England 71, 81, 88, 89 n11,
100.

United Nations 11, 52, 225, 226; Convention on Transnational Organised Crime 102; High Commissioner for Human Rights 1; the International Organisation for Migration 1, 4, 233; Protocols on Trafficking and Smuggling (the Palermo Protocols) 1, 53, 102 n17, 223.

Unthinking Eurocentrism (Ella Shohat and Robert Stam, 1994) 22, 38.

War 94, 99, 112, 218.

Wertheimer, Alan 102.

Wesh, wesh, qu'est ce qui se passe? (Rabah Ameur-Zaïmeche) 6, 142-7.

Welcome (Philippe Lioret) 94, 100.

When Mother Comes Home for Christmas (Nilita Vachani) 6, 73-4, 107, 114 n24, 134-41.

Work: in brothels 19, 20, 27, 31, 37, 63, 81, 85, 98, 163, 170-2, 174, 177; as dancers 84, 110 n23, 199; health and safety 67, 72, 78, 180; physical 12, 16, 31-8, 54; as prostitutes 9, 27, 63, 81-2, 84, 89, 92, 106, 107, 125, 130, 168, 191-3, 198-9, 202, 231; sweat shops 3, 19-21, 31, 37, 54, 78-9, 146; sex work 4, 81, 94, 193, 198, 227, 231.

World Bank 75, 76.

Žilnik, Želimir iv, 90, 99, 120.

Žižek, Slavoj 17-8, 33-4, 46.